# HISTORIC NELSON: THE EARLY YEARS

# Historic Nelson
## *The Early Years*

*by*

## JOHN NORRIS

oolichan books
LANTZVILLE, BRITISH COLUMBIA, CANADA
1995

**Canadian Cataloguing in Publication Data**

Norris, John, 1922-
Historic Nelson
Includes bibliographical references and index.
ISBN 0-88982-151-8 (bound)
ISBN 0-88982-150-X (pbk.)

1. Nelson (B.C.)—History.   2. Kootenay Region (B.C.)—History.
I. Title
FC3849.N44N67 1995     971.1'.6203     C95-910886-6
F1089.5.N44N67 1995

Publication of this book has been financially assisted by The Canada Council.

Published by
**oolichan books**
P.O. Box 10
Lantzville, B.C.
Canada V0R 2H0

Printed in Canada by
Best Books

*This book*
*is dedicated*
*mostly*
*to Shawn Lamb,*
*without whose beneficent presence*
*it probably would not have been written,*
*but also*
*to Ted Affleck, Henry Stevenson, and Alan Ramsden,*
*who greatly eased*
*the writing of it.*

*The writing of this book*
*was financially assisted*
*by*
*The Ministry of Small Business, Tourism and Culture*
*through*
*the British Columbia Heritage Trust*
*and*
*B.C. Lottery revenues,*
*and by*
*the Corporation of the City of Nelson.*
*It was sponsored by*
*the Kootenay Museum Association and Historical Society*
*to celebrate*
*the 1997 centennial of Nelson's incorporation.*
*The writer wishes to thank*
*Ron and Frances Welwood*
*and*
*Peter Chapman*
*for their assistance as early readers.*

# TABLE OF CONTENTS

# Present Day Map of the Area Chronicled in this Book

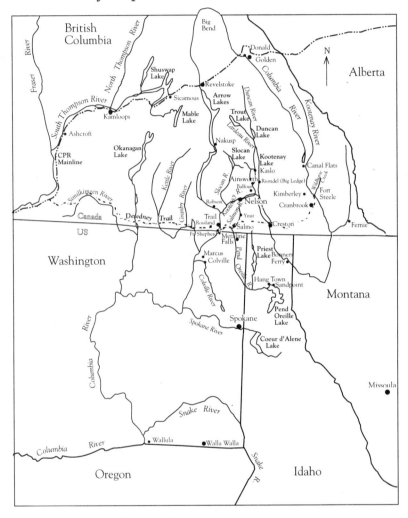

*This map and all others are by Selena Hudson.*

# FOREWORD

*In which we consider certain general geographical and
historical facts already well known, by means of which
review the author hopes not only to place his readers
in that philosophical frame of mind proper to the contemplation of history but also to provide them with an
adequate setting for our subject. Readers who resent
the somewhat pedagogical tone of Forewords, or those
who prefer to read them Afterward, may turn at once
to Chapter 1, although the author does not recommend
such disregard of proper order.*

THE MODERN-DAY MAP to the left of this page presents the
geographical setting for the story being told in this book. It is a
map so reduced that it shows only one of the landscape's primary
features—the watersheds. The mountains have not been indicated,
but we can imagine them easily. Knowing that British Columbia is
a "sea of mountains" and that water courses run along valleys,
most of us could fill in the mountains there, and even those below
the international border, with a fair degree of accuracy. We can,
therefore, assume that the landscape's second primary feature is
also a part of the map.

The map shows us that Nelson, the subject of this book, is a
town situated at the extreme western tip of the west arm of
Kootenay Lake; in fact, just at the point where the west arm becomes the lower Kootenay River. We can see that Kootenay Lake is
approximately at the centre of a large oval—"Kootenay country"—formed by two rivers—the Kootenay which rises in the

Rocky Mountains near the Alberta border, flows south into the United States of America, bends to the north, reenters Canada to form Kootenay Lake, and then continues westward as the lower Kootenay River; and the Columbia which rises in a lake very close to the upper Kootenay—a plain only about a mile and a quarter wide separates the two—flows northward to make the Big Bend, then moves southward through the Arrow Lakes into the United States and turns westward to reach the Pacific Ocean. The oval is closed on its western side when the lower Kootenay flows into the Columbia, and remains open on its eastern side. Once, however, as our story will relate, the oval was closed there, too, for a short time, when a canal was built across the plain to connect the upper Kootenay to the source of the Columbia.

The map makes it clear that the whole oval of Kootenay country is the northernmost branch of the Columbia River watershed—a really immense drainage system, especially when we take into account the vast territory emptied by its lower branch, the Snake River. We notice too that all the rivers of southern British Columbia west of Kootenay country drain southward across the border and into the Columbia. Only the mighty Fraser manages to reach the Pacific on Canadian territory. In contrast, only one American River, the Pend d'Oreille, flows "upwards" into Canada. That is why so many people driving from Nelson to Spokane along the Pend d'Oreille make the remark "That river seems to be flowing the wrong way."

Watersheds are the political units of nature. Their rivers serve as highways, people live in their valleys, and the mountains between them constitute boundaries. Only as we become more separated from the "natural" can we ignore them, climbing across mountains in our motor vehicles or flying over them in airplanes. Such was not the case for the original occupants of our land, or for the earliest European explorers of it. The first people in this history, for example, could not make a short hop across from West Kootenay to East Kootenay, from Nelson, let us say, to Fort Steele. The Selkirk Mountains were in the way. Those early travellers had to follow the Kootenay River as it wended its long way *around* the mountains. In following natural routes they became more intimate with the geography of the landscape than we denizens of the highways do in our enclosed vehicles.

If we take the "natural" view that watersheds are the real political units, then it is obvious that modern boundaries are often flagrantly at fault. The map makes it clear that "the natural political unit" of the Columbia River watershed has had its integrity violated several times by the international border along the 49th Parallel. That straight line crosses the Kootenay River twice, actually lopping off the southern end of the oval, bisects the Columbia itself, and continues wreaking similar havoc as it moves westward. One can imagine a space-alien examining our planet through a telescope and pondering on the strangeness of human beings who cut up their world in such an irrational way.

Actually, however, during the struggle between the United States and Great Britain over where the western boundary should be, the British presented a strong case for annexing all the territory west and north of the Columbia. That would have made a more natural boundary, one at least partially in keeping with the watershed concept. By an agreement of 1818 the international boundary had been drawn along the 49th Parallel only as far west as the Rocky Mountains. Beyond that point all the territory comprising much of what is now British Columbia and the state of Washington was designated "Oregon Territory" and was open to use by settlers of both powers. During that open period the Hudson's Bay Company fur traders established forts throughout the lower Columbia River area. Fort Vancouver, on the Columbia at the mouth of the Willamette River, was their headquarters. But thousands of American settlers were moving westward across the plains. These people saw the Hudson's Bay Company personnel as foreigners. The situation became untenable. In the parleying which was undertaken to settle the border once and for all, the decision went against the British, and in 1846 the line was drawn along the 49th Parallel.

The map makes very clear the problems that confronted the administrators of British territory north of the new border, problems not made any simpler by the fact that the administrators were in London, England. Those north-south watersheds form the only natural highways for the movement of people and goods, and would serve that purpose well during later gold strikes up in Canada. The simple addition of a horizontal line cutting across them to mark the border on a map certainly couldn't stop that natural up-and-down flow. Even after the border made its appearance in the real world by means of a clear-cut swathe and cairns, people ignored it and would continue to do so until customs men came on the scene. The British knew that preventing that north-south movement of men and goods was an almost impossible job because of the natural politics of the landscape. East-west movement was across the grain and very difficult, yet east-west movement there had to be if the constant danger of American economic—and, in spite of the border, even political—take-over was to be averted. Three things had to happen, and happen quickly: the territory had to be given a real political form (in 1858 the Hudson's Bay Company colony on Vancouver's Island became a Crown Colony administered by a governor in Victoria, and the mainland settlements became another, administered by a governor in New Westminster); the border had to be clearly marked (it *was* in 1861-62); and some means had to be found to promote the east-west flow of traffic north of the border (the Dewdney Trail was pushed through above the line to serve the gold-strike over in Wildhorse Creek in 1865). Nevertheless, for decades to come, gold continued to drain away into the States, American merchants continued to supply mines and prospectors in Canadian territory, and travellers from New Westminster to Kootenay had to take an American route via Tacoma and Portland, thence up the Columbia by steamboat, wagon road, and pack train to Colville or Bonners Ferry. A hope of improving this state of affairs dawned when British Columbia joined Confederation as a province in 1871. Actual improvement followed when the cross-Canada line of the Canadian Pacific Railway was completed in 1885. But even then it was so easy for American railroad companies to build spur lines up those north-south watershed valleys into Canada that the CPR felt continuously threatened. That threat was very strong in Kootenay country and played a role in Nelson's history.

Our story begins in the year 1882. At that time British Columbia has been a province of Canada for 11 years, but it is a lonely province, a wilderness, a sea of mountains separated from the rest of Canada by a vast, largely uninhabited prairie. Alberta and Saskatchewan do not yet exist as provinces and Manitoba is a fraction of its present size. The transcontinental railway that was promised back in '71 when British Columbia joined Confederation has not yet been completed, although survey crews are up in the Big Bend country of the Columbia. Below the border, Washington, Idaho, and Montana are only territories, not yet states. But the vigorous American nation is expanding rapidly, exerting a strong northward pressure.

# CHAPTER I

*In which that part of British Columbia known as West Kootenay is introduced to the reader at a time before it became settled by Europeans, and two white men by the names of William Adolph Baillie-Grohman and Richard Fry, along with a husband and wife of the Lower Kootenay Indian tribe, are observed preparing to visit it.*

IT WAS SPRINGTIME in the year 1882. West Kootenay country, like the rest of British Columbia, was undergoing the slow process of ridding itself of winter's snow. As it lay voluptuously responsive to the triumphant sunshine, it was a landscape empty of people and still largely unknown to the world outside. As early as 1826, a voyage—the first recorded one—had been made by an employee of the Hudson's Bay Company along Kootenay Lake and down the lower Kootenay River to the Columbia, but the account of that journey still lay undiscovered in company record books. The Gold Commissioner over in East Kootenay had made little or no mention of the area for some years now in his annual reports published in the *British Columbia Gazette*, and the provincial government which published that organ of communication had hardly given a thought to the Kootenays since the short-lived gold rush on Forty-Nine Creek in '68-'69. Across the Purcell Mountains in the East Kootenays, only a small population of settlers remained after the big '63-'64 rush on Wildhorse Creek. The Dewdney Trail built to link that strike with the seat of government in Victoria was not much used now, and had fallen into disrepair, particularly where it passed through the southern part of West Kootenay country. Up where the bending Columbia formed the northern border of this unopened territory, there was, however, much human activity. A survey party headed by a man called Rogers was searching for a pass through the high mountains that lie in the bend of the river. Already the transcontinental line of the Canadian Pacific Railway Company, which was going to use that pass, had reached the place that would be called Calgary. In a few months pack trains taking supplies from that centre would be struggling westward through the canyons of Kicking Horse Pass in the Rockies, commanded by one J. Fred Hume, a man who will in due time be a part of our story. Farther west, the rails that were being laid from the Pacific Coast to meet those coming from Calgary had already reached Fort Kamloops. But none of all that disturbed the springtime silence of Kootenay Lake, still, in 1882, as the marvelous natural events of unfolding millennia had made it.

Already the light-sleeping squirrels had left their winter nests; in a few weeks bears—the mothers with newborn cubs—would emerge from caves and hollow cedars to feed on multifarious stems and roots that awakening plants were quickly providing; deer and elk would leave their winter quarters on the flatlands near the lakeshore and follow the receding snowline to higher country. Summer birds would return, and the drum of the grouse would be heard throughout the land. Down in their wintering-grounds south of the border, the Lower Kootenay Indians—their population but a fragment of its former self after the 1862 plague of smallpox brought by Europeans—would feel the general awakening in *their* bones, too. They, like the animals, would respond to the ancient rhythms of rebirth by shaking off winter's lethargy and moving outward from confinement. Soon they would paddle northward onto the lake in their canoes, family by family, seeking out the hunting, fishing, and berry-picking locations allotted to each by tradition. Their activities, like those of the animals, would hardly ruffle the great flow of nature.

The coming summer would also bring other men, white men, as it had for a decade or two now. Kootenay Lake may not have been prominent in the minds of British Columbians, but the faster-growing population in American territories below the border still exerted a strong northward pressure: wagon roads had for a long time been replacing old prospector thoroughfares like the Walla Walla trail and bringing settlers in increasing numbers closer and closer to the Canadian border; the Northern Pacific Railroad—one of several pushing across the continent to connect eastern United States with its thriving cities on the west coast—had already passed through Missoula in Montana Territory, and two thousand Chinese labourers in the company's employ were laying steel at the north end of Pend d'Oreille Lake. Survey crews were busy along the last stretch to Sandpoint, where the rails would connect with others already carrying a heavy traffic up from Wallula in Washington Territory. And the Kootenay district of British Columbia had not been forgotten down there. Newspapers in Wallula and Portland extolled the mineral prospects north of the border. Each summer, parties came up the Kootenay River from Bonners Ferry or through the Salmon River valley from Colville for hunting and gold-panning. Because they had not yet made any big strikes, their incursions had remained gentle. Like their fellow creatures the Indians and the animals, they had not greatly disturbed the order of things.

But the year 1882 was a portentous one for West Kootenay country. Although the basking land had not yet received any sign that the coming summer would be an unusual one, a few of the Europeans who were going to initiate in earnest the destruction of its primeval serenity were already—unknown to each other—approaching the scene from widely different locations. Each of these men was bringing with himself the drives and ambitions that spring from the world view of a complex civilization. When they met on the West Kootenay stage in a month or so, they were going to enact a tale of money-lust, betrayal, revenge, flight, pursuit, capture, and punishment worthy of any opera.

William Adolph Baillie-Grohman was seated amidst a shipment of rails and live pigs on a flatcar (he called it an open truck) of the Northern Pacific Railroad. Over a month ago he had disembarked from a ship in New York harbour. Now, after four weeks of travel—not all that time with the pigs—he was nearing the farthermost western point that the rails had reached—a swamp at the northern end of a lake called Pend d'Oreille. Although aware of the incongruity of a man of his social position travelling with a load of hogs through the remote wilderness of western United States, he was not in the least unhappy. On the contrary, he was revelling in anticipation of the adventure ahead of him, all the while imagining the phrases with which he would describe the hogs for the pleasure of readers back in England when he wrote his next book.

Baillie-Grohman was still a young man, only thirty-one. He had been born in London, descended on his mother's side from Irish gentry, and heir on his father's to an estate in Austria. His paternal grandfather was a noted botanist, and his mother a cousin of the Duke of Wellington. That national hero, after defeating Napoleon at Waterloo, had lived to a very old age, visited by emperors and princes, followed by admiring crowds whenever he went riding in the park. His funeral, which had called forth the utmost pomp and splendour of Victorian England, had taken place when Baillie-Grohman was one and a half years old.

His destination only two or three hours away, B-G thought with satisfaction of the circumstances that had brought him here . . . the thrill of his first visit to the Rocky Mountains in the territories of Wyoming and Idaho . . . the trophies he had gathered to enlarge his collection of animal heads . . . the figure he cut back home as a romantic adventurer and big game hunter . . . his third book waiting to be published this year . . . already three visits to the wilds of America since his first one back in '78 . . . and now, in only a few hours he would be off this train and beginning his journey into the mountain wilderness of western Canada. Up there, he had been told, lived Indians called Kootenais or Flatbows, and part of their domain was a huge body of water, named after them Kootenay or Flatbow Lake. Around the northern end of this lake, rumour had it, lived a trophy that had so far eluded him in any respectable size—*haplocerus montanus,* the Rocky Mountain goat. Taking a deep, satisfied whiff of pig, B-G laid his head on a rail and closed his eyes. . . .

An hour or so later he was awakened by the stopping of the train. Rubbing the back of his head where it had been pressing against the rail, he sat up and looked around to find himself in the midst of a busy scene. Ahead of him the engine had stopped at a barrier set up at the end of the tracks. Beyond that, seemingly hundreds of Chinese coolies were at work carrying ties and rails, or loads of fill for a roadbed across the swampy ground. A few white men were directing the labour. To his right, several shacks were set amidst the debris of construction. To his left was the lake, where a small stern-wheeler bearing the name *Henry Villard* was nosed into the mud beside an improvised jetty. Removing his luggage from the flatcar, B-G approached the man who seemed to be directing the operation, and received the information that he could buy a ticket on the boat to a place called Sandpoint. The boat would be leaving in less than an hour.

A pleasant excursion along the northern shore of Pend d'Oreille Lake took B-G to Sandpoint. (Many of B-G's fellow passengers were indeed excursionists from Wallula, Portland, and other places on the western edge of the continent, making use of the new east-bound railroad whose terminus was Sandpoint to visit the wilderness of the interior.) Sandpoint was still only a very small community, but there was a hotel for B-G to spend the night in and a place to get his meals. He knew that to get to Kootenay Lake he must go through a place called Bonners Ferry. On inquiring where it was and how to get there, he was advised to catch the west-bound train next morning as far as Hang Town, only a few miles away. Hang Town had been a work camp when the railway was still being built, and many of the rough-and-ready workers still lived there. The old Walla Walla trail leading north to Bonners Ferry passed through it, and there B-G would easily find an Indian guide or two. The train would leave at 4:40 a.m.

According to B-G (who liked to thrill his English readers with the ruggedness of the life he was experiencing out west), Hang Town lived up to its name. The arrival of the monthly pay-train only the day before had turned, in his words, "the place with its two thousand navvies into a hell of lawless riot, with six-shooters going off all around one." Bristling with upper-class disapproval, he picked his way through this lively community—the last haunt of white men he was to see for several months—looking for guides and a horse or two. Horses were not available for either rent or purchase, but riotous Hang Town had many Indians of the Kalispel tribe hanging about in it and B-G had little difficulty in obtaining the services of two of these. He intended to get to Bonners Ferry as soon as possible and buy supplies there for the final leg of his voyage to Kootenay Lake. Late that morning the three set out— carefully groomed B-G and the two Kalispel men, "evil-looking" and "sultry" as he later described them.

The first part of their journey lay through heavily timbered country, recently burned over. It was not a difficult walk; a wide, flat corridor led them from Hang Town in a northeasterly direction to Bonners Ferry. Only occasionally they caught glimpses through the trees of distant mountains on either side. Well aware that he himself might often have to shoulder his gear, B-G had kept his outfit down to a minimum. Now, with two bearers, he carried almost nothing and was free to use his abundant energy for careful observation, for speculation regarding future literary ventures, and—most often perhaps—for indulgence in self-satisfied musing about the romantic adventure he was undertaking. At rest periods and especially during the preparations for the two nights they spent on the trail, he took pains to engage his companions in conversation so that he might pick up as much as possible of the "Chinook jargon" of this part of the Pacific slope, all without compromising his superior aloofness, of course, for he regarded the Kalispels as a decadent race, spoiled by contact with inferior whites.

Late in the afternoon of the third day they arrived at the tiny settlement of Bonners Ferry, situated where the north-flowing

23

Kootenay River moves temporarily in an east-west direction. We cannot do better than let B-G describe the scene himself as he remembered it many years later. The incisive and copious adjectives of his opening sentences clearly suggest the aesthetic appreciation he felt.

Paradise was no word to describe the contrast presented by the ravishing scene of sylvan beauty and peace that burst upon my eyes on reaching the Kootenay River. Under a huge cotton-wood on the edge of a vast meadow flanked by moderately high densely timbered hills, stood a small Indian encampment near which a few ponies were grazing, the waving masses of wild grass almost hiding them from view. A couple of teepees made of reed mats hung upon poles that converged at the top, leaving a small opening from which issued faint rings of smoke, occupied the foreground. On some trestles made of sticks near the river bank lay a couple of bark canoes of a shape I had never before seen, for both prow and stern tapered like a torpedo to sharp points, while their fine 'lines' assured speed. On some other trestles over a smouldering fire lay split salmon of goodly size, and near them some scantily garbed squaws were preparing buckskin by kneading deer skins with brain-matter. In the background one saw a great sweep of the majestic river glinting in the evening sun, the banks as far as one could see being overhung by the biggest cotton-woods I had ever seen. Our arrival, unusual as was the advent of a white man, created not the faintest trace of excitement; some stark naked, half-grown children and a barking dog or two were the only living things that as much as looked at us. The monotonous drone of voices inside the teepees revealed that also here the vice of gambling had its victims, and nothing short of a thunder-bolt in their midst would disturb the social calm of the redskins whilst thus engaged. Paying off the two Kalispels, who forthwith, uttering a grunt of satisfaction, disappeared into the teepees, it took me some time and the exhibition of a bright half-dollar to get one of the squaws to ferry me across the river to Fry's ranche in one of the canoes, which she deftly carried down the steep bank as were it of feather weight. The man I was in quest of was a half-breed named Dick Fry, so to speak the seigneur of his little world, which consisted of two or three log shanties, one of which was his store where he did his fur-trading with the Indians. A stream of naked brats of all sizes, whose swarthy skins betrayed no sign that they were quarter white, left no doubt that Dick was a squaw-man, while the fact that I discovered him playing poker with four Indians left little doubt that his reputation of being the poker player *par excellence* was lived up to by him, a very shiny, much handled, old-pattern Winchester lying on the table as the stake of the game.[1]

24

When B-G appeared at the door of the cabin, Dick Fry looked up from the game long enough to give him a welcome and then returned to the serious business of the table. Fortunately for B-G, who was impatient to talk to this man he had heard so much about, the game reached its inevitable conclusion in about half an hour. The Kalispels rose and silently trooped out. Giving B-G a wink and laughing heartily, Dick Fry stood the old-pattern Winchester in a corner and explained that he often had to win back goods and money that the Kalispels had won from the Kootenais.

"It's like stealing," he said. "They come up here from the Pend d'Oreille and rob my friends who can't play worth a damn for all the practice they get. And they never seem to learn! I spend a lot of time winning it all back. Gotta keep the cash in our own territory, ya know!"

B-G, in spite of his prejudice against "squaw-men," took an instant liking to his host, and Dick, whose brother Martin had been away for some weeks now on a packing trip, was pleased enough to see another white man. (B-G was wrong in his assessment of Dick as a half-blood. Small and lithe, his lean body dressed in Indian clothing, his hair worn like theirs, his habits no longer those of the typical white man—particularly of an upper-class Englishman—he was easily enough taken for the son of an Indian mother. Nevertheless, he was as white as B-G himself.) Since B-G wanted to leave next morning, they had only one evening together, but it was a very pleasant one, spent in talk of Kootenai country, hunting, Indians, and other subjects related to life in the wilderness. Dick promised to find two Kootenai guides for the trip to the lake, He said that he knew a fellow called Kan'kus'co whose traditional hunting territory was at the north end of the lake and included a high peak where goats were found in abundance. For one U.S. dollar per man a day Kan'Kus'co and his *clootchman* would guide and pack for B-G. At a late hour, having been fed and generally looked after by Dick's Indian wife Justine, they went to sleep. Rather than put up his tent (it was a very simple one—small and A-shaped), B-G bedded down on the floor of the cabin.

25

Next morning at breakfast B-G's journey was the subject of more discussion.

"Just go along with the Indians," advised Dick. "They know exactly where to go. It's their usual hunting ground, and they'd be going there in a few days anyway now that high water is coming. When you get to the lake they'll travel up the east side to the north end. Then after you've bagged your goat, they'll take you down the west side. They'll want to stop more than you want all the time, but don't forget you're paying them, so they have to do what you want."

"Too bad you won't be along," said B-G. "You must go up there quite a lot."

"Matter of fact, I *am* going up there in July," replied Dick. "Me and Justine are gonna do a bit a panning near the outlet sometime after Martin gets back to mind the post. Why'n't you meet us there? I'll tell the Indians where to find us."

"That would suit me very well," said B-G, pleased with the chance of being shown some of this wilderness by so famous a guide as Dick Fry.

After breakfast the two men got down to the business of B-G's supplies. The canoe, of course, came with the Indians, and they were already at work re-pitching it, Dick having talked with them long before B-G was even up. There would be lots of fish and game for the trip, not many berries yet, though. They finally decided on three fifty-pound sacks of flour and a little bacon and beans to vary the monotony of game on the six-week expedition.

While waiting for the Indians to appear, B-G made use of the time to write a few hasty letters to friends in England. As he explained his whereabouts—making his return address as romantic as possible—he pictured the thrill they would experience when they read this news from the colonial wilderness over their breakfast coffee. He gave the letters to Dick, who would include them in his next shipment to Walla Walla, due to go in about three weeks.

At last the two Indian men appeared, or one of them at least, a youngish fellow of handsome physique, his bristly, jet-black hair covered with the usual cone-shaped hat from which dangled many animal tails, his muscular chest adorned with the scars of a bear's claw. In one arm he carried his gun, cradled like a baby. Behind him, toting a canoe, came a much smaller female, no doubt his wife. Dick introduced the man as Kan'kus'co. As the diminutive woman carried the canoe down the steep bank to the water's edge, B-G turned to Dick. "Where's the other man?"

"What other man?" asked Dick, a strange smile on his lips.

"The *clootchman*. You said there'd be two men."

"There she is, Kan'kus'co's *clootchman*," replied Dick, pointing to the woman as she climbed the bank and went off to fetch the baggage. He laughed at B-G's discomfiture. "But don't worry! You'll see—she'll prove the better man of the two!"

Soon—it was still only a little past dawn—all three of them were seated in the canoe—B-G reclining in the middle, his back comfortably against the rolled-up tent, the woman at the front, and Kan'kus'co in the rear, where he could control the canoe's direction. The paddlers eased the canoe from the bank and out into the current. As it pulled them downstream B-G once again permitted himself to experience the "ravishing" and "sylvan" beauty of the scene. Turning back to give a final wave to Dick, he heard the trader call out, "See you in July!" In a moment they were carried round a bend in the river, and the wilderness engulfed them.

# CHAPTER 2

*In which we interrupt our narrative to hear the story of Richard Fry, a true man of the old American west. Readers impatient to follow B-G down the Kootenay River may turn at once to the next chapter and read this one later.*

IN THE YEAR 1849, Olney Fry[2], a man of New England descent, set out by ox-cart from Knox County in Illinois with his wife and eleven children ranging from infants to young adults. Like some Abraham moving his clan through hostile deserts to a land of promise, he led them in the company of other families on a migration across the plains of America and through the continental divide, until they came to rest in Oregon Territory not far from the Pacific Ocean. There they built a home and flourished. Of the four girls and seven boys who accompanied their parents on that perilous and hopeful journey, only two were brought by the accidents of fate into our story. They were Richard, who was eleven at the time of the journey, and Martin, who was six.

After the family had been settled in the Willamette Valley for six years, an Indian uprising occurred in the country around Walla Walla. Immediately the two oldest sons, Nathan and Alfred, wanted to go there for the excitement. Although still only seventeen, Dick begged to go along too, but his mother would not part with him. Looking at the small-framed, lean youth, his father thought differently. "Make a man of him," he argued. In the family discussion which followed, the male view prevailed. An officer in the military force that was being formed consented to take the lad with him as his private cook. So Dick got his way and left on the great adventure, not knowing that he would never again see his home except as an infrequent visitor.

Nathan was wounded during the fighting and returned home to convalesce; Alfred returned when the war was over; but Dick, his young soul drawn by some vague longing, decided to move farther northward through the wilderness. Having heard that many gold-seekers were panning successfully on the bars of the upper Columbia River near a place called Kettle Falls, he headed in that direction. Arriving there after a long journey, he found that there were indeed many prospectors at work on the bars and that more were arriving all the time. He also became aware of the resentment felt by the miners regarding the "bunch of furriners" at the near-by Hudson's Bay post called Fort Colville. (By the agreement of 1846, Hudson's Bay forts were continuing to operate in American territory even though the border was in place along the 49th Parallel.) This British company was raking in profits selling goods to American miners, goods brought up the Columbia from Fort Vancouver. In a precocious manifestation of that famous "Yankee know-how," young Dick decided he could do something about the situation. He opened a small trading post on the banks of the Columbia, near where the town of Marcus now stands, with the intention of bringing supplies by pack train from Fort Vancouver more cheaply than the Hudson's Bay Company was bringing them up the Columbia in *bateaux*. Soon, his trading post a success, he began to feel other yearnings.

Across the river there was an Indian village and in that village lived a man named Soqu'stik'en, better known to whites as Harry, the name he had received on his baptism into the Catholic Church. Soqu'stik'en had two daughters. Both were of marriageable age and one of them pleased the eye of young Dick. Her name was Justine, and in course of time she obligingly reciprocated and came to find the white man from across the river pleasurable to look upon. The two were married at St. Paul's Mission (which stands to this very day near the settlement of Kettle Falls). So Dick Fry found his beloved Justine, mother of his children and companion of his journeys throughout West Kootenay. She survived him by many years, but now they lie side by side in the cemetery at Bonners Ferry.

Large numbers of the gold-panners were migrating farther up the Columbia. Dick decided to move up to the mouth of the Pend d'Oreille and open a second post there. Accordingly, he wrote his brother Alfred a letter asking him to manage the first post while he and Justine went north to the new site, taking their small family with them. Soqu'stik'en visited them there.

One day, while Dick and Soqu'stik'en were panning in the river up at the second post, there was trouble for Alfred down at the first one. A group of Indians from the village across the river were making one of their usual visits to the post. A dog of theirs stole a slab of bacon from the camp of a miner, who immediately shot the offending animal. The Indians became angry and demanded payment. A hot exchange of words took place between them and the miners. Older tribe members finally persuaded the young braves to return home and wait to see if the miners would make payment. The miners, appreciating their vulnerability, decided that the trouble must be stopped before it became worse and hastily collected the sum demanded. Alfred Fry and another man were chosen to take the money across the river. As they were landing, a young brave—still too hot-headed to be entrusted by the elders with a Hudson's Bay rifle—killed Alfred with an arrow. While Alfred's companion fled back across the river, the village elders held a hasty conference, watched by the miners from the other bank. Soon a small party of braves was seen to embark in a couple of canoes and paddle upstream, while the remainder of the villagers, taking their dogs with them, disappeared into the teepees. To the watchers across the river the village suddenly appeared deserted; the body of Alfred Fry lay at the water's edge and a charged silence brooded over everything.

The miners came to two decisions: the embarking of the canoes upstream must mean that the Indians were intending to kill Dick Fry also, probably in the belief that he would seek revenge for his brother's death; and the disappearance of the villagers into their tents must be to give the miners time to retrieve Alfred's body. Accordingly, while a small party—armed but not showing their weapons—crossed the river to do that, another party was formed to hurry by land to the Pend d'Oreille to warn Dick. Meanwhile the miners at the post must stay together and remain armed until tensions eased, and the body of Alfred Fry must be buried.

The overland party failed to reach Dick in time to warn him. The Indians got there first. Leaving Justine and her baby untouched, they seized Dick and Monteur, a Frenchman who was his close friend. Only the presence of Soqu'stik'en prevented them from murdering their victims on the spot. Instead, they tied the two friends up and threw them into a tent to await execution.

Wily Soqu'stik'en, his mind frantically searching for a method of saving his son-in-law, began an extended parley with his fellow villagers, all men younger than himself, hot-headed braves but respectful of his position as an elder. Plea after plea failed and he became desperate. Addressing the leader of the group—a man not much younger than himself who he knew also had a favourite married daughter—he played his ace card.

"Very well. If it's murder you want, hear this. You kill my son-in-law and I'll kill yours!"

As he knew it would, this threat alarmed his fellow Indians and they began a conference among themselves. Making the most of his opportunity, he hurried over to his daughter and whispered instructions into her ear.

"I'll keep my friends arguing until well after nightfall. When it's dark, go to the tent and free the two men. Take them over the mountains to safety."

The parley resumed. As Soqu'stik'en and the other Indians continued the discussion—absorbed in their exploration of the interesting ramifications of Dick's proposed murder as only people who were not clock-watchers could be—it gradually became dark. No one noticed when Justine slipped away.

Finally the parley reached what clever Soqu'stik'en had foreseen would be its inevitable conclusion. His interest in talking at an end, the leader of the assassination party rose and announced that the two captives would be put to death immediately. The Indians trooped off toward the tent, followed by Soqu'stik'en, who was praying that his plan had worked and the tent would be empty. Angry shouts relieved his anxiety. Indians swarmed past him—they did not think to connect him with the escape—and rushed to the riverbank, bent on recapturing Dick, who they assumed had set out by canoe downstream. Watching their canoes disappear into the darkness of the swirling river, triumphant Soqu'stik'en smiled to himself.

And so it was that, on an evening in late April of the year 1861, Justine—carrying her baby on her back—guided her husband and his friend Monteur through darkness into the mountains, not daring to rest until they had put many miles between themselves and the post. There are no written records of where they went, but the oral tradition cites either the military post at Fort Colville or one of the Catholic missions.

By May 4th Richard had decided to travel down the Columbia as far as The Dalles. From there he could send a message to his parents informing them of the death of Alfred, and the long journey would give the Indians time to forget their anger. On their return he and Justine went back up to the trading post at the mouth of the Pend d'Oreille, stopping in the Fort Colville area only long enough to settle Alfred's affairs. They remained at the post for several years. The fact that it was in British territory was of little account. British Columbia was still only a Crown Colony and this part of it was a complete wilderness. Prospectors, hunters, or miners travelling to a strike crossed back and forth without concerning themselves with a border that was unattended and only recently marked.

We can surmise that during this period Dick and Justine made many expeditions north of the border. A glance at the map will reveal how close they were to Kootenay Lake. They had two easy routes to the lake from the post: up the Columbia by canoe past the mouth of the Kootenay River (which in those days ran through a gorge close to its mouth), then a lengthy portage along a well-established Indian trail up the valley of present-day Pass Creek and down into the valley of the Slocan River, then along that to its junction with the Kootenay, and finally along that river, past its rapids and waterfalls, to the west arm of Kootenay Lake; or eastward on foot along the canyon of the Pend d'Oreille to the mouth of the Salmon River, then a gentle walk northward along the valley of that lovely river to the swamps at its source, followed by a climb over the slightest of rises to a creek that would lead them down to Kootenay Lake at the outlet of its west arm (the future site of Nelson, in fact).

When Edgar Dewdney was at Fort Shepherd in 1864 searching for the best route for continuing his trail to Wildhorse Creek, he made an exploratory side trip onto Kootenay Lake. There, to his utter amazement, he came across "a white man firing at a mark with several little naked Indian boys." The man took him to some warm springs (later called Ainsworth). The man was Dick Fry.

Later that same year Dick and a man called Adam Boyd were commissioned by businessmen of the Colville area to explore the upper Columbia River to its source by canoe. The businessmen wanted to know if that was a feasible route for getting supplies to the recently discovered gold fields at Wildhorse Creek in the East Kootenay.

After reaching the lake that is the source of the Columbia, the two men carried their canoe eastward for a distance of under two miles over a very flat area of land until they came to the Kootenay River, with the intention of paddling down it to the mouth of Wildhorse Creek. They had no way of knowing it, but this was the very portage David Thompson had made back in 1808 on his first trip west of the Rockies, when, after erecting Kootenai House, he and his party had decided to explore southward. Like Dick Fry and Adam Boyd, Thompson had also paddled down the Kootenay River, although he called it McGillivray. And this same portage will again become a part of our story in 1883 when our friend Baillie-Grohman lays eyes on it.

After the two friends made their report to the Colville businessmen, Dick returned to Justine at the Pend d'Oreille post. But he was no longer content to remain there; the jaunt to East Kootenay country with Adam Boyd had sparked a desire for change. The summer of '67 saw him—accompanied by Justine and the family—at Forty-Nine Creek on the Kootenay River just a few miles below the outlet of the lake. The family spent that summer and the two following ones— in fact most of the duration of that short-lived gold rush—sluicing in Forty-Nine Creek.

---

LETTER TO J. FRED HUME FROM RICHARD FRY [3]
Dec. 2, 1893

Dear Sir:
    Yours of the 18th at hand and contents noted. I with several others worked on 49 Creek in 1867-8-9. We made from $6 to $12 per day. We worked with sluice and rockers, the old-fashioned way. Wages were $4 to $5 per day. Most of our mining was done on the creek where your company has located. The gold was coarse and some good crevices were found. I knew two men to make $1900. each in six weeks. I cleared $2500. the first summer. The Discovery Boys did their own work and cleared about $800. each. Flour was worth $25. per cwt., and everything in proportion. The largest nugget we found weighed $20; many others were from $2.50 to $12 and $18. We sold our dust for $18/oz. I am convinced if said ground is worked in a scientific manner that you have a good thing.

Yours very truly,

Richard Fry,
Bonner' Ferry, Idaho

---

During the first summer of their sojourn there, Dick and Justine had the opportunity of attending a gathering that, dear as it was to the heart of Justine, they had never been able to attend before. Every summer—every Indian summer, to be exact—the Colville (Lakes) tribes would ascend the Kootenay River into the country of their cousins the Lower Kootenay Indians, by portaging across the falls and rapids which formed the natural boundary between their respective territories. At some point near the lower end of the lake the cousin nations would meet for fishing, hunting, berrying, and visiting. The occasion was really a party that lasted for many days of feasting, courting, and gambling. Occasionally white men—there were usually a few camping at Warm Springs or Big Ledge up on the main lake even in those early days—would venture down the west arm of the lake and appear on the scene as uninvited guests.

This year, the site of the gathering was a sharp point of sand on the north side of the west arm, just at the outlet where the arm's smooth water assumed the roughness of the shallow river. Here, on the white sand at the water's edge and on the flats in the woods of the hillside, the tribes gathered and set up their camps. To Dick and Justine, living only a short distance up Forty-Nine Creek, the celebrations seemed hardly more than a stone's throw away. Dick agreed to attend, although he was aware that the villagers who had attempted to murder him a few years ago would probably be there. He reasoned that there was no danger now that a fair amount of time had passed by, and since he himself felt no desire for vengeance over the murder of his brother, he and Justine should attend and enjoy themselves. He was right. The pair were welcomed, and the Indians decided to complement their Christian wedding with the rituals and joy of an Indian one. When the gathering of the two nations broke up, the newlyweds returned to Forty-Nine Creek feeling as if they were beginning a second honeymoon.

After work there was over they left the post at the mouth of the Pend d'Oreille for good and moved over to Kootenai country where Dick began packing along the Walla Walla trail. As a packer Dick came to know the man called Ed Bonner who, soon after the strike on Wildhorse, had decided that the easiest way to make money was to build a ferry at the place where the trail crossed the Kootenai and charge the miners a toll. He made his fortune quickly, for the miners, a carefree lot, paid in gold dust and weren't too concerned about the amount. Sometime in the middle seventies, Bonner decided he was rich enough to make use of his money elsewhere, and Dick bought him out.

And that was how young Dick Fry and his Indian wife Justine found their home. There they raised their children, maintained the ferry and a trading post, established a pack-train business along the Walla Walla trail, carried furs and gold to the British Columbia coast along the Dewdney Trail, and in general established the first American business of the upper Columbia region. (It was said

35

of Dick at his death in that region many years later that "the first chapter in the history of the Kootenai Valley was the story of Richard Fry.") And today, if you go to Bonners Ferry you can visit a remote hillside cemetery and stand at their graves under the big trees there. All graveyards evoke the past, but in this one especially, the visitor seems to disturb the quiet of a former age. Standing there, looking at the panoramic view through the trees of that hilltop, you can spend a poignant moment wondering what it would have been like to be Richard Fry, a man of New England descent brought across the plains of America by ox-cart as a boy, who from his earliest adult life chose to live intimately with Indians in the wilderness in a way we can only with effort imagine.

Always the practical business man, Dick decided he needed to open another trading post just north of the border. By doing that he would have a base in Canada and avoid customs regulations regarding the furs he periodically packed to the coast. Accordingly, in 1876 his young brother Martin received a letter asking him to come to Bonners Ferry to take charge of the post. Martin, on reaching adulthood, had at first led a wandering life rather like his brother's, at one period working for wages at a new placer camp up in British territory where Rock Creek enters the Kettle River. Soon, however, he had returned south to the area around the mouth of the Columbia. Here, in territory that was fast becoming more and more settled, he married and became a schoolteacher. When Dick's letter reached him he was living on the coast, teaching school in the winter and carrying on a business in oysters during the summer. He decided to visit Dick and return for his family if he chose to stay. To reach Bonners Ferry he undertook a complex journey. A small tugboat took him to Astoria; there he boarded the first of several steamers which took him up the Columbia to Wallula, where he disembarked and took a twenty-nine-mile journey by narrow gauge (his first railway journey) to Walla Walla. Martin, who was uncertain where Bonners Ferry was or even how far he would have to travel to get there, now found himself short of money. He decided to walk the rest of the way and ration himself to one meal a day. After walking four days (about 120 miles) along the old Walla Walla trail—it was now a wagon road and Martin could have gone by stagecoach had he had the money—he fortunately fell in with one of his brother's pack trains, and by a stroke of even greater luck Dick was leading it himself. The remainder of the journey to Bonners Ferry was easier. As his visit there continued, Martin began to learn the Indian language and gradually came to feel at home.

Next spring, the brothers and a small party with ten horses took a load of furs along the Dewdney Trail to New Westminster. Leaving the pack train there, Dick and Martin crossed by boat to Victoria, where the furs were auctioned off. Dick bought supplies for the trading post at Bonners Ferry and returned with them to New Westminster to be loaded on the pack train for the journey home. Martin meanwhile went by steamer to Astoria, then by tug to his family. After settling their affairs as quickly as possible, he prepared for the journey with them into the northern wilderness. They retraced the route he himself had followed as far as Walla Walla, where by prearrangement they met another of Dick's pack trains. Travelling with them was their two-year-old son named Freddy Lee. Many years later, up in Canada, one of the West Kootenay district's most famous mines would be named after him.

And that is how the brothers and their families began their communal life in the little trading post at Bonners Ferry. Besides their usual business enterprises Dick and Martin took to guiding occasional visitors throughout the area. More than once they took big game hunters up to the mountains around Kootenay Lake or over into East Kootenay country. Martin and his wife undertook the education of the small population of Indian, half-blood, and white children. This was the idyllic community that William Adolph Baillie-Grohman came upon that evening in the springtime of the year 1882.

# CHAPTER 3

*In which Baillie-Grohman is taken by his Indian
guides to the north end of Kootenay Lake on a hunt for
the elusive* haplocerus montanus.[4]

STRETCHED OUT IN THE CANOE, his paid servants already settling into the rhythm of their paddling, B-G was thinking with pleasure of his romantic situation: the educated and successful Englishman being led into the unknown wilderness by a half-naked savage and his squaw.[5] They moved gently through the fresh spring day, over the brimming river hedged by newly leaved trees and bathed in deliciously cool air. Some other kind of man lying there might have thought differently about his companions, might have been moved by their mystery to wonder what their thoughts were, might have wanted to reach beyond their differentness to understand them as fellow human beings. But B-G was constituted in a different manner. He chose to acknowledge their humanity only so far as a literary cliche would take him. He named them Darby & Joan, thinking by that allusion to provide an adequate and amusing image for his readers back home.

They certainly couldn't have chosen a better time of the year to take a canoe trip down this lovely river, which serpentined in huge loops through table-flat country, its deep channel fringed with cottonwoods, willows, and other deciduous trees. B-G called it "bankful," and indeed the channel, almost empty in winter, was filled nearly to its top as the annual spring run-off rapidly increased in volume. B-G noted that the water level had risen even in the short time he had been at Bonners Ferry. Now, as they paddled along near the shore (the current was not strong because the river was falling very little over its almost level course, and the overflowing lake still many miles ahead of them was exerting a backward push), he could look over the top of the bank and see, beyond the fringe of trees, the luxuriant grasses already well grown, their coarse texture indicating that they were the varieties that live on flood plains. He surmised that in a short time the river would rise above its banks and flood over the whole valley.

Darby & Joan paddled a regular stroke for five hours until, at noon, they pulled up onto the shore at an inviting spot and made lunch. Five or six hours of paddling later, at the end of their first day, they set up camp and spent, as B-G afterward described for his English readers, "a memorably uncomfortable night on the banks of the river, where, in spite of 'smudges' and netting, one was simply eaten up by mosquitoes, which filled the air in masses the like of which I have never seen in any part of the world." A second day very much like the first brought the travellers in sight of the border by mid-afternoon. They could see the swathe cut on the nearby mountains by the British/U.S. Joint Boundary Commission in 1861. Shortly before crossing, however, they came to a dwelling on the river bank that Dick Fry had warned B-G to expect. It was a place called Ockanook, once the site of the Hudson Bay Company's Fort Flatbow until that fort had been moved farther north. The big company trading post of hand-axed logs was still there, its unglazed windows nailed up with rough-hewn boards; nearby was a much smaller log cabin, its one window covered with oiled paper. A few yards north of the trading post there was a large pyramid of stones which B-G surmised had been put there by the Border Commission in '61 to mark the 49th Parallel. Smoke issuing from the stone chimney at the back of the cabin indicated to B-G that it must be the home of the man Dick had told him about—a half-blood named David McLoughlin, son of the famous Dr. McLoughlin who had once been in command of the Hudson's Bay forts on the Pacific slope. In his own account of this journey, B-G does not mention stopping at Ockanook, nor does he mention David McLoughlin by name. He speaks only of seeing a log dwelling "owned by a man with a large Indian family." After leaving Ockanook, B-G and his Indian companions spent a second night on the bank of the now overflowing river. In B-G's own words, this night was "if possible worse" than the first had been.

In spite of the discomforts, B-G was becoming very interested in the landscape they were travelling through. He was impressed by the perfect flatness of the plain and by the richness of the soil, which he sampled during the hours they were ashore. He noted that some of the grasses were as high as a man or higher, and he observed the rings around the trunks of the cottonwoods, which indicated the level to which the flood waters had risen last year. They were the height of a man above the ground. What magnificent farming land this huge area would make, he thought to himself, if only it weren't covered by six feet of water at a crucial time of the year. Perhaps B-G had in him a streak of upper-class paternalism that made him want to do something for less fortunate sectors of society; or perhaps he felt a secret discomfort that big game hunting, though an interesting pursuit in the eyes of the reading public, did not make him worthy of respect in the minds of people of real accomplishment like his relative the Duke of Wellington; whatever the reason, the idea suddenly struck him that if he could think of some way of preventing the annual flooding of that land, it could then be used for settling the thousands of veterans that Britain's wars continually produced, and the empire would be forever grateful to him. It was an idle thought, and B-G soon turned to the contemplation of his next book.

A third day of travel brought them near Kootenay Lake, and after lunch they left the river bed and struck out in a northeasterly direction across the flooded plains. Well before evening, by means of this shortcut they reached the east side of the lake, a magnificent body of water about four miles across, with splendid peaks and ridges rising from its western edge. They continued to paddle northward to put as much distance as possible between themselves and the mosquito-laden swamps they had just left. That night they slept on a pebbled beach several miles north of the river's mouth. B-G noticed that on a nearby rock cliff the high-water mark was twenty feet above the lake's present surface.

They awoke in the first light of dawn to find another cloudless day of early June. Across the still lake the snow on peaks and ridges was red in the first rays of the sun. Long before its warmth reached down to them, they had travelled many miles along the eastern shoreline. Darby & Joan's knowledge of local geography kept them from wasting time by turning into the big inlet now called Crawford Bay. In what seems to us an unbelievable feat of paddling, they reached the northern end of the lake late that evening. Along the way, B-G trolled and caught "a goodly stock of fish—splendid landlocked salmon." About halfway to their destination they came to a rocky promontory with a steep bare face toward the water. It was streaked with large brown stains. Darby paused long enough to point it out to B-G and then touched with his paddle the Express cartridges in B-G's belt. Interpreting

## Kootenay Lake at the Outlet to West Arm

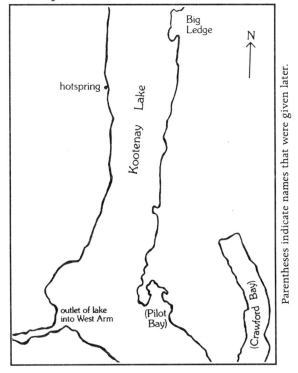

this sign language correctly, B-G concluded that lead was found there. Although B-G didn't know it, they were passing Big Ledge, a place even in those early days famous among the few prospectors who occasionally came into the region. It had been discovered many years earlier by Hudson's Bay Company explorers, who had taught the Indians how to extract lead from the rocks found there. And another thing B-G didn't know was that before a year had passed he himself would be involved in events that would make this place notorious all over America. Happily unaware of the future, he fished on, while the paddlers tirelessly pursued their course to the head of the lake.

The great peaks along the eastern shore became even more imposing as the travellers moved northward. On the far shore the mountains were lower, only occasionally a white peak showing in the distance, until, about mid-afternoon, they saw over there a large valley leading westward, and emerging from it the delta of a good-sized creek. From there on, the lake narrowed a little and became crowded with peaks on both sides.

On and on they went. The white peaks radiant in sunshine, the high crags shiny with melted snow, the rampant forests, and the great cliffs falling into the lake gave B-G the feeling that he was indeed plunging into the heart of some romantic dream. Well toward the onset of darkness Darby pointed to the largest peak of all those on the eastern shore and nodded his head, by which signs B-G understood that it was the mountain they would be climbing in search of *haplocerus montanus*. His excitement grew. A mile or so farther on, they found a sandy beach from which they could see where the lake ended in swamps and sandbars, and where a wide valley, dank with cedars and cottonwoods, ran into the mountains beyond. They made a hasty camp and retired to bed, for, if possible, the mosquitoes here were even more fearsome than those at the other end of the lake had been.

The hunters must have been very eager to encounter their prey. Next morning, their fifth day out from Bonners Ferry, they were up before dawn (perhaps the mosquitoes helped rouse them) and canoeing back to the base of the mountain that Darby had pointed out. Once there, they stowed the canoe and their gear in a safe place, taking as their first load whatever they would need for making camp up at the tree line.

At dawn they were ready to begin their climb: dapper B-G, encumbered by the clothes of a European, carrying his tiny "A" tent, his sleeping bag, and his rifle; "shock-headed" Darby, dressed—if we are to believe B-G—only in breechclout, moccasins, and a string of beads (his hat had been left at Bonners Ferry), carrying a very large pack on his back and his rifle in his hand; Joan, "slim and diminutive" in her moccasins and single garment made of the coarse sacking that Dick Fry imported from Walla Walla, carrying an immense load that appeared to be heavier than the seven stone (ninety-eight pounds) estimated by B-G as her own weight. After a mile or two through tangled brush and forest, which caused some feelings of despair in B-G, they came to a faint trail at the point where the mountain became steeper. Many hours later, having climbed just under 4,000 feet, according to B-G, they reached the timber line with barely enough time to set up camp before dark.

Next morning, the weather still favouring them, they again rose early. While the *clootchman* ("indefatigable Joan," B-G called her) returned to the lake for a second load, the two men, the cultural abyss which separated them now happily bridged by their mutual eagerness for the kill, set off to find *haploceri* farther up among the crags. After several hours of enjoyable exploration and searching, "the sharp-eyed 'Darby,' who of course knew exactly where to look, had soon spotted a band lying motionless like blocks of stone on a patch of green grass at the bottom of a couloir filled with snow about three-quarters of a mile off." The men separated and B-G lost sight of the prey as he crept up toward a ridge. When next he saw them they had moved much closer and were well within range. In spite of the bond of blood-lust that had formed between the two men, rational communication was still minimal. B-G had just decided that the group of animals did not contain a buck worthy of being shot, when Darby, thinking that the aim of the foray was to bag as many as possible, opened fire and shot four of them before they could make up their minds to run away. Caught up in the excitement of the kill in spite of himself, B-G aimed at the biggest buck and brought it down. Then, making an extraordinary effort at communication, he brought Darby to an understanding that what he really wanted was to bag only the biggest old males. Gathering what meat they could carry, the hunters began the homeward descent.

Meanwhile, indefatigable Joan had spent these hours returning to the lake, loading the remaining gear onto her back, and carrying it up to their camp. Unhampered by the retarding presence of B-G, she made much better time than the three of them had been able to make yesterday, and was able to reach camp before the men returned. It is the fervent hope of this historian that she got back to camp in time to take a long nap and thereby supply the furnaces of her indefatigability with the refueling they must so badly have needed. It is a hope so fervently held, in fact, that this historian, making use of the powers invested in him, is prepared to state that she *did* return in time and *did* take a long nap, and that, furthermore, the returning hunters made so much noise as they approached camp that she had time to awaken and allow them to find her indefatigably at work in her outdoor kitchen.

A couple of days later, luck favoured B-G and he "bagged what proved to be one of the largest Haplocerus I have ever killed, a fine old buck who weighed quite 180 lbs." He and his two guides remained at the head of Kootenay Lake for six weeks, he tells us, but without revealing what they did. We can imagine, however, that they hunted, fished, and explored that marvelously beautiful region, and experienced fully the mosquitoes that inhabited its swamps then and still do. We will leave them there for a time, while we direct our attention to two other groups of men who, unknown to each other and to B-G, had also chosen to disturb the primeval silence of Kootenay Lake in that spring of 1882.

# CHAPTER 4

*In which, after accompanying two prospectors, Robert Sproule and Gay Reeder, as they also journey to Kootenay Lake in that fateful spring of '82, we observe one John C. Ainsworth portentously at thought in Oakland, California.[6]*

MUCH OF B-G'S PLEASURE in his hunting expedition came from the idea that—barring Dick Fry, who was, after all, more than a hundred miles away—in all this vast and remote wilderness he was the only white man. It was just as well, then, on the day he was bagging his 180-pound goat, that he couldn't see back to the river he and Darby & Joan had canoed down less than a week previously. There, about half a day away from the lake, was a roughly made rowboat, and in it were two men, taking it easy as the current pulled them steadily northward. One of them, a man called Sproule, was leading his companion to Big Ledge, with the intention of restaking some claims he had made there the previous autumn and also finding some new ones in the name of his friend. As the two of them sat in the dappled sunshine of the river, Sproule was happily unaware that the train of events he was starting would lead to his violent death and make him one of the immortals of Kootenay Lake folklore.

Robert Evan Sproule had come originally from Weeks Mills, Maine. While still a young man, he went west to the mining camps, and was in Washington Territory during the 1870s, when a railway that would eventually connect with the Northern Pacific—the one we have already seen Baillie-Grohman and the pigs

45

on in '82—was under construction. Robert Sproule was one of two rival parties who laid claim to the discovery of coalfields that were needed by the railway. A prominent member of the opposing party accused Sproule of arson. In the subsequent trial, Sproule was cleared of the charge but left the territory. In the summer of 1880, he was working in Fort Colville. After wintering there, he went to Bonners Ferry and was hired by Dick Fry to assist in the building of a new barge for the ferry service. Both Dick and Martin Fry became friendly with the new workman. In one of their many conversations, Dick, who was interested only in gold at the time, told Sproule about the rich galena float he had picked up at Big Ledge on Kootenay Lake. In the late fall of '81, when the barge was completed, Sproule decided to see Big Ledge for himself. Dick lent him a rowboat and drew him a rough map; then, all by himself, Sproule set out on the long journey into the wilderness, knowing that even the Indians had left the lake and were back in their winter quarters near Bonners Ferry. At the Ledge, he staked three claims—uselessly, because the mining laws of the time required a prospector to record his claim within three days, and to get to the nearest recording office he would have to go back to Bonners Ferry and walk along the Walla Walla trail to Wildhorse Creek, a journey of about a week.

With winter in the offing, the return to Bonners Ferry from Big Ledge must have been cold and very lonely, especially the last ninety miles rowing upstream against the current, sluggish though it was at any time of the year. At this season the water level in the river would be at its lowest and the banks would rise steeply for twelve feet or more, isolating the solitary traveller from a view of the landscape beyond. Sproule encountered a snowstorm and arrived back at the post wet and sick. After regaining his health and spending at least part of the winter with the Frys, he travelled in the spring of 1882 down the trail to the Northern Pacific railhead, Sandpoint. There he hoped to meet up with Jacob Meyers, a friend with whose family he had lived a couple of winters ago when he was in Fort Colville. Perhaps, he thought, Meyers could be persuaded to accompany him back to Big Ledge.

46

Meyers was not to be found anywhere in Sandpoint, but one day Sproule got into conversation with a fellow standing next to him at the bar in the hotel. In reply to one of the usual questions with which strangers break the ice between them, Sproule admitted that he was headed north to Canada. "Hm," said the stranger, "I been thinkin' a takin' a trip up that way m'self." As the talk continued, the two men, taking a liking to each other, formally introduced themselves and carried their drinks to a table that had just been vacated. Gay Reeder, for that was the stranger's name, soon got Sproule to confide that he was a prospector and had already staked a claim on Kootenay Lake. "Not up't Big Ledge, I s'ppose?" asked Reeder, smiling broadly.

"You know about Big Ledge?" exclaimed Sproule. Hearing this chance acquaintance use that name as if it were common knowledge gave him a moment of extreme anxiety for the safety of his claims.

"Oh, I've heard rumours about't—only once, but the old guy doin' the talkin' sure seemed t'think't was somethin' good. But ya know what rumours are, there's always some fabulous strike that nobody ever can find."

"Yeah, there always is," said Sproule noncommittally. He was not yet eager to confide in his new friend. "And it's always funny how the guy who finds it never develops it himself. Always just talks about it."

"Well, ya know, ya can't develop a hard-rock claim w'thout some way a gettin' ore out and equipment in. There's gotta be steam—rails er stern-wheelers. Ya may not need that for gold, not mosta the time anyhow, but Big Ledge isn't gold, I hear. It's galena." Reeder watched Sproule narrowly. He was sure his guess had hit home. Sproule's claim *was* at Big Ledge, and the rumours he had heard were confirmed. He sensed Sproule's tension—the guardedness that was keeping him silent. He decided to jolt Sproule into confiding in him. "How 'bout *yer* claim?" He smiled more broadly than ever. "Has Big Ledge got steam to it?"

Sproule looked at the smiling face across the table, warmed to the mischief in the friendly eyes. "No, it hasn't, as you and I well know." He felt himself giving in to Reeder's demand for confidence. "But it will have soon, and I'm damned sure you've been thinking about that every bit as hard as I have!"

Reeder laughed. "Well, I can't deny that. Ever since I heard that rumour I been hankerin' t'get up there. All I've needed's a partner. Now that the railway's come t'Sandpoint, it's only thirty miles er so t'Bonners Ferry and easy goin' the resta the way by water. Seems like now's the time t'stake a few claims on Kootenay Lake."

"You're right," answered Sproule. "They'll build a spur line up to Bonners before too long, and it would be crazy to wait till it's built before getting up there. Now's the time, before every Tom, Dick, and Harry gets the idea. That's why I went up there last year and that's why I'm here now—looking for a guy I know to go back with me. Well, he's not here, so what d'you say you and I go."

"Sounds good t'me," answered Reeder, and the two men shook on it.

They left Sandpoint only a few days after B-G did, and may indeed have been there at the same time as he. In any case, they did not meet him there; nor, when they arrived at Bonners Ferry en route to the Ledge, did Dick Fry—whose experience had taught him that most of the people who passed through his trading post preferred that their journeys remain undiscussed—see fit to mention that anyone had gone north recently.

When the two men at last came out onto the lake, their hard work began, for the rowboat they now had to propel without benefit of current was really only a clumsy scow, thrown together at Bonners Ferry from whipsawed planks. They made their way up the east shore, taking turns at rowing and admonished to put forth their utmost effort by Robert Sproule, who was afraid someone else might get to the Ledge first, since the mining season had opened on June 1st and his claims of last autumn might be legally jumped in his absence. Their progress was much slower than B-G's had been over the same route a few days ago, propelled by the skilled paddling of Darby & Joan in their light craft. However, after one night of camping on a beach, they reached Big Ledge late the next evening. Nosing to shore in a small cove, they found, much to their concern, evidence of a very recent camp. It was obvious that whoever had been there was no longer around, and Robert Sproule hurried to find his stakes of last autumn. They had not been touched, but the fact that someone else must have seen them was a worry.

Next morning, after a breakfast of bannock and fish, the two men set about staking their claims, first locating the pieces of float that were lying around and then using the skills of the prospector to determine where the vein ran from which the float had broken loose. A few hours and the work was done—the pacing of the prescribed areas and the pounding of stakes. Sproule staked the *Bluebell* and Reeder the *Mogul*, contiguous with *Bluebell* on the south side. After lunch, the two decided to explore the area around the claims. During their wandering they discovered the remains of camps much older than the recent one they had seen on their arrival. Sproule concluded that this site must have been visited by other white men many times; in fact, there was evidence of other claims, very old and obviously undeveloped. He felt less concerned about the recent camp: since there were no new claimposts in the area, the recent campsite must only signify that some traveller had passed by, perhaps not even prospecting. Reeder, who had been thinking along the same lines, suddenly said, "It's kinda sad, all these old claims not bein' developed. Those guys were too early, ahead a the times. They didn't have a hope a gettin' ore outa this god-forsaken place. I wonder how many of 'em even bothered recordin' their strikes?"

"Not many, I'd guess," answered Sproule. "The mining laws being what they are, they couldn't even get to the recorder in time. After all, the nearest recording office is over at Wildhorse Creek and that's a lot more than three days away from here, more than a week at least."

"Yeah. Well, this looks like a rich strike t'me, but after a couple a days on the trail, if there wasn't much hope a developin' it I guess they'd just lose interest, not even bother t'make the trip t'Wildhorse. Too bad . . . but good fer us. We've struck our claims at just the right time, if you're right about that spurline."

"Yes, we have." Sproule was looking thoughtful. "If our hunch is right we're sitting pretty that way, but basically we've still got the same problem they had, and . . . "

"Ya mean gettin' t'Wildhorse," broke in Reeder.

"Yes. How are we going to get to Wildhorse Creek in time to file our claims within the three days limit?"

"Wildhorse Creek," echoed Reeder. "How we gonna get around that one?"

"Well, I don't know, but we're *going* to get around it. And until we figure out a way we're going to sit right here and renew the date on our claim posts every three days! And I'm going to sit here till the end of open season if I have to, because no lousy stinking claim jumper's going to jump this man's claim! Damned stupid law that says some bloody robber can come along and restake your claim just because you leave it for more'n seventy-two hours!"

The two men continued their walk in silence. Reeder was surprised at the way Sproule's voice had risen in anger during his last speech. It was the first time he had seen his partner in such a state. And Sproule himself was surprised at the anger he had heard in his own voice. Where had it come from? Searching for reasons, he suddenly realized he had been carrying it around ever since losing his chance at the coalfields he had been robbed of back in the States. He had pretended he didn't care, but now he saw that his loss was still rankling. Well, he wouldn't lose this one!

Back in camp at suppertime, the two men were in a better mood. Evening always brings with it the need for companionship and pleasant talk. It is the time of day when the human spirit seeks the contentment afforded by a quiet meal with one or more friends. Their own quiet meal over, Sproule and Reeder remained seated at the campfire, contentedly prolonging the lovely ritual of drinking many cups of tea and filling their pipes when they needed them. All their doubts of the afternoon were forgotten and each of them felt at ease with himself and with the other. Gradually, as the beauty of the summer evening worked its way upon them, they fell silent, each thinking his own thoughts and gazing across the great expanse of Kootenay Lake to where the sun was setting behind dark mountains.

"When d'ya think they'll build the spur from Sandpoint t'Bonners Ferry?" Reeder's question broke the silence so quietly it sounded as if his thought had somehow become audible on its own. "Maybe it'll be a few years before . . ."

"Maybe it'll be a few months!" interrupted Sproule. "I tell you, Gay, the word's out about this country. Down south the papers are full of talk about Kootenay. I wouldn't be even a little bit surprised if right now—in fact, I'll bet my bottom dollar on it that right now there's some railroad bigshot somewhere eyeing that forty-mile stretch between Bonners Ferry and Sandpoint and thinking that it would be a good idea to put a spur line there from the Northern Pacific."

Away down in Oakland, California, one John C. Ainsworth, financier and entrepreneur, banker, dealer in real estate, mining developer, and promoter of railways, was seated at his desk thinking. From his youngest days John C. had been set on becoming one of those clever business men who rule their own financial empires. Born in Ohio in 1822, he had gone to work early in life on the Mississippi steamboats, and by the age of twenty-five had achieved the position of master. Then, hearing of gold discoveries in California, he went there, not with the romantic idea of gold-panning, but with the hard-headed aim of getting rich in the steamboat service. During the gold rush on the Fraser River in the late '50s, when governor James Douglas was so hard pressed to prevent hordes of American prospectors and businessmen from taking over the Crown Colony of British Columbia, Ainsworth had taken his own steamer up to the Fraser and done a thriving business on that British river. By 1860, he was a leading figure in the formation of the Oregon Steam Navigation Company, which made its directors rich men. With the unerring insight of the born entrepreneur, he sensed the coming railways would make steamboats obsolete and sold out to the Oregon Railway and Navigation Company, an affiliate of the Northern Pacific Railway Company. Then, moving to Oakland, he began to play the game of high finance. Using all the methods of communication his time provided, he kept his eye on every business opportunity in his domain. One of his first involvements was the promotion of the railway from Wallula to Sandpoint for the Northern Pacific Company. Now, seated in his office thinking, he contemplated the rumours he had heard of riches in the Kootenay area of British Columbia; he contemplated the proximity of Sandpoint to Bonners Ferry and of Bonners Ferry to Kootenay Lake; he became aware that the time was ripe for a spur line from Sandpoint to Bonners Ferry and that if he didn't promote it someone else would.

But John C. Ainsworth hadn't got where he was by making unprepared decisions. He didn't mistake hastiness for boldness. Think it all out first and then act aggressively, that was his motto. There weren't many maps of the northwest lying around in those days, but he didn't need one. Staring blindly at the wall behind his desk, he began tracing routes on an inner map of his own construction. In his mind's eye he moved from Sandpoint, which he knew, slowly up to a place called Bonners Ferry, which he didn't know, and from there up to the place called Big Ledge on unknown Kootenay Lake in the province of British Columbia. Moving westward in that alien territory, he saw the Columbia River carrying steamers from the United States northward into the Big Bend country; and farther west, the Fraser on which he himself had navigated in his neophyte days, back in the times when British Columbia was still a Crown Colony under Governor James Douglas. And now, alongside that river and farther east, to Fort Kamloops—indeed by now far beyond that—workers laying rails that would meet those coming from the east. And southward, along the border, a tenuous line, the disused Dewdney Trail, which, he remembered, had given the British Columbia government so much frustration when it failed to draw commerce westward to New Westminster instead of southward to the States. A big smile slowly widened across John C.'s face. An idea had come to him, an idea that would bring him much more than a mere spur line from Sandpoint to Bonners Ferry would. He must act fast, though. But first, it was necessary to find out just how rich that new Kootenay country was. John C. Ainsworth came to a decision: it was time to send some of the boys up there on a reconnoitering trip.

Next morning Sproule and Reeder decided to set up separate camps, each on his own claim but in sight of the other. They spent the day preparing their camps and puttering about their respective locations. That evening, a few families of Kootenai Indians who were summering across the lake at a hot spring observed two fires on the far shore where there had been only one the night before. Sproule and Reeder likewise noticed *their* fires and speculated as to who might have lighted them. Resigned to a long wait guarding their claims, perhaps until October 31st when the close of the season would release them from the fear of being jumped, the two men took to their beds as soon as darkness fell.

# CHAPTER 5

*Being an account of further arrivals at the lake.*

JUNE CAME TO AN END, cool and wet in its last week, and the long, hot days of July began to pass slowly by. Somewhere at the north end of the lake, B-G and Darby & Joan, unaware that two other white men were only a few miles away at Big Ledge, continued their exploration and their fishing and hunting. Their supply of bacon and beans was long gone, while only a small quantity of flour remained to add variety to the meals of game and fish. Berries were beginning to appear as the season advanced, and the Indians were also finding roots and herbs to eat, some of which their companion liked. Despite the insects and other annoyances, B-G still felt elation over the adventure he was having. He intended to arrive at the rendezvous with Dick Fry about mid-month. Since Darby assured him the journey there would not take more than three days even if they stopped often, he wanted to remain at the head of the lake until about the twelfth. He was very interested in the swampland surrounding the great river that entered the lake at its northern end, and, in spite of the amazing number of mosquitoes breeding there, he insisted on exploring a good part of the huge area it encompassed. Once again, as he had on seeing the tableland at the southern end of the lake, he thought of the empire and the possibility of his serving it by devising a scheme to get rid of the water and make farmland of such swamps.

By the end of the first week of July, Dick Fry and Justine had already made the journey from Bonners Ferry and were living in their teepee on the shore of the lake's west arm, near the point where it became the lower Kootenay River. They had often camped here before and expected to do so many times again, unaware that in a few years this shoreline would be a busy place dotted with buildings, the first of many in the growing town of Nelson. They had erected the teepee at the mouth of a small creek which flowed from the woods across the pebbly shoreline. They could see its deep gully leading up a series of fairly gentle rises to the mountain in the background. Across the west arm (hardly wider than a large river here and in those days usually called one) and about a mile downstream, was, they knew, the sandy point where their Indian wedding ceremony had taken place fifteen years ago in the summer of '67.

On the first day after their arrival Dick decided to visit a trapline he often used when in the vicinity. Accordingly, he and Justine, taking a few new traps with them in case some of the ones in place needed changing for some reason, walked downstream half a mile or so to the mouth of a larger creek and began following it up as it ran smoothly over the flat ground. Soon they came to a waterfall and had to climb alongside a gorge until they reached flatter land again. Here the going was easier, as they came upon

## The West Arm at the Site Of Nelson

a well-defined trail (used by Indians and the parties of white men who sometimes came up from Colville in the summer). The light was dim as they followed the trail along the stream through the huge trees of the forest at the bottom of a narrow valley. After about four miles of walking they came to an oval-shaped mountain lake, the stream's source. It was small and dark, somewhat forbidding among the huge trees that grew all around its edge. On its western shore a mountain, burdened heavily with forest, rose precipitously from the water; but to the south the skyline above the trees gave promise that the valley was widening. They left the trail and climbed down to the east shore, at a spot where a feeder stream had made a tiny delta of muddy sand, the only beach around the whole circumference of the lake. Here Justine remained to build a fire and catch some fish for lunch, while Dick visited his traps, resetting them where they had lain idle since his last trip. After lunch they began the walk home, arriving there in mid-afternoon.

Next day they paddled over to the point where their Indian wedding had taken place and then, crossing back to the south side and carefully threading the rapids of the river, took a jaunt down to Forty-Nine Creek and walked up toward their old rockers and sluices of '67. Dick wanted to try some of the small tributary streams that he had not explored before. The following afternoon they returned to the teepee on the lake, carrying in their pockets a few gold nuggets for their effort.

Uncertain when B-G would arrive, Dick did not stray far from base camp. One day, while giving the traps time to catch something, he and Justine took a short trip eastward along the shore and followed another creek across the flats into a defile, partly to do a little exploring and partly to try their luck at panning. This time they found no gold. Late in the afternoon, as they were beaching the canoe in front of their teepee, Justine drew Dick's attention to a small tent on the shore about a hundred yards downstream. Leaving Justine at the camp, Dick strolled down the beach to see who had arrived. Up close the tent turned out to be merely a tarpaulin strung over stakes and a ridgepole, and the man sitting in it introduced himself as Bill Feeney.[7]

After the men had exchanged pleasantries and given each other basic information about themselves, Dick invited Bill to share the supper that Justine was preparing, and the two of them, liking each other, walked slowly through the cool evening air toward the fire she had lighted. During the meal and afterwards, as they all three sat drinking cups of tea and smoking some of the fresh tobacco Bill had brought with him, the newcomer told how he had found his way to Kootenay Lake.

"I was down in New Westminster looking at timber possibilities and starting to get a little bored. Too many people there. Then I started hearing about the Kootenay country, that there was gold up there, and I decided to take a look at it. Somebody mentioned that there was a fairly direct way to get there, the old Dewdney Trail. It wasn't too bad, lots of climbing up over mountains and then flat land in between."

"I know," said Dick. "It's still pretty good along that section. I've packed over it lots. It gets bad from here eastwards. What'd you do to get across the Columbia?"

"Oh, you mean that big river a couple of days back from here where the old fort is."

"Yeah," said Dick. "Fort Shepherd."

"I rafted over it. I went quite a way upstream and threw a few logs together, enough to get me across, and landed right where I wanted to on the other side. I'm used to crossing rivers. Did a lotta log-driving for the timber companies back home. There was another river coming into it just below where I landed."

"That's the Pend d'Oreille. It's lucky you didn't get caught in the big whirlpool there."

"Well, I kept following the trail just north of the Pend d'Oreille till I came to a smaller river emptying into it. Somebody had told me that would be the Salmon and after a few miles when the big trail veered off to the east I just kept along the smaller one following the Salmon upstream. Must've been a few people in here over the years. That's a pretty well-worn trail."

"Yeah," said Dick. "They come up from the States quite a bit."

"And then I came to where the Salmon petered out in swamps, just like they said, and I walked over a rise for a few miles and came to a lake and a stream that led me right here."

"I wasn't too surprised to see you," interposed Dick. "Every summer there's a few other whites in here. You interested in gold?"

"Oh, not much. Mostly timber. There's beautiful timber here. Actually, I'm on a scouting trip for a big timber company back east—R.C. Clarkson & Sons. That Salmon River valley really is beautiful country. I might come back and settle here."

Dick looked his new friend over. A fine handsome man, tall and big with it. And in the prime of life. He was impressed by the way Bill had set out on his journey alone and by the way he had so fearlessly crossed the Columbia. "What'd you do before you got to New Westminster?" he asked.

"I own a farm in Ontario. It's in a beautiful valley with a stream running through, an' only a few neighbours. In the winter I work on the river-drive. There's lots of timber there. I got one small boy, an' another on the way. And then this big timber company hired me to go west."

"How come you left your wife back home?" asked Justine.

"Well, I didn't figure I'd be here long enough this trip. I won't stay too long out here this time, an' if I really like it we'll all come out to stay."

"Will she be okay on the farm?" asked Dick.

"Oh yeah, she's strong and a good worker. She can manage."

Dick looked at Justine, then, grinning, turned back to Bill. "Bet she's not as good as a real Indian wife." His smile broadened. "You should get yourself one while you're out here."

Embarrassed, Bill glanced at Justine. "Well . . ."

But Justine was laughing at his discomfiture. Glowing with pleasure at the compliment she had received, she poured them all another cup of tea. Bill, suddenly glad to have something to do with his hands, took out his jackknife and began to make shavings from his tobacco plug so they could fill their pipes.

58

"Anyway," he went on, "I sure like this country. There's lots of work in the woods in the States, so I can earn money if I come back, an' if I decide to settle somewhere—maybe even around here—I can send for them. I like the timber in this country. I could make a good livin' here. Some day it'll open up and then there'll be transportation."

"You been working a long time in timber?" asked Dick. "How'd you get interested in that?"

"Well," answered Bill, "ever since I was a wee mite, I been helpin' my father cut wood. He used to be a sea captain, but to get away from all the hate and fightin' in Ireland he quit that job and came to America and started loggin' for masts and spars. He taught me to help him shape them. They had to be eight-sided and tapered, no axe marks. It was very fine, careful work, and they had to be exact as to size. It taught me a lot and gave me a lot of skills that've stood me in good stead ever since."

The talk and the ceremony of drinking tea and smoking went on until very late. Before Bill left to walk back to his shelter they had agreed that he would accompany Dick and Justine up to the lake next morning to collect pelts.

Next day they left early and reached the lake by mid-morning. While Justine lit a fire and fished from the little beach on the east shore, the men went to see what the traps had caught. By noon three marten and two muskrat pelts were packed away, and the three people were eating a lunch of fish.

"Hello, down there!" The voice came from the trail on the bank above them. It sounded friendly.

"Hello, yourself!" Dick glanced at the rifle lying a few feet away beside his pack. "Who all's up there?"

"Me and two buddies," said the voice. "We've come from Colville, and we're on our way to Kootenay Lake. Is it far? Can we come down?"

Dick looked at Bill. "Sure, c'mon. There's not much room here, but we can fit you in."

There was a noise of scrambling through brush and soon the three strangers appeared on the delta. Justine, Dick, and Bill rose to their feet, and introductions were made. The man who had called from the top of the bank was named Jerry O'Donnell. The names of his two friends have not come down to us. Dick, Bill, and Justine having finished their lunch and the delta being too small for any prolonged socializing, they all decided to head down the trail immediately. On the way back they learned that the newcomers had walked, over a long period of time and with many stopovers, all the way from the state of Wisconsin. Even at that distance they had heard talk of gold on Kootenay Lake. When they got back to the beach, Jerry O'Donnell and his friends set up a small tent near that of Bill Feeney.

And now, in that portentous July of 1882, there were three tents housing five white men on the shore of the west arm where Nelson would be in a few years; there were two more white men up at Big Ledge on the eastern shore of the main lake; and there was B-G somewhere on the flats at the north end of the lake. All these men had definite ideas about adapting this lake to their use, some modest and some not so modest. And there were probably others of whom history has left no record. Furthermore, there was one John C. Ainsworth sitting in his office away down in Oakland, California, mulling over very large plans indeed for adding this lake to his business empire.

# CHAPTER 6

*A long chapter, telling what happened when B-G kept
his rendezvous with Dick Fry, how Sproule and Reeder
fared during the summer, and what actions were taken
by the Ainsworth party when it came onto the lake; but
also containing digressions upon the beauty of the landscape, certain problems of the historian, and a cosmic
event.*

DURING THE FIRST DAYS of the enforced sit-out on their
claims, Sproule and Reeder found much to do. They explored both
sides of the lake and soon found that the Indians on the opposite
side were friendly, even to the point of letting them use the bath-
ing-pool. One morning they climbed the mountain behind the hot
spring, and there Sproule staked a claim which he named *Inca*.
Gradually, however, as the days of waiting became weeks, time
began to hang heavy. Their different natures made their constant
companionship oppressive, and they took to spending more time
apart. Sproule particularly began to be less communicative, staying on his claim at Big Ledge as Reeder continued his explorations.
He started construction on a stone building just outside his
boundaries, to be used as a powder house when the site was
worked. Actually, he had begun to brood about the recent events
of his life and had developed the feeling that this strike was his
last chance to make good. In coming west he had gone against the
common sense of his settled, affluent family and unless something
happened soon to change his luck they would be proven right; he
had been out west years now and had got nowhere. And that busi-

ness of the arson charge and the nastiness of the trial had shown him how ruthless people were in the pursuit of money. He had failed in the coalfield venture, but he must not fail here. If this was a rich strike, and he knew in his bones it was, then he wanted nothing more than to get to a mining recorder and secure his ownership. Meanwhile, work on the powder house gave him something to do and eased his tension.

On the twelfth of July B-G and Darby & Joan left their camp at the north end of the lake and began their journey to the rendezvous with Dick Fry. Travelling down the western shore, they came late in the afternoon to a warm little stream that entered the lake amid limey channels and lush vegetation. Darby & Joan were eager to stop here, where a couple of canoes indicated that other Indians were already present. Soon, while B-G explored the area, they were greeting their friends and stripping to bathe in the small pool that had gathered in a rocky hollow near a place where hot water gushed from the cliff-side. There was nothing to indicate to B-G that white men had ever been here. Any old campsites he came across he assumed to be Indian ones, and any evidence to the contrary he either failed to observe or unconsciously dismissed for fear of spoiling the romantic illusion he wished to maintain.

We can surmise with certainty that Dick Fry would happily have bathed with the Indians, but what about B-G? Did *he* strip off and join the Indians in a state of nature? Or, too aware of his dignity to strip among these uninhibited people, did he wait until dark to sneak hurriedly into the longed-for bath? Or did he scorn the communal warm water altogether and bathe in private at the lakeshore? In asking such questions and others related to them, we are indulging a curiosity that seems peculiar to our own age. Thousands of older books give us accounts of voyages, forays, battles, treks, migrations, and a hundred other human endeavours without taking into consideration that the participants in these events were daily faced with biological demands of all kinds that had to be satisfied in some manner. We are hardly ever told even what they ate. As readers in an age that seems to want everything private made public, we often find ourselves wishing older writers had given us more information along these lines. They did not, however, and in wanting answers to such simple questions as whether or not B-G bathed with the Indians, not to mention other questions of an even more intimate nature, we are faced with a wall of silence, and must refrain from speculation on grounds of a complete lack of evidence.

Knowing that it would please Darby & Joan, B-G decided to spend the night at the hot spring. When darkness fell—not until about ten o'clock at this season—they could see the light of camp-fires across at Big Ledge. Darby asked the Indians if they knew who was over there and received the answer that two white men had been camped there for a few weeks now. B-G was somewhat put out at this erosion of his uniqueness by unknown adventurers, and late next morning, when they again set off in the canoe, he did not insist that they go over to investigate. Throughout the hours of late morning and early afternoon they moved at a lei-surely pace southward past the steep banks and cliffs of the shore-line, coming at last to a spacious bay whose lovely open curve was in good part lined with a beach of smooth pebbles. Leaving the shoreline, the paddlers cut across the open water of the bay's mouth and reached the narrows through which the lake entered its west arm. Here, on both sides of the narrow outlet, stood many teepees. Indians were scattered along the shores taking advantage of the excellent fishing afforded by the shallow, swiftly moving water. It was an enchanting spot, and B-G decided, much to the pleasure of Darby & Joan, to camp for the night. Early next morn-ing they set out on the last leg of their journey to the rendezvous with Dick Fry—down the west arm about twenty miles to the point where it becomes the lower Kootenay River. The day was one of those perfect ones of mid-July, cloudless and hot, made to be spent deliciously floating on water or immersed in it. We can pic-ture our travellers taking their positions in the canoe: in the mid-dle, correct B-G wearing the clothes of a European, undoubtedly hatted against the sun and still looking impossibly dapper; at the front, indefatigable Joan in her indefatigable old sack dress; at the rear, bronzed Darby clad most sensibly for the occasion, according to our modern notion, in his beads, breechclout, and moccasins.

The west arm, in contrast to the main lake with its grandiose peaks and ridges, is lined with small, rounded mountains or hills, and has something of the gentle quality of a pastoral landscape. At intervals, creeks debouching on both sides have pushed great bars of white sand almost halfway across its expanse. These, covered to the water's edge with marvelously beautiful forests of cottonwood trees, form narrows through which the water passes swiftly over a sandy bottom. Between the narrows the arm widens to form deeper lagoons several miles in length, reflecting the rich conifer forests of the hillsides and dotted frequently with beaches of white sand. It is a landscape to bring joy to the artist, or to anyone who stops to contemplate it as a natural garden formed by the labour of ages. Today the northern shore (and much of the southern) of the west arm is crowded with houses all along its length, and yet it is so beautiful that the people living there wouldn't want to be anywhere else; we who can remember it as it was seventy years ago—its beaches remote and unpopulated in those days, and washed by the rising of the lake during the annual spring flooding—think of it as the vanished Eden of our childhood. What, then, must it have been like in that summer of 1882 for Baillie-Grohman, who saw it in its virginal state, shaped by the handiwork of aeons, uncluttered except by the artifacts of natural creation?

As anyone who has ever drifted in a quiet boat through such a landscape on such a summer's day will know, the souls of B-G and his Indian companions (deeply buried under incrustations of worldly ambition or habit) rejoiced that morning in the loveliness around them, while their bodies took equal joy in the warmth of the life-giving sun. And all of creation was also rejoicing. Over the last six or eight weeks a cosmic event had been taking place, unnoticed by B-G and other human beings except when it impinged on their practical concerns. As the tilted earth in its yearly orbit left the position of vernal equinox and moved toward that of the summer solstice, those rays of the sun striking its equator vertically began to move northward, tracing across its revolving surface a great ascending spiral which, somewhere around June 21st, would reach the Tropic of Cancer, 23.5 degrees N., before veering southward into a six-month descent to the Tropic of Capricorn, 23.5 degrees S. That northward spiralling was bringing spring to the northern hemisphere. The winter's snow melted, first slowly, then with a rush as the sun grew stronger. As we have seen, the process had already begun in the Kootenay River watershed when B-G and his Indian companions were leaving Bonners Ferry. As they moved northward on the river the advancing season accelerated the pace of melting on the great peaks around Kootenay Lake, and the deep masses of snow up there began to form torrents of water which rushed down valleys into its basin faster than the outlet could carry them away. The rising water began pushing upstream toward Bonners Ferry and caused the flooding B-G had predicted on the first days of his journey. Then, a week or two later—B-G was hunting goats on the crags now—spring reached the higher peaks of the Rockies far away to the east at the source of the river, and more water poured downstream to raise the lake and river even further.

As the waters rose, floods pushed into the tableland between the lake and Bonners Ferry, and into the swamps at the lake's northern end. Along the length of the west arm the white beaches were flooded to their innermost recesses among the trees and shrubs; the moving water cleansed them, scouring out the grasses and other plants that sought to take root, ensuring that the slowly wrought perfection of their sand would remain unviolated. The rising water poured into the hollow land behind spits and sand dunes and lay soaking into the earth, where it wakened myriads of life forms waiting there for this moment since the mud had dried last autumn. They hatched, expanded, grew, threw off protective coverings, exulted in the return of life, and moved upwards into the nourishing water. Weeks passed. Snow disappeared from the peaks, creeks became smaller, the lake's excess water poured out through the lower Kootenay River. Gleaming beaches reappeared, and sandspits, shining in the sunlight, once again reached out into the water.

As the level of the lake fell, the water that had flowed over spits and dunes became trapped and formed swamps, marvelously burgeoning with life in response to the light and warmth. Frogs, toads, salamanders, newts, turtles, leeches; all the water bugs—striders, boatmen, backswimmers; dragonfly, and damselfly nymphs, larvae of the caddis fly and a hundred others; marsh beetles, mud burrowers, minnows, planaria, hydra, worms; all water-rooted plants; all the attached and floating algae—Spirogyra, Ulothrix, Oedogonium, and a host of others carrying within their microscopic jungles the one-celled predators of the animal kingdom—the Amoeba and its cousins Difflugia and Arcella; Euglena, Volvox, and countless other flagellates—all these innumerable manifestations of the sun's energy mysteriously transformed into life began to display the frenzy of their short period of activity. This annual rebirth was earth's answer to the sun's message, a singing of the swamps about the blessedness of light and warmth; it was an age-old hymn of joy and thanksgiving tossed off into the vast, cold reaches of space, proclaiming to the universe the miraculous fact of life.

As a part of the miraculous fact of life, B-G was also a participant in that age-old hymn of joy, although he would probably not have interpreted his pleasant feelings on that wonderful day in quite such a manner. Indeed, his mind idly moving among thoughts about big game trophies, schemes for possible development of this new area, and plans for his new books, he was unaware of those life forms acting out their humble destinies in nearby swamps, did not even notice the millions of tadpoles[8] that poured from those swamps and were, as he paddled by, darkening the shores in unbroken lines half a mile or more in length; and certainly the idea that he and an amoeba or a spirogyra cell were fellow choristers in a hymn of joy would have seemed to him bizarre in the extreme. Unaware of them now, he was also unaware that before seventy-five more years had passed those creatures and those swamps would be buried forever under the pavement of parking lots and housing developments.

Paddling at a leisurely pace through that lovely morning and afternoon, Darby & Joan brought them toward evening to the place where Dick and Justine were camped beside the small creek. There they found the teepee empty, and also the two nearby encampments. Dick and Justine, however, were only over at the cliffs across the lake, and on noticing the arrival of the canoe they hurried back to greet the travellers. That evening Bill Feeney returned to his camp and Dick took B-G over to meet him. Had they been in the land of their parents, the true Irishman and the scion of Irish gentry would not have met at all. Here in the new world, although to each the accent and manner of speech of the other betrayed his origin, they met amicably. Jerry O'Donnell and his friends were off on a jaunt somewhere, and B-G did not meet them until another day or two had gone by.

B-G was anxious to explore the region in the company of Dick Fry. Accordingly, he went on the next expedition to the trapline and learned about the valley of the Salmon River as another avenue of entry to Kootenay Lake from the States. He was most interested, however, in the lower Kootenay River. He and Dick canoed downstream to the first of the waterfalls, and he saw at first-hand the difficulty this river presented as a direct route to the Columbia River with its steamer traffic to the States. The following day he asked Dick to accompany him once again down the river, this time only a mile or two below camp to a place he had observed the day before, where a creek (it would one day bear his name) pushed a delta of gravel into the river, thereby narrowing it considerably. B-G had not forgotten the vague idea he had had about reclaiming the tableland between Bonners Ferry and Kootenay Lake and again when he saw the swamps at the lake's north end. It now seemed clear that all this gravel at the creek mouth was what mainly prevented the excess water of the spring melt from escaping rapidly enough to prevent flooding of the flat land at both ends of the lake. There might be a possibility that if this gravel were removed and the river channel deepened, the empire's war veterans could be settled in homesteads on those remote flatlands. Further examination of the river bed above the creek revealed the presence of a ridge of solid rock stretching not far below the surface from one bank to the other. That settled it. This ridge could easily be blasted away and the gravel later as easily removed. Excess water in the lake would flow away quickly, the tablelands far away at the ends of the lake would remain dry during the spring floods, and William Adolph Baillie-Grohman's reputation as a man of vision and accomplishment would be assured. It was an audacious vision and B-G was proud of it. He began at once to think about the plan that was to obsess him for the next several years. There was no longer any reason for him to remain in the area. His hunt had been successful—he had the trophies to prove it—and now he had found a new interest of much more importance than chasing after big game. He must get to the centres of civilization and begin the task of winning other minds to the furtherance of his scheme. A few more days spent here, or a week at the most, he decided, and he would head back to Bonners Ferry and from there to the railhead at Pend d'Oreille Lake.

As the weeks of summer passed by up at Big Ledge, Sproule and Reeder continued to sit out the long wait until October 31st. They saw less and less of each other. Their supply of flour and other staples was getting low; fish and game were abundant, but the diet was becoming boring. Both men longed for a change of food and of company. Reeder often went off alone and sometimes stayed away two or three days. Sproule doggedly kept on working at raising the walls of his powder house. It was heavy work, and more than a little pointless, since he didn't have the tools to finish it; however, it filled the long days and let him think that at least something was being accomplished. It was obvious to both men that some resolution of their dilemma had to occur soon. Singly and together they pondered the problem many times, and we too should now review it, in order that we may understand it clearly. The mining laws of the time stipulated an open season (from June 1st to October 31st) during which time if a prospector left his claim for more than seventy-two hours it was considered abandoned and was subject to being "jumped" by someone else. During closed season (November 1st to May 31st) it was safe to leave a claim because it could not legally be jumped. The law also stipulated that claims must be filed within three days of staking. From Big Ledge, the nearest recording-office was over in Wildhorse Creek, a journey of much more than three days. The problem was augmented by the fact that even recorded claims, if unattended, could be jumped in open season.

Our narrative has reached a point where this historian must make his readers aware of a difficulty that has arisen. It is a difficulty common to historians. The source books from which the fraternity gathers its facts may be said to be of two kinds: secondary sources, which are other histories already written by authors whom we assume to have made careful and painstaking investigation into their subject, or other accounts which have used these first histories as their source books; and primary sources, which are record books whose entries give irrefutable dates and times put down on the very day of the event's occurrence, or eye-witness accounts of the event. It is clear that both kinds of sources are liable to error but that the liability is much greater in the secondary sources. Often, as the secondary sources assume the dignity of age there is less and less probability that their truth will be questioned, and it becomes very tempting to latter-day historians to accept them as primary sources without hesitation. In that way, the mistakes of the original histories are perpetuated, and the veils which separate us from the ever-receding past remain inadequately pierced.

To return to our narrative, record books of the mining recorder in the year 1882—a primary source of unassailable integrity if there ever was one—give us a hard fact: on July 31st, the *Inca* and *Bluebell* were recorded for R.E. Sproule, and the *Mogul* (on the south end of the *Bluebell*) for Gay Reeder. Secondary sources— among which a letter dated Victoria, January 26th, 1909 from William Fernie to S.S. Fowler is perhaps the most interesting[9]— fail to give us any indication of how Sproule and Reeder solved the problem of getting to the recording office, thereby making it necessary for this historian to indulge in conjecture. Two probabilities present themselves. The first is that Gay Reeder, not as tied to his claim as Sproule and already active in sorties and forays away from the site, decided to boat back to Bonners Ferry and from there make his way up to Wildhorse Creek, on the speculation that the recorder would, considering the circumstances, allow him to record both his and his partner's claims. (The possibility of Sproule making the journey and leaving Reeder to guard the claims does not seem probable to this historian, considering the way we have seen Sproule acting lately.) The second probability is that the mountain came to Mahomet; that is, neither of the two men went to the mining recorder but the mining recorder came to them. For reasons contained in the 1909 letter from William Fernie to S.S. Fowler—with which I will not bother the reader—it seems very reasonable to assume that the mining recorder (whose name was William Fernie) made, in the company of his brother, an unofficial sortie to Kootenay Lake and arrived at Big Ledge, quite by chance, on July 31st of the year 1882. Here he listened to the complaints of Sproule and Reeder and decided to relieve their concern by recording their claims on the spot. He also listened to Sproule's offer to sell him or his brother a half-interest in the *Bluebell*. (Sproule obviously thought the claim was rich enough to share and thought selling half of it a good way to make some working money.) However, as Fernie mentions in his 1909 letter, the offer was not accepted.

This historian favours the second probability and therefore, with the authority vested in him, and with the full knowledge of his readers, is prepared to state that on the 31st day of July William Fernie, the mining recorder, accompanied by his brother, arrived at Big Ledge and recorded the claims of Sproule and Reeder. Shortly after that, Reeder, perhaps feeling that his claim was now safer as it was recorded, and that, in any case, Sproule was on the site to protect it, left Big Ledge and headed to Bonners Ferry and points south.

August passed slowly by. Down at the end of the west arm, B-G said goodbye to Dick Fry and Justine and to his acquaintances in the other two camps and set off, propelled by his faithful paddlers, up the arm to the main lake and southward to Bonners

Ferry. There Darby & Joan, not even remembered by their right names, pass out of our story. B-G must have owed them by this time nearly two hundred dollars, a lot of money in those days. We hope they did not lose it all to the wily Kalispels, or that if they did Dick Fry won it back for them. They remain in our memories as figures much more shadowy than the more prominent persons of our story, but in parting from them we may take a moment to hope that the rest of their days were happy ones.

Not more than a week after the departure of B-G, Jerry O'Donnell and his anonymous partners also broke camp. Being interested only in gold and having decided there was none on Kootenay Lake worth the trouble of looking for it, they headed toward fresh fields and out of our story. Bill Feeney also decided to move, but only a few miles. He went back to a location in the Salmon River valley that had taken his fancy on the trip in, and settled there to do a bit of cruising for the company.[10] Once again only passing Indians broke the stillness of the beach where Nelson would one day stand.

As summer ripened into autumn, Sproule, left alone at Big Ledge, continued his obsessive work on the powder house. We can imagine his feelings: his loneliness, his sense of being abandoned, his despair at the thought of the long wait until October 31st, his rising panic at the thought that other prospectors might come at any time and surround his site with claims of their own, his boredom, which daily must have grown more acute. One day his worst fears were realized. Canoes loaded with white men, their Indian guides, and supplies, came along the shoreline from the south. Observing his camp, the white men ordered the canoes beached and came ashore. Sproule's answer to their greetings was curt, suspicious, and unfriendly. Repelled by his animosity, the men returned to their canoes and continued toward their destination, the hot spring across the lake. Breathing heavily, his hands trembling, Sproule watched them cross the water, wishing he had his partner here to talk to.

As the reader may have guessed, the intruders were the party sent by John C. Ainsworth to explore the area and bring him a report on its economic value. Its principal members were three white men: Thomas Hammill, miner and man-of-all-work for John Ainsworth; E.W. Blasdel, business friend of John Ainsworth; and C.J. Woodbury, reporter for a Spokane newspaper. When they arrived at the hot spring, Blasdel told the guides to find out from the Indians camped here all they could about the man across the lake. "That guy sure must think he's sitting on something valuable," laughed Hammill, looking over at Big Ledge.

"Yeah," agreed Woodbury. "He sure didn't want us around."

"Well," said Blasdel, "he just might be sitting on something good. That's gotta be the Big Ledge we've been hearing about over there."

"Yeah. Well, we'll check it out in a couple a days," said Hammill. "Right now, let's give this hot spring here the once-over. This might do for that land the boss wants to buy."

A few days later the Ainsworth party did go over to Big Ledge for the purpose of "checking it out." Robert Sproule could do nothing but watch as they nosed aggressively around the borders of his and Reeder's claims. That first day they left without doing more than look, but next day they returned prepared for action. Woodbury staked the *Comfort* at the north end of Sproule's *Bluebell*, and Blasdel jumped Reeder's *Mogul*, renaming it the *Kootenay Chief*. Then, leaving poor Sproule in a very unhappy state, they returned to their own side of the lake, where they were busy staking more claims. Next day Woodbury, accompanied by two of the Indians, set out for Wildhorse Creek. He reached there on October 5th, and recorded the *Kootenay Chief* and the *Comfort*. He also persuaded William Fernie to accompany him back to the hot spring to—in the words of Fernie himself in the 1909 letter— "confer with him in regard to developing the mineral resources of the Lake region." Perhaps impressed with the credentials of the Ainsworth party, Fernie listened sympathetically when Hammill drew his attention to the fact that "Sproule had not properly done the assessment work on the *Blue Bell* but had been fooling his time away in building a stone powder house outside of his location." We can imagine the feelings of Sproule as he watched the mining recorder hobnobbing with these powerful intruders.

In time William Fernie went back to Wildhorse Creek, the Ainsworth party paddled across the lake to Hot Spring and returned no more, and Robert Sproule was left to his lonely thoughts. October passed by, day following weary day, as Sproule became more and more lethargic under the burden of his depression. He became ill, unable even to make the effort to obtain food for himself. Finally, on October 25th, only six days before the end of open season, he fastened a note to one of his claim posts. It said that he was forced to leave before October 31st because of ill health and lack of food. Then he got into his boat and began the journey to Bonners Ferry. His departure was observed by the watchers over at Hot Spring. Next morning Thomas Hammill rowed over to Big Ledge and restaked the *Bluebell*, naming it the *Silver Queen*. A few days after that, the Ainsworth party also left for Bonners Ferry. On November 15th the *Silver Queen* claim was recorded in Wildhorse Creek.

Once again the land lay empty. The Indians too had returned to their winter quarters near Bonners Ferry as the wilderness of Kootenay Lake prepared for months of cold. Majestic peaks at the north end of the lake became snow-covered; humble life forms shrank into protective cases buried in mud as the swamps of the west arm dried up; deer and elk straggled down from high country to their wintering-grounds along the shorelines; bears once again sought their hibernation dens. Only a few posts with writing on them at the hot spring and others at the place white men called Big Ledge gave any indication that things were no longer as they had been.

# CHAPTER 7

*A very short chapter containing weighty matters which the author hopes his readers will peruse with due care and attention on the promise that Chapter 8 will move us once again out into the fresh air and sunshine.*

IN THE YEAR 1883 the *British Columbia Gazette,* printed weekly by the government at Victoria, began—as a direct result of the events we witnessed on Kootenay Lake in 1882—to refer more and more to the West Kootenay. As early as January 4th it contains—among its usual notices about legislative matters, business, land sales, incorporations, etc.—an item of great interest to us. On page 8 of that issue there appears a notice dated at Victoria, December 21st, 1882 that clearly indicates the speed with which that arch businessman John C. Ainsworth acted after receiving a favourable report from his reconnoitering party in late autumn of 1882. As a matter of fact, he had probably begun lobbying in Victoria well before he received their report. He had a detailed plan and knew exactly how to set about getting what he wanted. We recall him having his first idea of it in Chapter 4. The plan involved the British Columbia government, but John C. Ainsworth was not afraid of that: he was an empire-builder, not at all hesitant about attempting to manipulate governments, even foreign ones, for the furtherance of his aims. Sometime during the autumn of '82 he approached government members with a proposal, and the notice entitled "Private Bill" shows us what that proposal was.

He, his son George, and his friend Enoch Blasdel would form a company to run steamboats on Kootenay Lake and would also construct and operate a railway from the junction of the lake and its west arm (in present-day terms, from the site of Balfour) to the Columbia River, about fifty miles to the west, and from there run steamers up and down that river. John Ainsworth knew that government members would be delighted with his proposal, would, in fact, regard him as a saviour. He carefully pointed out to them that a rail link from Sandpoint to Bonners Ferry was almost certainly in the promotional stage, and that once it was built it would be tied in with a steamboat service on Kootenay River, able to haul ore from Kootenay Lake mines upstream to Bonners Ferry. Supplies for the mines would then come north from the States, and ore would go south to American smelters. All this could be prevented by his proposal, which would allow Kootenay Lake ores to reach the Columbia and then move northward to the transcontinental railway now nearing its completion. The transcontinental railway would unite Canada, and with Kootenay Lake linked to it as a result of Ainsworth's proposal, the constant threat of economic invasion from south of the border would at last be ended in British Columbia. Members of the government and prominent coastal merchants—the "establishment" of British Columbia—were duly alarmed by the threatened new spur line and not only enthusiastically accepted the proposal but also acquiesced in the demands which accompanied it.

Those demands were immense, but the notice of January 4th didn't give any hint of what the Ainsworth company wanted in return for building the Columbia and Kootenay Railway. The general public had to wait a few months to receive that knowledge. Meanwhile, in the *Gazette* of January 25th another notice appeared, stating that George J. Ainsworth (John C.'s son) had, on September 5th, 1882, applied to purchase certain lands, already surveyed, "situate at Kootenay Lake." One of these was for a township at Hot Spring.

In the *Gazette* of May 23rd, 1883, the public finally received complete knowledge of the agreement between Ainsworth and the British Columbia Government.

---

## PUBLIC NOTICE.

### KOOTENAY DISTRICT.

NOTICE IS HEREBY GIVEN that, in consideration of the provisions of the "Columbia and Kootenay Railway and Transportation Company Act, 1883," the following described tracts of land are hereby set apart and reserved from sale or pre-emption for the purposes of said Act, viz.:—

All the vacant unoccupied land situated within a tract or tracts of land commencing at a point on Kootenay River or Lake, fifteen miles from the southern boundary line of British Columbia, thence down the said river or lake, and through and throughout the said lake and its navigable tributaries; and also a tract or tracts of land from the outlet of Kootenay Lake to the junction of the Kootenay and the Columbia Rivers; and also a further tract or tracts of land commencing at that point where the southern boundary line of British Columbia intersects the Columbia River, and from thence to the head of navigation on the Columbia River. Such reservation shall extend to a depth of six miles on each side of the rivers and lakes above mentioned.

WM. SMITHE,
*Chief Commissioner of Lands & works.*
*Lands & Works Department,*
*Victoria, B. C., May 23rd, 1883.*

---

We observe that the government of British Columbia, rendered myopic by its preoccupation with immediate economic aims, was intending to grant to this foreign company a vast acreage encompassing the whole of Kootenay Lake and its associated waterways, all in return for about forty miles of railway. While indulging in a quiet smile of victory, John C. Ainsworth must have longed for more challenging opponents in the economic chess game.

He soon found them. Members of the general population, looking at the situation from a different perspective, now began to raise a hue and cry. Let us leave for a time the ambitions of John C. Ainsworth and the British Columbia government transfixed by that public clamour, and return to William Adolph Baillie-Grohman, who has been, if possible, even busier than Ainsworth during the winter.

We recall that when B-G left the valley he did so with the intention of interesting other people in his project of flood prevention on Kootenay Lake. He returned to England, where he was able to arouse the interest of several wealthy friends. Then, on the 10th of May, 1883, he embarked from Liverpool on the S.S. *Germanic*, White Star Line, and reached New York ten days later. On board he became friendly with one W.H. Barnaby, Barnaby's friend and neighbour M. Clive, and his brother-in-law A. Mitchell. These men were tourists, bent on seeing America in comfort. Barnaby has left us an interesting book telling of their travels. B-G and his new friends parted in New York City, but Barnaby tells us in his book that when he and his two companions reached Victoria in early July and signed in at the Driard Hotel they found B-G once again.

B-G, of course, had journeyed to Victoria to lobby the government regarding his plan for the reclamation of the flatlands at the south end of Kootenay Lake. The result of that lobbying can be seen in two notices reproduced from the *Gazette* for July 12th, 1883.

---

PROVINCIAL SECRETARY'S OFFICE,
*10th July, 1883.*

HIS HONOUR the Lieutenant-Governor has been pleased to place the following gentlemen on the Commission of the Peace, viz.:—

EDGAR CROW BAKER, M. P., and NOAH SHAKESPEAR, M. P., Esquires, for the Province.

WILLIAM A. BAILLIE-GROHMAN, and EDWARD KELLY, Esquires, for the Electoral District of Kootenay.

---

We observe that in the space of one day William Adolph
Baillie-Grohman was granted a reservation on a large piece of the
flatlands at the southern end of Kootenay Lake and became a Justice of the Peace for the Province of British Columbia. We further
observe that in the space of a few months two of the intruders onto
Kootenay Lake in the summer of '82 had, by their combined ambitions, laid claim to every acre of the most desirable land of the
lower Kootenay watershed north of the border. Government officials, greatly interested in the proposals of both B-G and the
Ainsworth party, decided to send their own representatives to
investigate the new territory. They chose two men: Gilbert
Malcolm Sproat, who was, among other things, a writer on Indian
life and had from 1876 until 1880 been a member of the Indian
Land Commission; and Arthur Stanhope Farwell, a surveyor working with the Department of Lands and Works.

It is of interest that the Jno. Robson, Provincial Secretary, who
signed the letter to Sproat, later became the Premier of British
Columbia and had the present-day town of Robson named after
him.[11] That being as it may, it has become time to end this chapter.
We leave Sproat, Farwell, and B-G (whom the government officials
had asked to act as their guide to Kootenay) preparing for their

## INSTRUCTIONS TO GILBERT MALCOLM SPROAT BEFORE
## LEAVING FOR KOOTENAY

Victoria, B.C., 12th July, 1883.

Sir,

You are instructed to proceed at once to Kootenay, in company with Mr. Farwell, for the purpose of examining and reporting upon that territory, or as much thereof as may be possible within the necessarily brief period at your disposal.

The primary object of the expedition is to obtain such a descriptive report upon the areas covered by the Ainsworth scheme, and the Baillie-Grohman reclamation scheme, as will enable the Government to form correct conclusions respecting the value of the country for farming, grazing, mining, and other economic purposes; but you will, at the same time, give as extended a description of the country drained by the Kootenay and Upper Columbia Rivers, lying within the Province, as may be compatible with the time and means at your disposal.

In addition to such a general description of the country, and its advantages as a field for settlement and the employment of capital in mining and other industrial pursuits, you will also report upon the Indian population and indicate approximately what lands (if any) may be required for the purpose of Indian reserves.

In point of time, your first duty will be to report upon the Kootenay River lands intended to be leased for reclamation purposes, in order that the Government may be in a position, at the earliest possible date, to complete the lease.

It will scarcely be necessary for me to enjoin upon you the utmost economy in time and expenses, as the Government have only a very limited sum at their disposal for the exploration.

I have, &c,
Jno. Robson,
Provincial Secretary.

## INSTRUCTIONS TO ARTHUR STANHOPE FARWELL BEFORE
## LEAVING FOR KOOTENAY

Lands and Works Department,
Victoria, B.C., 14th July, 1883.

Sir,

That the Government may be possessed of full information in regard to certain lands in Kootenay District, situated on the Kootenay River and lying between the International Boundary and Kootenay Lake, I have the honour to instruct you to proceed, with all convenient dispatch to the place in question. You will there make such surveys as may be necessary to enable you to report upon the extent and character of the valley on each side of the river, the approximate area of the lands subject to overflow, and the average depth of flood water, and upon the nature and magnitude of the operations necessary to reclaim the submerged lands, together with any information bearing on the subject which you may gather.

You will also report particularly upon the number of Indians (if any?) who, by usage, may have claims for grazing or other purposes, upon the lands proposed to be reclaimed, and generally upon Indian requirements in the locality.

G. M. Sproat, Esq. who will accompany you to Kootenay, charged with a separate service, will render you such assistance as may be in his power.

A cheque for $250 is herewith enclosed as an advance to be repaid by voucher. The remuneration for your services will be at the rate of $150 per month, together with travelling and living expenses, represented by voucher. It will be necessary that you exercise the strictest economy in the matter of your expenses, and that, at the earliest date practicable, you return to Victoria with your report upon the reclamation scheme.

I have, &c.,
Wm. Smithe,
Chief Commissioner of Lands and Works.

trip in those early days of July, 1883, while we go back a month or two to observe the activities of Robert Sproule as he prepares to return to his claims on Kootenay Lake. And we also leave John C. Ainsworth, who, seated in his office in Oakland, California, very annoyed at the interference of the general public of British Columbia in his private affairs, is still hopeful that the clamour will be quieted and that he will have his way.

# CHAPTER 8

*A dramatic chapter which tells what happened when Robert Sproule, accompanied by Jacob Meyers and Jesse Hunley, went back to Big Ledge in the spring of '83 and was followed there by the Ainsworth party.*[12]

SICK AND DISHEARTENED as he had been when he left the lake on his solitary journey southward in the last days of October, 1882, Robert Sproule nevertheless reached Bonners Ferry safely and slowly began to recover under the care of Dick Fry and Justine. When the Ainsworth party came by a few days after his arrival he remained out of sight for the few hours they stayed. Then, a few weeks later, much recovered physically but still not his former self emotionally, he felt the desire to be near the Meyers family in Fort Colville, where he had been so happy two winters ago. There he would renew his friendship with Jacob Meyers and perhaps persuade him to accompany him on his return to Big Ledge in the Spring.

Getting to Fort Colville from Bonners Ferry was made easier by the presence of the Northern Pacific Railroad. Sproule, carrying a little cash borrowed from Dick Fry, first walked along the trail to Sandpoint, then got on a west-bound train, getting off at a stop not very far north of Spokane where the mountains gave way to fairly level plateau land. From there, after a short walk, he picked up the western branch of the old Walla Walla trail, now a wagon road. This led him in a northwesterly direction along the Colville River valley, at the end of which was Fort Colville on the Columbia River. He may have walked all the way, or, depending on how much cash he had left, flagged down a passing stagecoach.

Reunion with old friends speeded Sproule's recovery, and he spent a happy winter in Fort Colville. Jacob Meyers was pleased to see his old pal and soon introduced him to another of his friends called Jesse Hunley. Meyers and Hunley already had jobs, and, Fort Colville being a busy centre, Sproule himself soon found work. During the course of the winter, he told his friends of the tribulations he had undergone last summer at Kootenay Lake, but also extolled the virtues of Big Ledge as a rich staking site. He told them he was determined to get back there as soon as possible after spring break-up and would welcome their company as allies in fighting off the Ainsworth party. Meyers and Hunley, eager to see the new country, did not need much persuasion to agree to make the journey with him. Thinking that they should get an early start and arrive at Big Ledge before anyone else, they decided to leave just before May 1st. Sometime that winter, Sproule, on the lookout for a person of education and position to help him in his fight with what he regarded as the superior forces of the Ainsworth party, met a government official from Helena, Montana and offered him a good portion of the *Bluebell* in exchange for his help against the Ainsworths. The man refused but kept the matter in his head.

Sproule and his friends spent several pleasurable hours that winter discussing the route they should take in getting to Big Ledge. From Fort Colville there were four ways of getting to Kootenay Lake. They could go up the Columbia River to Fort Shepherd, then take two routes: either follow the Columbia farther north to the mouth of the Kootenay and then follow that river up to the lake, or at Fort Shepherd move onto the Pend d'Oreille River and follow the Dewdney Trail as far as the Salmon River and then follow that northward to Kootenay Lake. Both those routes would take them to the lower end of the west arm, a place we have already visited in Chapters 5 and 6. They could also strike out almost due west of Fort Colville and cross over the mountains using a route that is today called Tiger Pass to reach the Pend d'Oreille

River, which they could then follow down to the mouth of the Salmon, and once again follow that river up to the pass at what is now called Apex, then down what is now called Cottonwood Creek to the west arm. The three men were tempted by these routes but finally rejected them because of the difficulty of getting to Big Ledge from the lower end of the west arm, and chose to go over to Bonners Ferry by retracing the route Sproule had used to get to Fort Colville in the autumn.

Accordingly, next spring sometime before the 1st of May, having judged that winter would be well over at Kootenay Lake, they set out for Bonners Ferry. Arriving there, they bought supplies and remained a day or two visiting the Frys. Then they started on their trip down the river and along the lake to Big Ledge. This time Sproule was carrying tools purchased in Sandpoint so that he could properly develop his claims. The other two men were likewise much better prepared than Sproule had been on the '82 trip. Happy in the company of his companions, Sproule could not help contrasting his present optimism with the feelings of loneliness and despair he had experienced last autumn.

Late one morning a week or so later, they were approaching Big Ledge. Sproule, who was eagerly looking ahead in anticipation of their arrival, suddenly spotted a column of blue smoke rising out of the trees. He felt a spasm of pain in his stomach. Someone had beaten them here! Oh, God! Don't let it be Hammill and that bunch! He cautioned Meyers and Hunley, who quickly moved the boat closer to shore and slowed down. Then they eased along the shoreline until Sproule could see the source of the smoke. It was a campfire. Nearby, facing the lake, was a small tent, and in its opening a man was seated looking out at the fire. The camp was close to them, well south of the spot where Sproule knew he had staked the *Bluebell*. There were no signs of other human beings. The solitary man got to his feet. With a surge of relief Sproule recognized him.

"Reeder! Hallooo! Reeder!" While Sproule stood at the prow waving his arms, Meyers and Hunley eased the boat from the shore and began to move it forward more rapidly, drawing closer and closer to the camp. Reeder, waving his hand and shouting a greeting as he recognized his erstwhile partner, ran down to the waterline and waited to assist them in landing.

It was a happy reunion. Sproule and Reeder had much to catch up on, and after introductions were over with Meyers and Hunley they talked steadily during the unloading of the boat and the setting up of camp for the new arrivals. Reeder, of course, knew nothing of the Ainsworth party, and listened raptly while Sproule informed him of their arrival on the lake and subsequent invasion of Big Ledge.

"So it was one a them who jumped my claim! Some guy by the name of Blasdel. Pulled my stakes out and got 'is own name there instead."

"That's the bastard, all right," answered Sproule, remembering the bitter moment that day last summer when he had stood and watched Blasdel do it.

"Ya better come an' see yer own claim," said Reeder. "The *Bluebell* stakes er pulled and some guy named Hammill got a post there namin' it *Silver Queen*." Sproule made no reply but his face was flushed with anger. The two men left Meyers and Hunley to finish setting up camp and walked silently along near the shore toward the *Bluebell* site. When they came to Reeder's *Mogul*, Sproule, still saying nothing, looked at the new post with Blasdel's name and *Kootenay Chief* on it, then walked on.

When they arrived at the *Bluebell* Reeder stood watching Sproule as he looked down at Hammill's name on the claim post, his features dark and heavy with the anger he was feeling.

"Filthy bastard." Seemingly forgetful of his companion, Sproule stepped back a pace, raised his right leg, and began to hammer blows with his foot against the post halfway up its length. The post began to lean. Sproule suddenly stopped kicking it and turned away. "Let's go on. I want to have a look at Woodbury's stake." Reeder followed without a word. A few hundred yards farther north they came to another claim post.

"Here's Woodbury's *Comfort*." Sproule seemed once again fully aware of his friend. "While Blasdel was stealing your claim, this guy staked this one here. They had me hemmed in, but now that they've jumped me too they've got the whole block." He looked down at the stake for a moment. "Well, let's get back to camp."

Sproule's brief communicative spell was over. As they retraced their steps, he again fell into a morose silence. Coming alongside Hammill's stake at the *Bluebell* site, he stopped and looked at the partially dislodged post. Suddenly he bent over and, grunting with the effort, lifted a large boulder up to his chest; then, taking a step towards the post, he smashed the rock against its top end. The post gave way and fell to the ground, sending the small boulders of the cairn which had supported it flying in all directions. It lay with its whittled writing-surface upward, bearing the names *Hammill* and *Silver Queen*. Again and again Sproule lifted the rock and smashed it down. Finally the writing was obliterated in a mass of pulp and the post was in splinters. Then, without a glance at Reeder, Sproule began walking toward the camp.

An hour later, lunch over and the four men reclining on the beach enjoying a smoke, Sproule's mood had improved. In answer to questions from the others Reeder was explaining how he felt when he discovered that his claim had been jumped.

"Well," he admitted, "I w's purty mad. But what c'd I do? It's like the law says, I left m' claim in open season, some other guy come along an' jumped't."

"And you're just gonna lay down and take that?" commented Meyers. "You're too easy-goin."

"Well, the way I look at't," answered Reeder, "is what's the use of causin' a big fuss? The law's on his side, an' all I had to do was restake right close by. Who's t'say? Who really knows where the vein runs? Maybe m' new position's a lot better'n my old one. An' anyhow I already made the trip to Wildhorse and recorded it on May 4th."

"Yeah, but you and I staked the best sites last year, and now they've got them. I'm not going to give *Bluebell* up without a fight, in fact, I'm not going to give her up at all." Sproule was sounding angry. "And you should keep *Mogul* too. That way we'd have a big block with nobody between us."

"Yer prob'ly right," remarked Reeder, "but I guess we'll jest have t'do what we each think best."

"An' I think it best that we all get up an' take a walk," interjected Hunley, deciding it was time to change the subject. "I'm ready to see what this Big Ledge looks like."

Anticipating that the Ainsworth party might arrive any day, the four men wasted no time digging themselves in at the site. They intended to present the appearance of being well in possession when Hammill & Co. or anyone else appeared. Sproule went to work immediately on the *Bluebell*, simply ignoring the fact that it had been jumped. To fulfil his obligations as a claim owner he began to build a shack in which to live, knowing that work on a residence constituted under the law proper "miner-like work" for the holding of a claim. Reeder, true to his stated belief, made no effort to repossess the *Mogul* but continued maintenance work on his new claim, the *Silver King*. Meyers staked a claim for himself, the *Ruby*. As for Hunley, he had an idea that he would wait to see when the Ainsworth party arrived. If they weren't back by June 1st, the day open season began, he would jump the *Kootenay Chief* (which Blasdel had jumped from Reeder); meanwhile, he would explore the area around Hot Spring over on the west side of the lake.

There were now four men in four separate camps at Big Ledge, all fast friends according to the exigencies of the mining game. They would indeed present a solid front to any would-be interloper. They all, from time to time, made exploratory sorties around the countryside, especially the mountains behind Hot Spring; but never all together or for very long. They wanted to be seen in possession when the enemy arrived.

Playful fate, as if in imitation of some transcendently inventive Sophocles, chose to arrange the movements of the Ainsworth party in such a manner as to display the utmost amount of irony. Thinking that to arrive on June 1st would be time enough to take possession of their claims before anyone could jump them, they arrived, alas, in mid-afternoon to find those claims already restaked. That morning Hunley, according to his earlier intention, had jumped the *Mogul/Kootenay Chief*, renaming it the *Lucy Long*. Meyers, caught up in the jumping craze, had taken the opportunity to restake Woodbury's *Comfort* in the name of a friend of his, one Hudnut, calling it the *Gem*. The original block of claims was once more in the hands of the Sproule party.

This year the Ainsworth party's principal members did not include Blasdel. Hammill and Woodbury were there, accompanied by two new members, Maxwell and Brown. Captain Brown was a well-known mineralogist and assayer from San Francisco who had been summoned to the scene by the thorough and aggressive John C. Ainsworth. When they beached and stepped ashore at the *Bluebell* site, Sproule and the others busied themselves at the far end of the property, apparently taking no notice of the arrivals. Hammill and his companions walked around to ascertain the true state of affairs. Then, realizing the seriousness of the situation, they wisely retreated across the lake to Hot Spring, where they set up camp. Sproule and his friends were in possession of Big Ledge, but next morning a canoe carrying two couriers left Hot Spring on its way to Bonners Ferry and Sandpoint. From there a telegram could be sent to John C. Ainsworth down in Oakland, California. About ten days later the two men and the canoe returned.

The days of June went by, some very hot and some dreary with cold and rain as is usual in that month at that place. The two camps watched each other from across the lake and waited to see what was going to happen. The men at Big Ledge kept very busy with development work on their claims, and the Ainsworth party were likewise engaged. They had furthermore the pleasure of planning the layout of their townsite, for, as the source books tell us, their application for the purchase of this land was authorized that very year. Sproule and his companions did not venture across the lake any more, or for that matter anywhere else, but remained guarding their possessions. Incidentally, we can no longer imagine the scene on Kootenay Lake as sparsely populated as it had been in '82. As Sproule had remarked to Reeder earlier on, the word was out about Kootenay. From the beginning of open season until the close on October 31st, prospectors in ever greater numbers came into the valley, many of them staking in the slopes above Hot

Spring. Between the summer of '82 and the spring of '83, William Fernie had been succeeded as Gold Commissioner and mining recorder at Wildhorse Creek by Mr. Edward Kelly. When Mr. Kelly sent his report for the year 1883 to the Minister of Mines, he ended it in the following manner:

> The mineral locations, or quartz claims, at Kootenay Lakes, have increased in number, since last year's report, from four to nineteen.
>
> From the prospects I saw at these mines, when I was there in October last, I am convinced there will be, in two years from hence, an extensive mining camp, where capital will be expended in labour and otherwise.
>
> Ledges or lodes of the ore found in this district are numerous. Prospectors on the mountains about these Kootenay Lakes, have had very little trouble in finding claims.
>
> Two claims recorded at these mines, this season, were bonded, or sold conditionally, for $20,000. I have, &c.,
>
> (Signed) EDWARD KELLY.

As the days of June continued to pass uneventfully, it became apparent to Sproule and his friends that the Ainsworth party was not going to return to Big Ledge, at any rate for some time, and that if they remained on the site no enemy action would be taken. Meyers and Hunley were anxious that they make their jumping of the *Comfort* and *Kootenay Chief* final by recording them over at Wildhorse Creek. The group decided that it would be safe for them to sneak away, get their recording done, and return as quickly as possible. When they were gone, Sproule and Reeder would guard their claims by lighting fires in their campsites and generally making it appear to the watchers across the lake that all four men were present at Big Ledge. It had become known to the group that there was an Indian trail starting a few miles to the south of Big Ledge, climbing to a pass in the mountains, and following a large stream down to the upper Kootenay River quite near Wildhorse Creek. It is likely Meyers and Hunley opted for this route since, apart from the fact that it was a shortcut lopping off hundreds of miles of travel, it would obviate any need to take the boat (whose absence might be noticed by the enemy), and would furthermore

# The Disputed Claims at Big Ledge

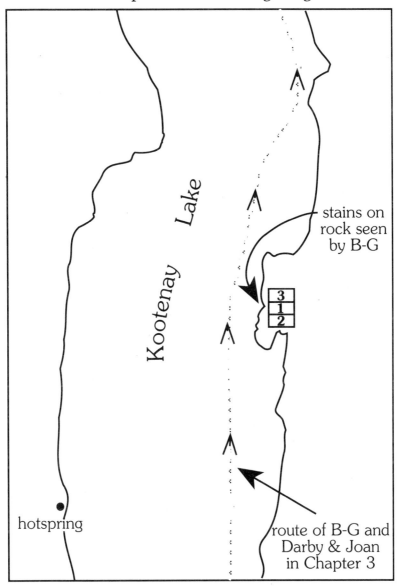

stains on
rock seen
by B-G

3
1
2

Kootenay Lake

hotspring

route of B-G and
Darby & Joan
in Chapter 3

be a much more secret route. In any case, whatever their choice, they got to Wildhorse Creek, filed their claims on June 13th, and returned without having been missed. A month later, there still having been no harassment by the Ainsworth party, Meyers, this time with Sproule, again used the same ploy and made the hurried return journey to Wildhorse. There, on July 16th, Meyers recorded the *Ruby* and Sproule re-recorded the *Bluebell*.

Readers may remember that in the first pages of Chapter 1 they were promised "a tale of money-lust, betrayal, revenge, flight, pursuit, capture, and punishment worthy of any opera." The writer wishes now to remind them that the stage is set, the scene is laid, and the plot can begin unfolding toward its final catastrophe. The diagram on the previous page shows us the situation in a nutshell: a small disputed bit of land in the wilderness of Kootenay Lake; on it three claims staked, restaked, and staked again; two parties of armed men with much to lose waiting in uncertainty for an unknown resolution coming from the outside, all of them nourishing the seeds of violent emotions: hope, desire, frustration, hate, bitterness, anger, fear, vindictiveness. There are no sopranos in this opera to offer relief; only tenors, baritones, and basses to play out the dark emotions to their inevitable conclusion. And now, our tale having somehow climbed to this high dramatic note, we must avoid the strain of sustaining it there by ending the chapter.

# Chapter 9

*In which Sproat and Farwell are brought by B-G to Kootenay Lake, and we learn what they did there; but also giving an account in B-G's words of the hearing to settle the dispute between the Ainsworth and Sproule parties for the claims at Big Ledge.*

W HILE IN VICTORIA lobbying and waiting to escort Sproat and Farwell to Kootenay Lake, B-G visited frequently with Barnaby, Clive, and Mitchell, his tourist friends whom he had met on the boat from England. He gave them such exciting accounts of his adventures on Kootenay Lake that Clive expressed the desire to be taken there. Accordingly, B-G arranged to meet him at Sandpoint on July 13th or 14th. On July 6th the Barnaby party said goodbye to B-G and got aboard a steamboat en route for Tacoma, Washington, whence they would continue by rail to Portland and eventually Sandpoint. Meanwhile, B-G continued to prepare for his trip to Kootenay with Sproat and Farwell. Since the only connection from Victoria to Kootenay through British Columbia was the disued Dewdney Trail, the simplest route to follow was through the United States. Because of his obligation to meet Clive at Sandpoint on the 13th or 14th, B-G left Victoria several days before Sproat and Farwell, arranging to meet them at Sandpoint on the 19th. We do not know what route he followed, only that, having been detained somewhere by the sickness of a friend, he reached Sandpoint on the 15th, a few hours after Clive, tired of waiting, had left to find his friends farther east.

On the 16th—the very day that Sproule and Meyers were at

Wildhorse Creek recording the *Ruby* and re-recording the *Blue-bell*—Sproat and Farwell left Victoria by steamer early in the morning and later that day arrived at Tacoma, where they spent the night. (They left us a fairly complete itinerary of the trip.) In the evening of the 17th they arrived at Portland and spent the second night there. At 7:30 a.m. on the 18th they left Portland on a railway belonging to the Oregon Railway and Steam Navigation Company. At Wallula they changed to the Northern Pacific Railroad, and finally, at 8:00 a.m. of July 19th, they reached Sandpoint to find B-G—Cliveless—awaiting them. B-G had everything ready for a quick departure for Bonners Ferry and they left that very day. Besides B-G and the two commissioners, the party consisted of three men, one boy, and about a dozen mules and horses. At the normal rate for a pack train of around twenty-five miles a day, they reached Bonners Ferry in the early afternoon of the 20th, having camped one night on the trail. After a stay of two days at Bonners Ferry the party left their horses under the care of the Frys and embarked in two heavy, hand-hewn Hudson Bay *bateaux* on the journey down Kootenay River to the lake; all except B-G, who—if he can be taken at his word (after all, he may have been ornamenting his tale for the delight of his English readers)—chose to travel reclining on a couch of buffalo robes in a canoe propelled—as he put it—by two half-naked bucks, arriving at the lake a full two days ahead of the officials he was guiding, and later describing his trip in winged prose.[13]

In whatever fashion—B-G either dutifully *en bateau* with Sproat, Farwell, and the luggage, or joyously *a l'indigene* with his two bucks and the buffalo hides—the party reached the lake and then proceeded in a leisurely manner to Big Ledge—"the Mine," as Farwell later called it in his written report to the government. Arriving there, perhaps on the 26th of July, they found Sproule, Reeder, Meyers, and Hunley in residence and working on their claims. In addition they found Captain Brown of the Ainsworth party along with two assistants busy—just outside the Sproule party sites—collecting ore specimens for removal to Hot Spring, where they would be assayed. Sproule and his friends were unfriendly at first but warmed up when they learned that the new arrivals were not a further threat to them. B-G and his companions noticed that there was no communication between the Sproule and Brown parties but did not learn the reason until the next day when they went across to Hot Spring and talked to the men there. Meanwhile they found Captain Brown the most interesting of those at the Ledge. Farwell in particular enjoyed talking to him, and was pleased to learn that the assayer held the opinion that Big Ledge was a rich site and that the orebody probably extended well beyond the Ledge itself. The two men even discussed the possibility of a smelter near the location. Brown spoke of the abundance of timber in the area and mentioned that he had found in the vicinity a large bed of clay containing kaolin, ideal for the manufacture of fire-brick. They also talked about the prevailing mining laws and their unsuitability for minerals found in lodes and veins. Brown remarked that he personally knew of over a hundred prospectors who would already be on Kootenay Lake were it not for the archaic mining legislation in Canada. When the two men parted that evening, Farwell was left with a most favourable impression of Kootenay Lake as a region for economic development. Next morning the government party embarked on the four-mile trip across the lake to Hot Spring, leaving early to be sure that they would arrive well before the heat of the day could generate a storm or wind. There Sproat and Farwell talked at length to Hammill and the other members of the Ainsworth party and also spent much time examining the country, each according to the mandate he had been given in the letter of instruction. B-G, finding himself increasingly affected by the mining activity around him, decided that within the month he would talk with Sproule about an idea he had. After a night at Hot Spring, they set out on a leisurely journey down the west shore of the lake toward the west arm, retracing the very route that B-G had taken with Darby & Joan almost exactly a year ago. Sproat and Farwell were eager to examine the rapids in the lower Kootenay River where B-G had said the blockage was.

Late in the afternoon of the 29th, they arrived at the lower end of the west arm and, looking for the best spot to set up camp, chose the very place at the mouth of the small creek that Dick Fry and Justine had selected during the events of Chapter 5. Next morning Farwell and B-G set off down the river to the mouth of the creek that would one day bear B-G's name. There they spent the day examining the terrain and discussing the feasibility of deepening the river bed.

Meanwhile, Sproat remained at the campsite. Like Farwell, he too was convinced that the mountains around Kootenay Lake would someday yield large quantities of ore. The whole area might become economically important to the province, and if that happened there would have to be a town, a "capital city," to function as a centre of distribution, of governmental bureaucracy, and of law. In his mind he formed a map: over to the east, the Columbia and Kootenay Rivers rising close to each other, one flowing north to make a large bend southwards, the other flowing south into the States and making a huge bend northwards, the two of them joining in the west to make almost an island, a huge oval island; in the middle of this oval a range of high mountains separating the eastern half from the western. One day, if Kootenay Lake did indeed become economically important, there would have to be two districts: Wildhorse Creek was much too far away. It or some other town could be the "capital" of the eastern district, while a new town would be needed to serve the same purpose over here on the western side of the mountain range.

"I might as well make it a part of my mandate while I'm here," said Sproat to himself, "to choose a site for such a town and reserve it; in that way, whether the Ainsworth proposal goes through or not, it'll be here waiting for whatever develops."

He looked around at the site he was standing on, the site that had sparked all this thought. Then, thinking to get a better view from the other side of the lake, he asked one of the men to row him across. Once there, he could see the whole shoreline from the place where the lake narrowed to become the river to where, eastward, the mountains came too close to the lake to allow for settlement, a distance of perhaps three miles. It was indeed, he decided, a very favourable location for a town, divided into two sections by a spur of the mountain which ended in cliffs not very far from the water about a third of the way from the eastern end. On his left, the eastern section consisted of a gently sloping plain, partly formed by the delta of a creek which debouched from a mountain ravine, running a distance of about two miles up to the mountain. To the right of the dividing spur a much larger and steeper plain ran a greater distance before arriving at the mountain, and even then not really ending because it continued out of sight through a wide pass which led southward, Sproat had been told, to the Salmon River valley. (B-G had told him how, almost exactly a year ago, he had gone with Dick Fry up that pass to the small lake where Dick kept his traps, and also how Jerry O'Donnell and his two friends had come up the Salmon River from the States.) Any town put here, Sproat thought, would be a hilly one, but there was no better location on the lake as far as he knew. The hilliness was more than offset by several advantages: the site was at the junction of two valleys, one—the Salmon River, just over the rise a bit beyond the small lake where Dick Fry had his trapline—giving easy access to the States and, more to the point, the other leading downstream to the Columbia River from which commerce could connect with the nearly completed trans-Canada railway. A town here, then, would be ideally located to steer business away from the States and into Canada where it belonged, especially if the railroad that Ainsworth was proposing got built. Furthermore, this site was more central to the western half of Kootenay than others which were possibilities. There was, for instance, already the small settlement called Second Crossing or Big Eddy forming where the trans-Canada railway was going to be bridged across the Columbia River as it flowed south not far after making the Big Bend. That could conceivably be an administrative centre for west Kootenay, or perhaps some other place farther south on the Columbia, like the little boat-stop near the north end of the Arrow Lakes. In Sproat's mind these sites were not central enough, the first one too far north and both too far west. After all, the Columbia was nearly forty miles west of Kootenay Lake, and in between was the unex-

95

plored country where the Slok-kum or Slocan Lake was said to be. No, clearly the present site was the best one. Sproat ordered his oarsman to get him back to camp as quickly as possible so that he could set about the job of marking off the site. He spent the remainder of that day and most of the next one walking along the shoreline and tramping through bush to place markers on the boundaries he proposed for the townsite reservation, starting at the little creek at the eastern end (the very creek, incidentally, that Dick Fry and Justine had unsuccessfully panned for gold a year ago that very month) and taking in the whole area he had viewed from across the lake. And that crude survey was the first in a series of actions which would cause Gilbert Malcolm Sproat one day to be called "the father of Nelson."

Sproat and Farwell did not leave us a detailed account of their itinerary after they reached the lake, and the only dates we have are those already cited and a few more that will appear as the story unfolds. We know that they travelled up and down the Columbia from the border to Eagle Pass up near Shuswap Lake, examining all of the territory demanded by the Ainsworth Syndicate. We can surmise that once back on Kootenay Lake they explored it extensively and interacted considerably with the Sproule and Ainsworth parties. In an article in the Nelson *Tribune* of October 9th, 1887, Sproat says "Mr. R.E. Sproule told me in 1883, as we sat on a log on this reserve [the one we have just seen Sproat mark out], that he believed that these mountains and over by the Ymir (now so called), were mineral bearing, and that he proposed to prospect them." During all their wanderings Sproat and Farwell made careful observations and kept notes for the reports they would prepare when they returned to Victoria. B-G sometimes accompanied them and sometimes went his own way.

Around the first week in August he began paying frequent visits to Sproule and his party at Big Ledge, and he had a good reason for doing so. Sometime in the Spring, perhaps at Sandpoint, he had met the very government official from Helena whom Sproule had asked for help the winter before. This man (the source books do not mention him by name) had, on learning where B-G was headed, recalled his meeting with Sproule and suggested that B-G might help him. B-G had replied that he would do so if, on looking the property over, he found it of any value. Now, having met Sproule and ascertained that the property might be extremely valuable, he decided it worth his while to talk to Sproule. This was a way of obtaining some valuable property and also becoming a player in the mining game going on so rampantly at Big Ledge.

Meanwhile the Ainsworth party had returned to Big Ledge and built a few small buildings. Now the rival parties were working side by side, avoiding open conflict only by keeping out of each other's way, since any chance meeting invariably resulted in threatening language. However, news had come that a solution to the conflict was on the way. Probably owing to the activities of John C. Ainsworth down in Oakland, California, there was to be a hearing presided over by Gold Commissioner Kelly (the successor, as we already know, to William Fernie). Sometime in late August "Judge" Kelly would arrive at Big Ledge from Wildhorse Creek to set up his court.

It was obvious that in this contest the Ainsworth party, with its financial backing and more educated membership, would have the advantage. Indeed, a prominent lawyer had already been engaged for them at the coast, and was expected to arrive in good time for the hearing. After several long conversations with Sproule, B-G either suggested or brought Sproule to the point of suggesting that he defend Sproule in court. In return he would receive a good share of the *Bluebell*.

On August 18th, Sproat and Farwell left the lake, headed upstream to David McLoughlin's at the border. Leaving there on the 21st, they continued on up the Kootenay River, and along the old Walla Walla trail into upper Kootenay country. Their main purpose in going there was to examine the strip of flat land—only about a mile across—between the source of the Columbia and the south-flowing Kootenay River. It was here that the most audacious part of B-G's plan to drain the flatlands south of Kootenay Lake was to unfold. He was proposing nothing less than a canal between the Kootenay River and the lake at the head of the Columbia (which was about eleven feet lower). Through this canal excess water during the spring melt would drain from the Kootenay into the Columbia. This drainage, coupled with the increased flow which should result when, about three hundred miles away along the watercourse, the stream-bed at the outlet of the west arm was widened and deepened, would prevent the annual flooding of the flatlands and allow settlement there.

The August 18th departure of Sproat and Farwell was hardly noticed on the lake, where there was much activity. Ainsworth's Hot Spring, as the prospectors were beginning to call it since Hammill's announcement that the townsite was now the legal property of the Ainsworth Syndicate, had been adopted as a centre of activity by the score or more of miners who were busy at their claims on the mountain behind it. Small rowboats plied the four-mile stretch of water over to Big Ledge, the second reference point on the miners' map, while many canoes gave evidence that the Indians were curious about the sudden goings-on on their lake. At Big Ledge itself an air of quiet brooding seemed to have taken hold, as Sproule, Meyers, Hunley, and Reeder worked, or gave the appearance of working, close to the Ainsworth party, whose members were also busy making sure that the rival party saw them in possession. Meanwhile, the hot August days slid by, bringing the arrival of Judge Kelly closer. One day he did at last arrive, and for a description of that event, and of the trial that followed, we will call upon B-G himself.[14]

Judge Kelly, a genial old timer, whose silvery locks and quaint Irish humour soon gained him the respect of all concerned, arrived in due time. It was a somewhat memorable scene. The canoe bringing him had been sighted from the enemy's camp, for the little cove in which it lay faced the south. Forgetting for the moment all the dire threats exchanged by the two camps, Winchesters and six-shooters were laid aside, and the inmates of both camps streamed down to the shore to receive the representative of the law. We were a motley little crowd, six or seven on our side, for some necessary witnesses had arrived, and twice that number in Hammil's party. The two camps had each built themselves a log cabin or two, which, by the way, were the first houses in West Kootenay, there being no others within

100 miles. Hence it became unavoidable that Judge Kelly should take up his quarters in one or the other of the rival camps. "Now, boys, " he addressed the crowd, "I think it will be fair to both camps if I grub in the one and sleep in the other, so just let me know who has the better grub outfit," a little joke which was greeted with merriment. A hasty exchange of information concerning our respective culinary possessions between Hammil and myself, left no doubt that the enemy's grub box was far better stocked than ours. Molasses, onions, and canned stuff, of which we had none, decided the question in which camp the judge would take his meals. Every morning and evening he was escorted to and fro from one camp to the other by one or more of his late hosts, the distance being a few hundred yards.

The largest of the three shanties in the two camps was selected as the court-house, where the trial took place. Every soul except the judge was, of course, deeply concerned in the issue of the litigation; millions, we all thought, were at stake, and feelings therefore ran very high, for Sprowle's intense animosity had communicated itself to his witnesses as well as partners. That in such a rough crowd, composed to a great extent of men who had passed their lives in American mining camps, where men very frequently take justice into their own hands, a trial lasting for some weeks was not marred by a single affray was, under the circumstances, very creditable to the man who had to decide the issue. The Court opened on Aug. 31, and the first thing Judge Kelly insisted on was that all revolvers were to be deposited in a box at his side so long as the court sat, a precaution which, alas succeeded only for the time being to save the life of one of the two persons most concerned. The litigation had resolved itself into four distinct cases, for each of the two parties had taken up the same four claims on the big ledge. As several important witnesses were absent, two or three short adjournments became necessary, and it was only on Oct. 16, 1883 that Judge Kelly gave his judgement. All four were decided in our favour! Judge Kelly was an old miner himself, and knew little of law; hence he took the view which from the first I had recognised as the saving of our case, namely the commonsense interpretation of the actions of men who, from causes beyond their control, found it impossible to comply with the strict letter of the mining regulations.

B-G goes on to tell us that a fairly large number of Indians watched the trial. We can picture them seated on the floor, or on the ground near the doorway, watching the interesting proceedings of the white men as they argued their case. Sproat and Farwell had returned to the lake on October 6th, well before the trial ended, but we don't know whether or not they attended all or parts of the proceedings. In any case, they soon left the area, probably accompanied by B-G, and reached Bonners Ferry on October 28th, Sandpoint on October 30th, and Victoria on November 3rd.

We can imagine the exultation of Sproule and his friends when Hammill and the rest of the Ainsworth party were banished to their townsite across the water. We can imagine Sproule walking alone on the shoreline, thinking of all the troubles he had undergone a year ago, all the worry and despair he had felt for so long. And now that was all finished; the law had given him the victory he deserved. But over at Ainsworth's Hot Spring Hammill and the others, though licking their wounds, had not given up. A messenger was on his way south with the news, and plans for an appeal would soon be under way.

October 31st came, and with it the closing of the season. November, always an unpredictable month in which winter can inflict a severe warning, made the men at the lake think of moving south. Secure in the knowledge that their claims were safe until next June, the prospectors began, one by one or in small groups, to head up the lake to the river, perhaps to spend the winter in Sandpoint or nearer the coast. We can guess that the Ainsworth party made what preparations for winter were needed at their townsite and left for home fairly early, leaving the enemy still working at Big Ledge for a few weeks longer. The Indians, obeying the impulses of their ancient cycle, also headed south. Once again, perhaps for the last time, Kootenay Lake lay anticipating the primeval silence of winter.

# CHAPTER 10

*A short interruption of our narrative, offering specu-*
*lation about a journey we know B-G must have taken*
*to the source of the Columbia in 1883, the year of the*
*previous two chapters; and also presenting certain*
*doubts about the reliability not only of B-G's books as*
*primary source material for our use in piercing those*
*veils which hide the past but also of B-G's own hon-*
*esty. Those readers not interested in the difficulties*
*historians experience may turn at once to Chapter 11*
*in which the tale continues.*

KOOTENAY FOLKLORE has always named Baillie-Grohman
as the first man to conceive the idea of preventing the annual
spring flooding of the flatlands at the south end of Kootenay Lake.
Taking B-G at his own word, all written histories, including this
one, have given him the credit. As readers know, the present historian has shown B-G over the course of his travellings slowly developing the idea and finally, in Chapter 6, coming to a decision
about realizing it.

And yet, this historian has been unable to find anywhere a
description of, or an actual date for, B-G's first visit to the flatlands
between Columbia Lake and the south-flowing Kootenay River—
present-day Canal Flat. There must have been such a visit if he was
to conceive the most audacious part of his scheme, the building
of a canal there to drain away Kootenay River water during the
spring melt. We saw, in the previous chapter, Sproat and Farwell
going there for the purpose of checking on B-G's proposal. That

means that B-G himself, in order to conceive the proposal, must have gone there in either 1882 or very early '83. There are a few months unaccounted for in early '83, after B-G's return from England and before his July rendezvous at Sandpoint. That may well be the period in which he went, and, indeed, in one of his books he mentions that he made his first trip to upper (east) Kootenay country in 1883. But there is no record of it, and that troublesome hiatus leads one to a suspicion: perhaps B-G did not make that first trip at all, and if he didn't, it must be that he did not need to make it, having already received the complete scheme—the draining of the southern flatlands by building a canal at present-day Canal Flat—from someone else.

Hidden away all these many years in the musty pages of a forgotten newspaper—marvelously preserved from water, mice, fire, and all the other dangers inherent in the passage of time— was evidence that someone else did indeed conceive of the idea before B-G, and not only conceived of it but also laid it out in a lengthy and very well-written letter which appeared in the Spokane *Chronicle* of September 14th, 1881. The writer of that letter was David McLoughlin.[15]

Readers may remember that away back in Chapter 3, B-G, on his first trip to Kootenay Lake in 1882 accompanied by his guides Darby & Joan, stopped briefly at the border to visit a half-blood named David McLoughlin whom Dick Fry had told him about. Some readers may have wondered at that time why this historian so carefully made the point that B-G neither described the visit nor named the man, but made brief reference to him as "a man with a large Indian family." If such readers there were, the time has come to resolve their wondering. Why didn't B-G mention David McLoughlin by name, and why didn't he record something of their conversation? It must have been worthy of mention, if only to express the strangeness of meeting so educated and literate a man in the wilderness. It is hard to believe that David wouldn't have talked about the flatlands and given his opinion of their economic value when he learned where B-G was headed. And why did B-G write so denigrating and patronizing a report of David when he again visited him in 1884? On that second visit, while giving David his due as a man of superior intellect, he took pains to leave the reader with a negative impression, calling David an "interesting old character who lived Indian fashion in a miserable hovel," a "squaw-man" who had "long relapsed into the dirt and savagery of Indian life," and was "constantly preyed upon by his squaw's numerous relations, who sponged on him with the callous persistence of their race." Descriptions by other people of David's home are much more pleasant.

Can it be that B-G had indeed received a full account of David's drainage scheme on that first visit in 1882, then later, appreciating its feasibility, decided to appropriate it as his own? That would explain why, in the books he later wrote, he found it necessary to minimize David McLoughlin, to portray him as a person incapable of conceiving such a scheme—all unsuspecting, alas for him, that in a newspaper file down in Spokane was lying the evidence that would reveal his duplicity more than a century later to people not yet born, and tarnish the reputation he was so studiously seeking to enhance. History has its delicious ironies.

Out of fairness to our friend B-G we must remember that the above aspersions are no more than mere suspicions. We have not proven that B-G was dishonest; we have only suggested the possibility. The history of intellectual development shows us that ideas both great and small seem to have their time and occur simultaneously to several minds. Darwin and Wallace—only a couple of decades before 1882—had both had the idea of evolution, each quite unknowing of the other. Why, then, should we not believe that B-G had *his* idea quite independently of David McLoughlin? After all, the idea of canals was definitely in the air: the Suez Canal had been opened only thirteen years before, and work had already begun on the Panama. And there is evidence that yet a third party had the idea of flood-prevention on the southern flatlands. In the *British Columbia Gazette* of January 18th, 1883, there is a notice that John C. Ainsworth, his son George, and Enoch Blasdel are applying for incorporation as a company for reclaiming the overflowed lands along the Kootenay River and "for turning the said river into the Columbia at a point known as *Kootenay Crossing* near the Columbia Lakes," although nothing seems to have come of it.[16]

In all this discussion of B-G we are looking through one of those open doors that historians continuously encounter—doors opening onto receding vistas of other rooms through which we must not wander, great as the temptation may be, because exploration of them is alien to our purpose. This is not a history of B-G. So far he has figured prominently in our chapters, but after only one more he will be dismissed from the stage, or rather will remove himself to the wings, to reappear from time to time only as our story makes passing references to him. He is, however, worthy of a whole story of his own. Perhaps other writers, their curiosity fired by the pages of this book, will give us an exhaustive look at Baillie-Grohman. Until then we must wait for the further research that will reveal whether or not his honesty is to be questioned in the matter of David McLoughlin, and for the more careful study of his works which will determine why they present such difficulties to historians who wish to use them as source books. Meanwhile, we will, as others have done before us, take B-G at his word and return to our tale.

# CHAPTER 11

*In which we resume our story by recording the events of 1884.*

THE AINSWORTH SYNDICATE was quick to file an appeal for Hammill after his loss of the *Bluebell* to Sproule. Down in Victoria at the Supreme Court of British Columbia, Chief Justice Matthew Begbie presented his deliberations concerning the case on March 25th, hardly before winter was over up in Kootenay. In the matters of Woodbury v. Hudnut and Woodbury v. Meyers for the *Comfort/Gem* claim, and Blasdel v. Hunley for the *Mogul/Kootenay Chief/Lucy Long*, he reversed the decision of Kelly and decided in favour of the Ainsworth party. In the matter of Hammill v. Sproule he confirmed Kelly's decision in favour of Sproule. (The reader is reminded of the diagram near the end of Chapter 8.) Judge Begbie made it clear that he considered Hammill nothing but a claim jumper, and near the close of his deliberations referred to B-G's part in the proceedings:

> It is impossible not to be struck with the fact prominently put forward in the printed documents before us, that the whole of this wearisome, expensive, and mischievous litigation has been caused and fostered by the unauthorized intrusion of a stranger, who seems to have succeeded, before the Gold Commissioner, in raising such a cloud of irrelevant statement and controversies, as to entirely obscure that officer's view of the few material facts in each case. This interference, it is scarcely necessary to state, is entirely illegal. The gentleman in question may have conceived himself to be impelled by the highest motives.[17]

One would expect Sproule to have been very pleased at Begbie's decision; instead, he was just the opposite. That was because he—he and Meyers and Hunley, that is—now owed B-G for his services at the Kelly hearing. The claims that had already, either wholly or in part, been conveyed to B-G as payment were now in the hands of the Ainsworth party. Furthermore, Meyers and Hunley, having lost their claims in the appeal, now owed court costs for the Begbie hearing.

According to B-G, reviewing the case in one of his books, Sproule's anger was directed mainly at him, because he, having gone to England soon after the Kelly hearing, had been unable to assist in preparations for the appeal before Begbie. So angry, in fact, was Sproule, that after B-G's return from England, he pursued him through the bush near Sandpoint, taking shots at him. However exaggerated this story may or may not be—the reader is already aware of the reservations this historian holds concerning the reliability of B-G, who, in all fairness, was writing with other purposes in mind than those of historians and should not be judged according to their standards—it does indicate a stage in the psychological deterioration of Sproule that eventually led to his own death. In any case, the quarrel between Hammill and Sproule, one of the central stories in Kootenay folklore, is an extremely complex one, and we must avoid pursuing it beyond its relevance to our own tale.

B-G would have to wait until nearly the end of '84 to learn whether or not the government favoured his proposal and would grant him the lands he wanted. Meanwhile, he was optimistic and went about preparing for the event. His trip to England had been partly to form the Kootenay Lake Syndicate for raising funds, and partly to obtain a boat. One of the British Columbia government's conditions for granting him the land was that his syndicate place a steamboat on the navigable part of the lower Kootenay River (i.e., from Bonners Ferry to the rapids downstream from the lake) by the end of 1884.

After obtaining prices from boat builders in Portland, Oregon, B-G concluded that he could get a second-hand boat in England more cheaply. Accordingly, while there he obtained one from Venables Kyrke, an investor in the Kootenay Lake Syndicate. This boat was the steam-launch *Midge*, famous in Kootenay lore as the first steam-vessel on the lake. When it arrived at Montreal strapped to the deck of the S.S. *Polynesian*, customs officers demanded a large amount of duty. Knowing that "settlers' goods," including second-hand agricultural machinery, were duty-free, B-G hit upon a plan. He told the customs men they would have to wait a few days, and set out for Ottawa, where, in his own words, "as I had letters from a member of the Cabinet at home to Sir John MacDonald [sic] and others in high official positions, I thought I would test their efficacy." Although anxious to please their guest, the high officials had to abide by regulations. During a discussion of the problems, B-G joked that since the lands he was acquiring were flooded, it would need a steam-launch to pull the plough. "Smiling benignly" at this solution, the relevant official agreed to sign a permit. A few days later B-G handed it to the astonished customs officers, who were obliged to clear *Midge* as an agricultural implement. B-G was proud of this coup, and later someone told him that it "deserved being put in a `glass case.'" The present author is pleased to indulge B-G across the gulf of more than a century by placing his little coup in the glass case of this history.

From Montreal, "by taking advantage of the artificial and natural waterways that penetrate into the heart of the continent," *Midge* was finally put on two flatcars of the Northern Pacific Railway (piecemeal, for her working innards had been removed to facilitate transportation) and carried from Duluth, Minnesota to Kootenai Station, a railway stop a few miles east of Sandpoint, Idaho. The most challenging part of her long trek into the wilderness of Kootenay now lay ahead—the thirty or so miles from Kootenai Station to Bonners Ferry. In Sandpoint during preparations for this final leg of the journey, B-G accidentally met up with a young adventurer called Arthur Fenwick, whose family he knew in England, whose father in fact had shares in the Kootenay Lake Syndicate. Delighted at having met up with a trustworthy person whom he knew to be of "good family," B-G decided to relieve himself of the necessity of accompanying *Midge* to Bonners Ferry. He proposed that young Fenwick take charge of getting her there so that he himself could go to Victoria, where he had much to do. Arthur Fenwick accepted the job offer.

From Kootenai Station to Bonners Ferry there was only the same trail that B-G had walked over in '82, its upgrading to a wagon road still a full year away. Ten or twelve white men, aided by tackle, pulleys and "a large force of Kootenay Indians," at first seemed unequal to the task. For the greater part of the thirty miles they simply carried *Midge* bodily along the flat terrain, spelling each other off and resting frequently, no doubt kept both lively and amused by enthusiastic Fenwick. On hills they attached ropes to her and, making use of trees and pulleys, hauled her up on rollers supplied by the forest, then let her down the other side in the same manner. Finally, after three weeks of labour, they reached Bonners Ferry and put little *Midge*, who had formerly plied the fjords of Norway, into her new home, the Kootenay River. There they reinstalled her boiler, firebox, and other working gear (all of which had been carried separately), not forgetting the fat little smokestack that to our eyes gives her such an endearingly early-industrial-age look, and in general made her ready and presentable for her maiden voyage northward to Kootenay Lake.

The Indians loved *Midge* at first sight. Her initial appearance on the water created the "most profound surprise" among them, and, for a long time after her maiden voyage, whenever groups of them heard her approaching they would dash down to the water's edge to welcome her. They loved to watch the thick smoke that belched so wonderfully from her fat smokestack; they loved to rope their canoes to her and be pulled miraculously along without effort; they loved to pull the string on her whistle and hear the shrill blast that resulted. And they were more than willing to leave stacks of cut wood for her firebox at intervals along the banks. Opportunistic B-G later provided a bucksaw—it also pleased them as a novelty—and let them pull the whistle string or be towed as often as they wanted in return for the wood. "This was an economical way," B-G comments, "of solving a difficulty which besets most pioneer steamers navigating the waters of un-inhabited countries . . . " The Indians have left no recorded comments, but we can be sure that, like anyone else in similar circumstances, they enjoyed the novelty to their utmost ability and did not mind paying for it.

All the while B-G's crew were undertaking their Herculean labours to bring *Midge* onto the lake, Ainsworth's Hot Spring and Big Ledge had been the scene of much activity. The townsite at the hot spring was rapidly becoming a small settlement as more and more prospectors made it their headquarters. Robert Sproule, having come north onto the lake much earlier this year, was in residence at Big Ledge, working on the *Bluebell*. As we have seen, confirmed possession had not made him happy; he needed money and could see no way out of that difficulty, except to go south and find a job. To add to this discomfort, he was alone, Meyers and Hunley having gone elsewhere after Judge Begbie's decision to award the *Comfort* and *Kootenay Chief* to the Ainsworth party. Even Gay Reeder was not around anywhere. And, of course, to make matters worse, Hammill & Co. were back at Big Ledge every second day or so, working the claims which were now legally theirs. The enemies avoided each other, and there wasn't any outbreak of hostilities. Just in case there might be, however, the government had seen fit to install an Acting Sheriff in the area, one J. Hope Johnston.

By the first week in May, or even earlier, Sproule decided to find a job and made his way south to Sandpoint. There he had good luck and became the Road Commissioner for the Third District of Kootenai County, Idaho. He did not lose touch with his *Bluebell* mine, however, and made frequent journeys north to Big Ledge. He was still concerned with the problem of developing his property and was on the lookout for a prospective partner with money. One day he met a likely prospect in Sandpoint. As this man is one of the chief figures in Kootenay folklore, he must be introduced in a paragraph of his own.

The Northern Pacific Railroad, at its headquarters back east, was interested in raising its profits by inducing tourists to visit the wilderness around Sandpoint. One of those who responded to its advertising was a medical doctor named Wilbur A. Hendryx. Dr. Hendryx's brother Andrew was a wealthy manufacturer of bird cages and other brass artifacts in New Haven, Connecticut, a fact whose significance will become apparent later. Early in the spring of '84, Dr. Hendryx took a vacation from his practice in Grand Rapids, Michigan for the purpose of viewing the newly opened wilderness in the west. In Sandpoint, on a day in June, he met Robert Sproule and was taken by him to Big Ledge.

The doctor had never before experienced at first hand the mining fever in full bloom, and he quickly became flushed himself—infected with the excitement that was everywhere in the air as the active community of prospectors and developers went about their business on the lake and its environs. A close inspection of the *Bluebell* and other claims on Big Ledge seemed, even to his unpractised eye, to confirm the optimism that everyone felt. Long conversations with Sproule and others completed the inoculation, and Dr. Hendryx succumbed, a willing victim of the fever. Who could resist the talk of riches in the offing? Who could feel otherwise than lucky to have discovered this place at a time when, since no real development had yet occurred, there was still a chance to become involved oneself? If Dr. Hendryx had set out on this vacation to the western wilderness motivated solely by romantic and aesthetic values, he was now firmly in the grip of monetary ones. Having made an agreement with Robert Sproule, he went home with but one aim—to talk his brother and others into forming a partnership for the exploitation of Big Ledge's ore deposits.

The summer wore on. One sunny morning, somewhere about the first day of August, little *Midge* came around the bend and into sight of the workers at Big Ledge. One can imagine the impact she made on that busy community, how surprised they were when the smoke belching from her fat pipe first hove into view, how glad the whole of the lake's population felt on those first days when, far across the water, they would see the plume of smoke that announced her friendly presence. Steam had come to Kootenay Lake! It connected the mines more firmly to Bonners Ferry and Sandpoint, and made the men feel secure in the belief that what they were doing here in the wilderness might indeed develop into something permanent. One can imagine also the practical advantages *Midge* brought. Errands, deliveries, visiting—all these were made easier by her presence. If Sproule had been there that first week of her arrival, he would surely have remembered Reeder's ironic question on that day in '82 when they had first met in Sandpoint—"Has Big Ledge got steam to it?" Perhaps he would have felt satisfaction that only two summers after that question steam *had* come—even if it was only in the form of tiny *Midge*.

Sometime about the middle of August, B-G, having completed his business in Victoria, was again in Sandpoint. He was to rendezvous there with two of his chief backers: Mr. Bates, a successful Welsh brewer, and Mr. Forbes, president of the Bell Telephone Company in Boston. He intended to impress them with the feasibility of his reclamation scheme by showing them the sites of his two proposed undertakings. First they would visit the narrows at the lake's outlet down at the end of the west arm, where he proposed to dredge; then they would travel by pack train to the flatland between Columbia Lake and the Kootenay River, where he proposed to build his canal. The two wealthy backers were very pleased to be participating in this adventurous journey into the Canadian wilderness. Mr. Forbes brought his son and his nephew, boys about seventeen years of age. Also along on the trip was Mr. Leslie Hill, an engineer whom B-G had met in Wyoming several years earlier.

The source books for this episode, though both technically primary sources, contradict each other. One is the work of B-G himself, and, as the reader knows, doubts have already been cast on his reliability. The second, namely the 1946 *Memoirs* of Arthur Fenwick, also contains serious internal evidence of dramatic aberration from the truth. For that reason, this historian, not wishing to assume the responsibility of passing on error second-hand, will let Fenwick relate the events himself. As the first paragraph of the quotation shows, Arthur Fenwick seems to corroborate B-G's story that Sproule had been gunning for him at Sandpoint.

. . . I had a pack train and a lot of saddle horses and had all arrangements pretty well made. Grohman paid me $5.00 a day to see he didn't get killed. The simplest way was to run Sproule and his toughs out of Sandpoint, which I did with the promise to shoot on sight if I met any of them again, so we had a little peace . . .

. . . Grohman's people arrived about the middle of August, 1884. I had the pack train and horses all ready in Sandpoint, but they had to stay there overnight whilst we made up the packs, as it was a big outfit: Mr. Forbes, Mr. Bates, Forbes' son and nephew (boys about 17 or 18 years old), a Mr. Owen and Leslie Hill as engineer, so there was a lot of baggage as well as food supplies. They put up in a new 3-room cabin with 3 double beds in it situated across the railway tracks from Mrs. Baldwin's Hotel, to which it belonged. I slept in the hotel. Between 2 and 3 in the morning I was awakened by a burst of gun fire. I jerked my boots on and saw a freight train pulling out and gun flashes coming from a boxcar and shooting straight for the 3-room shack, and gun flashes coming back. I bolted across the track behind the train which was pulling out and stumbled over a man lying in the doorway of the shack from which shouts were coming. I shouted it was me coming, went in and struck a light and looked around. They were all under the beds or under the mattresses, but while the wash stand jugs were broken and the beds hit, no one was hurt. They were all for going back to Boston on the next train. I told them it was men trying to steal rides to Spokane, and train men standing them off. I had to go and look after the man outside the door, as he was bleeding a lot, but it was only a flesh wound. Another had a leg broken . . .

. . . As it was by now getting daylight, I got the packers and horses up and we pulled out for Bonners Ferry where I had the *Midge* and the two big boats. It was 45 miles, but we all arrived in the afternoon and went down the Kootenay to where Nelson is now to look at a bad ridge of rock running right across the river just below Nelson. Leslie Hill afterwards tunnelled under it and blew it all out—the first reclamation work that was done . . .

It is unfortunate that the last two lines of this quotation do not give an exact date for Hill's blasting of the ridge. Does "afterwards" mean that very year or several years later? That being as it may, the party then travelled in *Midge* to the boundary where horses were waiting and journeyed by land over to the canal site. There B-G convinced them of the feasibility of his plan to drain water from the Kootenay River into the Columbia. They saw with their own eyes that the Columbia was indeed about eleven feet lower than the Kootenay. As they journeyed to the site they stopped occasionally for hunting and fishing. On their return, the party refused to pay another visit to Sandpoint, having had enough of being shot at (we can imagine the eagerness of the two boys to tell their friends back home of the wonderful "wild west" adventure they had had in that town). Instead, Fenwick led them to Ravalli, Montana, where they could board the Northern Pacific. They stopped to hunt big game on the way, "Grohman," Fenwick tells us, "posing as a mighty hunter." He goes on to relate, with relish, how B-G, identifying "a lot of beardigging" that Fenwick himself knew was merely the rooting of domestic pigs, caused the party to bag an old boar, which cost them a pretty penny when the farmer heard of it.

It should be mentioned that on their way down to the lake from Bonners Ferry, B-G had stopped in at David McLoughlin's for his second visit. At that time, for ninety dollars in cash and a fifty-pound sack of flour, David had sold him the old log building that had once been the Hudson's Bay Company's trading post known as Fort Flatbow. This B-G could make use of as a storage place and general headquarters whenever he was in that part of the country.

Summer became autumn. B-G, Sproule, the Ainsworth party, Dick Fry and Justine, David McLoughlin, the Kootenay Indians, and all the other characters in our tale went about their separate businesses within the large area of our stage, stretching from Sandpoint, through Bonners Ferry, to the wide expanse of Kootenay Lake. Back east, Dr. Wilbur Hendryx was not finding any difficulty in convincing his brother, the bird cage manufacturer, that a company should be formed to develop the *Bluebell*. Bird cages of fine quality are made of brass; brass is an alloy made partly of zinc; zinc is one of the components of galena; galena was the ore found at the *Bluebell*. By late autumn a company—the Kootenay Lake Mining & Smelting Co., Ltd.—was well advanced in the process of its formation. Sproat and Farwell—their reports on the journey of '83 all finished and submitted—were either working in Victoria or travelling in upper Kootenay and Big Bend country. B-G, now more than ever caught up in his land-reclamation scheme, was preparing to remove himself either to England or to upper Kootenay country for the furtherance of his canal plans—well off-stage for the time being.

Once again winter was coming and human beings prepared to leave Kootenay Lake; most of them, that is, for it seems likely that, although Sproule and the Ainsworth party left, a few of the prospectors around Ainsworth's Hot Spring decided to remain over the cold months. Game would be plentiful when deer and elk came down to the shoreline. Flour, molasses, baking powder, and other staples would already have been obtained from Bonners Ferry.

As for the Lower Kootenay Indians, their fate was being decided in Victoria and elsewhere. Farwell, in his report, had assessed their numbers in detail: 35 men, 34 married women, 39 boys, 32 girls, 4 widows with 6 boys and 3 girls, and 4 widows "without encumbrances," adding up to a total of 157. He had also spoken of their accelerating decline, and finally recommended that, in the event of B-G's reclamation scheme being successful, they should be removed to a reserve of perhaps 1,000 acres of grassland near the border.

Meanwhile, as the land prepared for winter, they straggled southward to their wintering-grounds, now, according to Farwell, near David McLoughlin's rather than Bonners Ferry. While peaks regained their ancient snows and life forms prepared for their age-old cycle of hibernation, those animals that wintered near Ainsworth's Hot Spring adapted themselves, if some of the prospectors did indeed stay over, to an alien presence.

December came. Winter deepened along the lake, and the

prospectors at Ainsworth's Hot Spring held to their cabins, almost, like the bears, in a state of hibernation. Two hundred miles to the northwest, the busy railway town of Kamloops took notice of Kootenay. On the 11th its newspaper, the *Sentinel,* reported the following:

> ...J.C. Rykert, Collector of Customs for Kootenay District, reports that a New Haven Company of 65 men have secured mineral land on Kootenay Lake. They plan to build a smelter in 1885, having bought out Sproule and other miners. They will run a steamer on the lake...

# CHAPTER 12

*In which our tale presents the revenge, flight, pursuit,
and capture that were promised in the first pages of
Chapter 1; but also gives passing mention to an event
of fundamental importance to Canada.*

DR. WILBUR HENDRYX, like John C. Ainsworth, allowed little time to elapse between an idea and its realization. And, like John C., he too thought things out very carefully before acting. Not for *him* fell the Shadow

> Between the conception
> And the creation
> Between the emotion
> And the response . . .

By the early spring of '85, his Kootenay Mining & Smelting Co. Ltd. had a portable sawmill erected at the Northern Pacific Railroad stop called Kootenai Station, a mile or so east of Sandpoint; and a crew working under Robert Sproule was busy converting the old trail from there to Bonners Ferry into a wagon road, just a year late for the convenience of B-G's men hauling the *Midge*. Lumber for building at the *Bluebell* and a road to carry it to Bonners Ferry—all that was needed now was a boat to haul it to Big Ledge down on Kootenay Lake. And that was in the planning. By summer the *Surprise*, a closed-in steamer—something between *Midge* and a tug-boat—would arrive at Dick Fry's ready to be put onto the river. With the thoroughness that characterizes the born entrepreneur, the doctor had brought his wife to live at Kootenai Station and was himself directing the directors of his operations.

On Friday, May 29th, Robert Sproule, now both a shareholder and a wage-earner in the Kootenay Mining & Smelting Co. Ltd., arrived at Big Ledge accompanied by three men he had hired at Sandpoint: a fellow called Charles Howes, and two half-blood brothers named Adam and Charles Wolfe, variously described as "sinister" and "sleazy." They settled in and began work on the *Bluebell* claim.

Already settled in its townsite across the lake was the Ainsworth party led by Thomas Hammill. This year the party was a large one. Besides Hammill himself, only two of its members concern us—a man called Duncan and one called Velnoweth. Also present at Ainsworth's Hot Spring was Constable Harry Anderson from Wildhorse Creek, who had succeeded Acting Sheriff Johnston of the previous year as the law's representative on the site.

On Sunday, May 31st, Sproule left Big Ledge and rowed across to the hot spring camp to see Constable Anderson on some business matter or other, interrupting him at lunch with Hammill. Later that afternoon the weather turned sour, and Sproule, not wanting to venture back across the lake, stayed for the night at the cabin of a friend. Very early next morning, he rowed over to the *Bluebell*. Not long afterward, Hammill, Duncan, and Velnoweth also set out for Big Ledge. By 8 o'clock in the morning the seven men of both parties were at work on their claims: Hammill at the *Kootenay Chief*, Duncan at the *Comfort*, Velnoweth at the *Ruby*, Howes and the Wolfe brothers at the *Bluebell*, and Sproule filing a saw at his cabin.

It was clear that the law's intervention in their dispute, while settling who owned what, had not quelled the varying degrees of dislike or hatred that members of each party felt for those of the other. And new party members had been infected by the older ones. Like neighbours who have fought over poor fences, they worked within hailing distance of one another, each aware of the activities of the enemy and pretending not to be, their hearts gnawed by the bitterness that was spoiling every hour of their lives.

Between 9 and 10 o'clock, Sproule approached Duncan and asked, "Where is Hammill?" Receiving no definite answer, he shortly afterward went away. Between 10 and 11 o'clock, Velnoweth and Duncan heard a rifle shot, but thought nothing of it. About noon, Velnoweth and Duncan walked toward Hammill's cabin. Nearing their destination, they discovered Hammill lying on the path, moaning and writhing in agony from a bullet wound. They carried him, almost delirious with pain, into the cabin, where he died without naming his assailant.

Duncan left immediately to fetch Harry Anderson from the camp at the Ainsworth Hot Spring. By 2 o'clock he was back with Anderson and two members of Hammill's party, as well as a few independent prospectors. *Midge* was not available during this emergency. Her skipper Arthur Fenwick was busy on another job for his boss B-G. He was leading a pack train to Canal Flat, carrying supplies for the furtherance of B-G's scheme there.

Sproule was immediately assumed to be the murderer. Everyone knew of his hatred for Hammill and many people had heard him make threatening remarks about his rival. He was not at the scene of the murder, and the Wolfe brothers said he had left in his rowboat for Bonners Ferry. They further stated that he had borrowed Adam's gun earlier in the morning. Anderson made an examination of the body and recovered a bullet that had lodged in the spine near the pelvic region. Then he authorized that the body be buried.

At least three hours had gone by since the time of Hammill's murder, as indicated by the sound of the gunshot. It was obvious that if Sproule was to be captured before he reached the border, there would have to be some speedier means of travel than a rowboat. A canoe was the only hope. As luck would have it there were no Indians at Big Ledge on this day, but Anderson knew there were always a few camping and fishing over at the entrance to the west arm. Rowing over there would mean a further delay of an hour or more, but even considering that, a canoe was the only hope of catching Sproule before he reached the safety of the United States. Accordingly, Anderson and a few assistants threw some supplies together and set out, rowing as fast as they could, to find the Indians. Reaching the west arm, they obtained two canoes with Indians to paddle them and began the pursuit southward, first crossing the lake to the eastern shore.

The Indians paddled tirelessly and the canoes sped southward, keeping fairly close to the shoreline but cutting across bays from headland to headland to save time. However, as the hours passed by, clouds massed in the sky and big whitecaps impeded progress. It became necessary to get relief from the storm by hugging the shore and following the curves of the bays more closely. All the time Anderson kept his posse busy scanning the thin line between water and forest for any sign that Sproule might have landed. At length, very late in the afternoon and close to the end of the lake, they spied a boat pulled up on the shore. No attempt had been made to hide it, but they almost missed seeing it, for it had been beached in a tiny cove almost invisible from the water. Anderson's men easily identified it as Sproule's. They looked around. There were no trails leading anywhere, only the desolate, unknowing forest staring back at them. Wherever Sproule had gone, there was little hope of finding him here; it was uncertain even how long ago he had landed. After a short consultation the men agreed with Anderson that Sproule, daunted by the storm, must have decided to abandon the clumsy rowboat and make for the border on foot. He would have a hard time of it, slogging through the brush, and could not possibly cover the many miles still left to reach the border before nightfall. The best thing the posse could do would be to paddle south as far as they could before dark then camp for the night. After all, Sproule too would have to sleep. Then, tomorrow morning they could reach the border in a couple of hours and wait for him there. Even if he was watching them right now from some hiding place, he could hardly avoid them by returning to Big Ledge or the west arm, where Hammill's friends would be waiting. They returned to the canoes and set off southward.

They waited right at the border, in fact on the swathe that marked it, which had been cut a score of years before and now was overgrown with brush. Half a mile to the north was the small house of J.C. Rykert, the new customs man appointed only the year before, and beyond that the disused Dewdney Trail; a few hundred yards to the south was David McLoughlin's home. Anderson decided that the posse should be divided, half the men on the east side of the river and half on the west. Particular watch was to be kept on the small trail that crossed the swathe on the east side, heading from the Dewdney Trail to the old Walla Walla trail farther south.

They waited in concealment. Anderson gave orders to the posse, including the Indians, that there was to be no gunfire. On the morning of the following day, Sproule walked down the trail and was seized as he began crossing the swathe.

There is a story about the capture, perhaps authentic, perhaps one of those decorations with which inventive time colours the fabric of the past, enhancing the bald truth of those first occurrences with myth and legend. It states that one of the Indians, forgetful of Anderson's proscription, fired at a bear. Nearby, Sproule, hungry and tired, heard the shot and reacted in a manner opposite to that anticipated by Anderson. Instead of being warned to retreat, he hurried forward without caution, perhaps having decided that, since no waiting posse would be so foolish as to give notice of itself, the shot must have come from the rifle of an Indian who would feed him. And so, ironic fate delivered him into the hands of the law only a few yards from safety.

He offered no resistance to his captors and indeed seemed surprised that they were after him. He seemed surprised also when he heard of Hammill's death, and continually protested his innocence.

"If you're innocent, why were you running away?" asked Anderson, not taking Sproule's apparent surprise as anything but good acting.

"But I wasn't running away from anything," answered Sproule. "I set out that morning to visit my boss in Sandpoint. I wanted to talk to him about . . . "

"How come nobody knew you was goin'?"

"An' how come you borrowed Adam Wolfe's rifle?"

"I did tell Adam Wolfe where I was going, and his brother, too," answered Sproule, "and why should I borrow his rifle when I've got one of my own? If you think I shot Hammill with Adam's rifle, you're crazy! Why should I borrow a rifle when I've got my own?"

"Yeah, well, if you wasn't runnin' away, how come you beached your boat an' took to the woods?"

"You oughta know as well as I do a big storm came up that afternoon. I thought the boat was gonna swamp. I figured it'd be easier to walk the resta the way till I met the trail to Sandpoint."

"Ya sure got your story all figur'd out. But no one's gonna . . . "

"Well, boys," interjected Anderson, "let's not keep this wranglin' up too long." He turned to look at Sproule. "You're goin' with us, and the law can decide what to do with you. And I've got the bullet that'll prove whose gun shot Hammill. Now let's get some grub into us and head back to Big Ledge."

"But I wanna go to Sandpoint," said Sproule.

"I've no doubt you do. That's because you think you'll get off in your own country," answered Anderson. But you committed your crime in Canada, and that's where we're gonna keep you." He turned to one of the posse's members. "Bill, you and Jack get Vowell to come over to Big Ledge and hold a hearing on the site of the murder. Try to get him back there as quick as possible. We'll keep this guy coolin' his heels in a cabin till he gets there."

Back at the *Bluebell*, Sproule was confined in one of the cabins and heavily guarded. After several days Gold Commissioner Vowell—he had recently taken over Kelly's position at Wildhorse—arrived and began his examination of the suspect. He concluded that the case was very strong against Sproule, strong enough to warrant his being sent to gaol in New Westminster, pending a trial conducted by proper justice authorities.

There was, of course, no possibility of taking the prisoner to the coast by the usual route through the States, but now a fairly easy all-Canadian route other than the disused Dewdney Trail had been opened up. Accompanied by a small party of volunteers, Anderson took Sproule first down the west arm and as far along the river as possible before reaching the waterfalls. From there, making use of what Indian trails there were, they walked westward to the Columbia. From its shore they flagged the sternwheeler *Kootenai*, which was on a steady run that year from the States up to Second Crossing, the point where the CPR crossed the Columbia River a second time in its journey westward. There, on the west bank was the tiny stopping-place called Big Eddy. Directly across the river on the east bank was another tiny settlement called Farwell, because our friend of that name had surveyed it, and, indeed, was still surveying on the site. He had gone there soon after his jaunt on Kootenay Lake with B-G and Sproat. (In a few months, the CPR would establish a railway station contiguous with Farwell on the downstream side and name it Revelstoke, after a CPR director who had been elevated to the English peerage.) The *Kootenai* deposited Sproule and his captors at Big Eddy. We may pause to wonder whether or not Farwell, who must certainly by now have heard of the murder, was aware that day of the proximity of his disgraced acquaintance from Kootenay Lake.

Farwell and Big Eddy were seething with activity as crews of men, both white and Chinese, laboured to hurry the laying of the trans-Canada rails from the east to their meeting with those from the west, now only five months away. As the Anderson party proceeded westward along Eagle Pass wagon road from Big Eddy to Eagle Pass Landing (present-day Sicamous), their progress was frequently impeded by the gangs of men at work changing the right-of-way into a railroad. That busy entrepreneur John C. Ainsworth had a gang contracted for a part of the work along the route. We can hope that poor Sproule did not have to suffer the bitterness of knowing that the forces of his enemy were even here.

At Eagle Pass Landing the party got on a sternwheeler which carried them along Shuswap Lake and down the South Thompson River to Kamloops, itself a booming labour camp as crews worked at top speed to bring rails from the west to meet those coming from the east. Work trains were frequent between Kamloops and Port Moody, the western terminus, and on one of these the party reached the coast. From Port Moody a short wagon ride took

Sproule to the prison at New Westminster where he would wait for the day of his trial, when he would be taken by steamer to Victoria.

Up on Kootenay Lake, work continued at Big Ledge, which people were now beginning to call "Hendryx Camp." Down in Kootenai Station, Wilbur Hendryx quickly found a new foreman to replace Sproule, a man by the name of Taillard. When Taillard arrived at the Ledge in mid-June, he took a look at the niggardly amount of work that had been done on the *Bluebell* site and immediately fired Howes and the Wolfe brothers, who at once left for the States, safe from any investigation that might subsequently occur regarding the murder of Hammill.

Summer wore on. At the mines of Kootenay Lake the excitement of the murder faded quickly while the routine of work continued. Meanwhile, in the world outside, the Hammill affair had given Kootenay an attractive notoriety. More and more miners flooded up from below the border, and curiosity was bringing many Canadians—both French- and English-speaking—into the area, either by the old routes from the States or by new ones opened up by the nearly completed trans-Canada railway. As investigation of the murder and preparation for the trial continued, newspapers south of the 49th began to report the affair, especially when Sproule's family became concerned about getting him returned to his own country. The *Surprise* appeared on the lake to join little *Midge* in making life easier and more convenient. Hendryx Camp became rapidly larger now that lumber and other supplies could reach the lake by steam.

Autumn brought the closure of the mining season as usual on October 31st. But the big event of the year occurred on November 7th, when in a much publicized ceremony a few miles east of Eagle Pass Landing at a spot named Craigellachie, the rails from the east met those from the west, and a dignitary drove the last spike in the trans-Canada line of the Canadian Pacific Railway Company. The great dream of uniting the province of British Columbia with eastern Canada had been realized, and, furthermore, there was now a close communication link to newly opening Kootenay.

This year, winter definitely did not bring with it the primeval silence to which Kootenay Lake had been accustomed through long ages. Both Ainsworth's Hot Springs and Hendryx Camp doggedly defied nature and retained a stubborn presence throughout the cold months. They were aided in no small degree by the technology of steam. *Midge* and *Surprise* either stayed on the lake the whole season or waited until very late in the year to leave for their respective winter quarters at David McLoughlin's and Bonners Ferry before the river froze over. Only the animals and the Indian people obeyed the ancient behest of the season and made their annual migrations to the wintering-grounds of their choice.

Down at the coast, in the settled and secure bastions of humankind, the drama of Hammill's murder reached another stage in its progress toward the inevitable outcome. On December 7th, the trial of Robert Sproule took place in Victoria, Honourable John Hamilton Gray being the presiding Judge. There was evidence to suggest that Sproule was not the murderer. At 4:40 in the afternoon the jury retired; at 9:45 in the evening they returned to the courtroom to say they could not reach a verdict; after further instruction from the Judge, they again retired, and returned at 11 o'clock next morning with a verdict of guilty. They recommended mercy. The judge sentenced Robert Sproule to be hanged on January 5th of the following year.

# CHAPTER 13

*In which the pressing needs of our tale oblige us to move to Colville, Washington. There, after taking notice of the economic and meteorological situations of that region in the year '86, we meet the Hall party and follow it on its journey to a mountain from which its members can look down on the west arm of Kootenay Lake near the place where Sproat marked out the prospective townsite in Chapter 9.[18]*

WHEN THE CANADIAN PACIFIC RAILWAY Company completed its trans-Canada line at Craigellachie on November 7th, 1885, the general rejoicing felt by Canadians did not manifest itself below the border. For a good two years the Colville Valley had done *its* rejoicing while supplying food to the hordes of men employed on the railway moving westward from the Rockies. Now, the line finished, the CPR began laying off the construction workers who had been hungrily consuming produce from Colville Valley farms and market gardens. The movement of food and also, of course, other supplies, had been the business of the sternwheeler *Kootenai* that Anderson's party had been able to flag on their way to the coast with Sproule. As bunkhouse after bunkhouse began closing down up north, the Colville area fell further and further into a slump. In addition, Chinese miners along the Columbia south of the border had taken their hungry mouths elsewhere owing to harsh treatment. Even the miners up in the Big Bend area of British Columbia no longer depended on river boats from the States. The CPR could now supply them with what they needed.

The Colville slump deepened as all businesses began to feel the results of the farmers' lack of income.

Even nature itself saw fit, that summer of '86, to enter into cahoots with the CPR in plaguing the good people of the Colville Valley. It provided inclement weather all summer. In the words of Charlie Brown, an old-timer of the area who in '86 was operating his father's ferry at the little settlement of Marcus on the Columbia, "The crops were not worth harvesting and the stock was not worth feeding." To farmers, the need to find money for paying taxes and providing for winter living became a serious matter. But farmers are resourceful people, and many of the menfolk had been prospectors and gold-washers before settling down on land of their own. Nothing was more natural for them in this crisis than to resort to their old trade. Prospecting parties up to Canada increased that summer.

Among those who took to the hills in search of gold were the menfolk of the families of two brothers—Osner and Winslow Hall. These brothers were the sons of a sea captain in Maine. During the early days of gold-rushing on the Pacific Coast, they had come west, Winslow settling immediately in the Colville River valley where he married an Indian woman, Osner going first to California and following his brother to Colville country later.

This year, as with all their neighbours, the talk at mealtimes in their homes was largely about the weather and the sensational murder up in British Columbia. They knew the place where it had happened, for some of them had been up that way a few times, washing for gold in the Salmon River and its feeders. The newspapers had been reporting the case steadily, and it was being built up into an international sensation. The outcry caused the judiciary to think twice and a stay of execution had been granted to March 6th, to allow a Supreme Court review of the case. Demands for life imprisonment instead of hanging were being voiced. Sproule's family were attempting to have him returned to the States. The execution was again postponed, this time to May 6th. On May 1st a protest meeting was held in Victoria, B.C. The American Consul intervened on behalf of his government.

At the eleventh hour, on May 5th, another temporary reprieve was ordered to July 6th. (We can imagine the emotions of Robert Sproule.) As legal arguments continued, a provincial-dominion power struggle developed over jurisdiction, and British Columbia threatened to appeal to the Imperial Privy Council. The execution was postponed to October 1st.

One morning in August, Winslow Hall said to his sons at breakfast, "Things aren't gonna get any better here. Why 'n't we go up to Canada and do a bit a prospecting? The Salmon's pretty well cleaned out, and so are its feeders, but nobody 's far as I know, has ever gone looking for the lodes that supplied the nuggets in the creeks." He turned to his wife. "You womenfolk can look after things here fer a few months till we get back with tax 'n grub money, can't you?" As the sons, including the youngest, still in his mid-teens, expressed their enthusiasm for the idea, Winslow added, "There's one p'rticilar creek, though, that might bear some panning. It's the only one I've never been to. Always had a hunch there might be somethin' there. It's way up near the top of the Salmon valley, almost at Kootenay Lake, I think. Comes in from the west side."

In spite of the fact that, as Charlie Brown later remarked, the crops were not worth harvesting, they waited until it was time for gathering what there was, and when that was done, sometime in early September, they were free to leave. It was to be a rather large party of men. Winslow Hall, a full-blood white man 48 years of age, was leader. Coming with him were his five half-blood sons: Bobby, Will, and Tommy from his first wife; along with Charlie and Albert from his second. (On the death of his first wife, Winslow had married her sister.) Winslow's brother Osner had his 15-year-old son Oscar with him. Then there were three cousins of the Halls: William H. Oakes, 30 years old, and his two young sons, Mel and Henry. Willie White, a man who was said by some to be Winslow Hall's adopted son, was also one of the party, as was Will Miller, a half-blood friend of Bobby Hall and one of the most venturesome of the prospectors and river-men in the area. Two full-blood Indians completed the roster: Narcisse Downey and Dauney

Williams. These young men had been invited along because of their skills as guides and hunters. Their job would be to keep the party in fresh meat.

The plan for beginning the trip was that the stronger members of the party would load the food staples and other supplies into boats at Marcus and row up the Columbia about 40 miles to the mouth of the Pend d'Oreille, where they would meet the younger members who meanwhile had ridden pack and saddle horses up to the rendezvous. Then the full party would proceed eastward along the Pend d'Oreille and north on the Salmon.

We must speculate about the trail the younger members would use to get from Colville to the rendezvous, and we must also ask, why not load the horses directly at Colville? There was certainly a trail up the west side of the Columbia to Fort Shepherd and beyond, but if they used that how would they get across the river to the mouth of the Pend d'Oreille? By 1886 there may have been a series of connected trails up the east side of the Columbia, but that route would necessitate that they cross the Pend d'Oreille to its north side; and the Pend d'Oreille flows through a deep canyon along all its length in Canadian territory, the very canyon whose turbulent waters had stopped David Thompson[19] when he tried to follow that river to its mouth in earlier days. There was only one trail that could be used to reach a crossing of the Pend d'Oreille, and that was a very old one. It had been made back in the '60s as an access route for miners leaving Colville for the gold fields during a short rush on the Salmon River. It crossed from Colville to the Pend d'Oreille River through Tiger Pass, more or less in the position of the highway that motorists use at the present day. At a point near present-day Metaline Falls there was a ferry. After crossing that they could follow the Pend d'Oreille past its junction with the Salmon to the rendezvous at its mouth, load the supplies from the boats onto the horses, and then the whole party could return on foot to the Salmon River and begin the journey northward toward Kootenay Lake. And now a possible reason for using boats instead of loading the horses directly at Colville becomes evident. The decision-makers of the party may have decided that the great length of the trail—a very roundabout route—made it more sensible to row the luggage forty miles up the river than to slow down the horses with it on their long journey.

It was a splendid group that assembled at the farm of Winslow Hall on the morning of departure, a busy gathering of men and horses. Fifteen men of ages ranging from half a century down to a decade and a half—all in the prime of life, the oldest still vigorous and eager to pit their experience against the challenges to come, the youngest joyful in anticipation of testing their new-felt strength and manhood in this, their first great adventure. We can imagine their feelings—the pleasurable male-to-male bonding that this fellowship was bringing about, the pride of fathers in their strapping sons, and of sons in being accepted as worthy participants in a manly undertaking. It was a joyous occasion. The womenfolk who had gathered to watch the men saddling horses and tying loads onto their backs must have taken pleasure in the eagerness of their sons and brothers. Mothers were pleased that their younger boys would have the protection of the experienced elders in such a large party. And all the women, like the men, were feeling a pleasurable anticipation of the coming time to be spent in the company of their own sex—and in greatly relaxed households.

In thinking about that scene from the past, we are tempted to colour it with descriptive details pleasurable to our senses and feeding our desire for the exotic. Surely, in this company so largely made up of Indians and half-bloods, we can assume a display of fur and feather. Surely Narcisse Downey and Dauney Williams, the full-blood Indians of the party, dressed themselves in buckskin and were adorned with beads around their necks and a tail or two dangling from their hats. And, granted that the staid elder full-blood whites probably disdained any Indian display, surely the young half-bloods, dressed at least partly in the same material as Narcisse and Dauney, cocked a feather or two in their hats, or displayed a bead here and there, if not on their own bodies at least on those of their horses. In the absence of hard proof, we can indulge ourselves by adding exotic colour—each to the degree that he or she sees fit—to this scene of the departure for Canada.

After the divided party had journeyed northward by boat or by horse, the two halves were reunited at the rendezvous and moved eastward on the Dewdney Trail and up into the valley of the Salmon River. That lovely wide valley through which the Salmon meanders so gracefully today must have been quite different when the Hall party journeyed through it; now, it is largely cleared of the first growth forests of cedar and hemlock that undoubtedly darkened the trail considerably when that early company saw it. Even then, of course, there were vistas of open land created by the forest fires which rampaged unchecked in those days. In fact, forest fires were a constant feature of summer in former times. Sproat and Farwell mentioned that the air was continuously thick with smoke all throughout the journey they made to Kootenay Lake in Chapter 9.

Always aware of the approach of cold weather—they had left Colville very late in the year for such a journey—the company made good time toward its destination near the source of the Salmon. They worked hard cutting brush from the old trail or making new side trails to explore the hills along the many small feeder streams coming down from the mountains. They enjoyed their strenuous activity, and avoided much of the friction that might have marred the pleasure of a smaller party. The group was large enough that members could avoid personal differences simply by moving to new positions within the group until whatever trouble there was worked itself out. Younger members enjoyed the companionship of their peers, leaving the wiser and more stable elders to make decisions. It is pleasant to imagine their mealtimes: Narcisse and Dauney, ranging far from the group as it made its daily progress northward, supplied fresh meat or fish when it was needed; bannock, molasses, tea, coffee, and other staples would be added to that fare. What numbers of their campsites, and those of other early parties, must lie under the farms and roads of the present-day valley! How often, we might ask, do present-day inhabitants walk over small heaps of buried white ash from the fires on which those early travellers cooked their meals?

The autumn weeks went by, and the company neared its destination. Finally, almost when it was time to hurry back home before their food supplies gave out, they reached the tributary creek that Winslow Hall had had in mind all the time, the creek that one day would be named after him and his brother Osner. A feeling of dejection had gradually come over the party as day after day their search for outcroppings of gold-bearing rock had revealed nothing. The hours of following will-o-the-wisp trails of float, fruitless trenching, and removal of overburden in likely places had been wasted work. And now this final creek, almost at the very source of the Salmon, represented their last chance of returning home with the gold they needed to see them through the winter. It led westward, behind a mountain that Winslow Hall knew faced onto the west arm of Kootenay Lake at the point where it became the lower Kootenay River. Reaching it just at dusk, they set up camp among the tall trees on the flatland where it emptied into the Salmon.

Very early next morning they broke camp and prepared to begin their exploration of the new creek. They couldn't see much through the thick forest of the flatlands, but it was apparent that the creek was coming from a surprisingly wide valley, almost in fact as wide as that of the Salmon itself. Furthermore, the valley was not inclined sharply, and the creek flowed gently. There was, of course, no telling what would develop a few miles farther up. They set out with the aim of spending the day moving the whole party, the horses included, upwards along the creek-bed, cutting trail where necessary and stopping frequently for exploratory panning.

At dusk a weary and disappointed company, only a few miles upstream and still without a strike, made camp and bedded down for the night. The forest had thinned, and the side of the mountain which lay between them and the Kootenay River had a series of open slopes leading upwards. By reason of having continually gained altitude, first by their ascent of the Salmon and second by following the creek even higher, they seemed already a good way up that mountain, which, had they viewed its other side from the much lower Kootenay River, would have seemed a great deal taller.

Talk around the fire that night was all of heading for home. Food supplies were unpleasantly low and winter not far off; the elders had no desire to be wandering about in the wilderness, cold and without food. Winslow Hall, giving utterance to the general opinion, ordered that early next day Narcisse and Dauney would make a foray for game while the others prepared for the journey back. Meanwhile they could forget their disappointment in sleep. Leaving the horses free to forage on the nearby slopes, they got into their bedrolls.

Next morning, one of those lovely bracing days of late autumn, they got up, had breakfast—a decreased ration of bannock for each man—and thought about leaving. The horses were not in sight, so one of the elders told a couple of the youths to find them. A quarter of an hour later the pair returned to say the horses were nowhere about.

"Well," said Osner Hall, addressing his nephew Tommy, "those slopes all look gentle enough. Maybe they've gone all the way up. Why'n't you and your brother Willie 'n' Willie White go on up there 'n' look for 'em. Narcisse 'n' Dauney can go up that way too. Looks like good deer country up there. Take your time 'n' look around good. You'll find 'em."

While waiting for the boys the remainder of the party began a little panning. As hours passed they went farther and farther upstream, absorbed in their search, and, well conditioned to life in the wilderness, not at all alarmed at the time the boys were taking. By mid-afternoon they were on their way back to camp, aware that they would now have to spend another night here, but expecting to find the boys and the horses waiting for them.

Meanwhile, Tom and the two Willies, accompanied by the hunters, had set off up the slopes, expecting to find the horses in a short time. They divided into two groups so that they covered both edges of the open areas, where the horses might be resting in the shelter of the impinging forest trees. On two or three occasions they saw droppings, but not fresh ones. The horses must have enjoyed the open slopes and the not-too-strenuous climb, for they seemed to have gone a long way up.[20] Gradually, under the influence of the lovely autumn day, the boys' spirits revived; soon they were enjoying the climb for its own sake, and, like the horses somewhere ahead of them, began to revel in the freedom of the open country. Before many hours had gone by, the slopes had led them, almost without their being aware of it, to the mountain top. The open country became more predominant, with large areas of thickly treed forest interspersed here and there. In the distance to the northwest a big rocky peak glistened in the sunlight, surrounded by lesser rock juttings amid the open country. They were walking on a carpet of grass, moss, and small deciduous plants, rich with autumn colour. Around them were large sparsely situated spruce trees of the kind that grow in high places. Gentle slopes invited them to walk farther and farther until they seemed to be moving downwards to the other side of the mountain. Turning back to the east, they soon came to a place were the ground fell away precipitously. Standing on a mossy ledge amid rock ferns and small red-leaved bushes they found a panoramic view lying below them. To their right they could see the long, flat valley of the Salmon up which they had come; to their left, a narrower, steeper valley leading downward—to Kootenay Lake they guessed—a triangular patch of which they could see in the distance. Directly below them, the mountain plunged a few hundred feet, flattened out for half a mile or so, and rose again into a rocky, well-treed hump before making its final descent. Behind that hump, out of their sight and knowledge on the valley bottom, was the tiny lake around which Dick Fry had his trapline. Draining that tiny lake, a small stream, hidden by the dense forest around it, ran down the steep valley and emptied into Kootenay Lake. About half a mile east of its mouth, on a stretch of shore already known by readers of this history, there was now a log cabin, built and occupied by Dick Fry's son-in-law, Arthur Bunting. This also was out of the sight and knowledge of the boys standing on the mountain; nor did Arthur Bunting, on his part, have any inkling that day of the nearby presence that was going to affect his life.

The exhilaration the young men felt as they stood on their viewpoint was suddenly dimmed by their realization that the sun was getting lower in the sky, that they had not yet found the horses, and that they were hungry. Furthermore, Narcisse and Dauney, while always looking out for game as a matter of course, had as yet failed to undertake a definite hunt. Depressed and anxious once again, the boys moved away from the ledge and followed the open slopes back the way they had come. They decided that Narcisse and Dauney should make a quick foray of half an hour or so while Tom and the two Willies waited where they were; then, having failed in their mission to retrieve the horses, they would hurry back to camp where surely the others were beginning to wonder what had happened to them. Accordingly, Narcisse and Dauney walked off on their hunt, while their companions lay down on the carpet of colourful mosses and other plants and fell asleep.

Shortly afterward they were awakened by the returning hunters, who sat down beside them and announced their failure to find game. What followed has been told many times. It is the most fateful event in our story and as such has become ornamented with legend. The source books—not one of them, alas, a primary source of unassailable integrity—have several versions. There they sat, the five of them, on a colourful mossy carpet amid sparsely situated spruce trees on the flat plateau-land of a mountaintop, and it is well that we should repeat their names: two half-blood brothers, Tommy and Willie Hall, younger sons of Winslow Hall of Colville, Washington Territory, U.S.A.; Willie White, their young half-blood friend and possible distant relative; Narcisse Downey and Dauney Williams, two full-blood Lakes Indians whom the others had known all their lives.

The afternoon of a late-autumn day had almost passed, the sky had darkened with cloud, and the air was heavy with the feeling of coming snow. Sitting there, the five young men were all experiencing the sense of urgency to return to shelter that always comes with late afternoon in the mountains. But they were reluctant to move; the dejection they felt seemed to have drained away their energy. Testy and grumbling as they reclined against the small outcroppings of weathered rock that lay about them, they worked off their frustration by digging their heels into the moss. Those wearing boots instead of moccasins had the satisfaction of pushing larger and larger amounts of the ground-covering into little piles, thus exposing the rock underneath. A squirrel skittered by, moving from one spruce to another. Annoyed by its chattering, one of the boys (some versions name him) loosened a chunk of rock from the outcropping nearest him. Throwing it aimlessly in the direction of the squirrel, he then turned to pry off another. What he saw caused him to forget the squirrel (or, as some versions have it, the grouse). In the space from which he had pried the chunk of weathered rock there was now a gap, and in that gap glittered the jewel-like colours of peacock ore, iridescent even in the failing light.

"Hey, you guys, look at this!" Suddenly alert, he got up and began pulling at the rock and the vegetation around it as the others caught his excitement and gathered round to see. None of them had ever seen peacock ore. "It's gotta be gold!" "Nah, it's only fool's gold." All five of them were now digging at the weathered rock around them, trying to pull off chunks to expose the fresh surface underneath. "Hey, look where we were scuffing!" The rock, although it had been buried under two or three inches of earth and vegetation, had been acted upon by the atmosphere, its surface a dull black, streaked or patched with brilliant green and blue, startling to the unpractised eyes of the boys. Very excited now, they moved about in a wider area, loosening rock to find good pieces. Then they gathered together again to examine their samplings.

They were holding pieces of richly mineralized rock in their hands. Besides a good quantity of quartz, there were mainly the copper sulfides bornite ($Cu_5FeS_4$) and chalcopyrite ($CuFeS_2$). On the freshly exposed surfaces of the pieces the boys had broken off and were now crumbling in their hands, these compounds presented the lovely iridescent colours of "peacock ore." On the surface of the weathered rock exposed during the heel-kicking episode, the bornite and chalcopyrite had been broken down chemically and their copper united with a carbonate radical to form the bright green and blue of malachite and azurite. Silver, gold, lead, and zinc also were present in much smaller quantities. Of all this chemistry the young men knew nothing, but they were well aware that they had hit upon something unusual and probably valuable. Their minds were on gold, and the rocks in their hands looked to them as if they might well contain good amounts of it.

"Well," said one of them as he peered closely at a patch of chalcopyrite on the complex surface of the rock he was holding, "this sorta looks like fool's gold, but it's sorta not quite the same."

"Yeah, it does," said another, "but this one"—he ran his finger over a nearby patch—"looks more like the real stuff—I mean real gold—t'me."

"Well," volunteered someone else, "all we hafta do is use the test." Taking out his knife, he ran its point along the whole surface of the piece of rock. The others crowded round, watching for the black streak which would prove that the metallic mineral they were looking at was not gold. The results were inconclusive. There was some black dust, but the rock surface was too varied for them to tell just where it came from and where it didn't. The young men did not lose their elation.

"I bet there's real gold in there!"

"It's gotta be gold. What else could shine like that? Sure, there's prob'ly some fool's gold too!"

"This could be a mother lode, where the stuff that's in the creeks comes from!" The unfound horses no longer seemed to matter now that they had such an exciting report to take back to camp. "Let's get outa here," said one of the Willies, "back to camp before it gets dark. And everybody take a couple a pieces of the rock." Recovering the sense of urgency they had had before, but now felt more strongly, they made good time hurrying down the mountain and reached the campfire just as complete darkness was falling.

As they had hoped, the elders were greatly impressed by their find, and questioned them closely about the extent of the outcropping. "We'll go up there early tomorrow morning and take a look. An' we'll take the shovels and mattocks," said Winslow Hall. "This may be a big one, boys."

Will Miller held a piece of the rock up to the firelight. "Yeah, this looks purty good to me. It's not gold, young fellahs, but it's darn near as good. It's peacock ore—lotsa copper, and silver too, I'll bet." The iridescent rock glittered in the firelight as if in agreement with his statement.

"Well, let's eat an' hit the hay," said Winslow. "We'll get up there early tomorrow. An' we'll take another look fer the horses too."

# CHAPTER 14

*In which we accompany the Hall party as it investigates its discovery on the mountain and returns home.*

THE ELDERS WERE out of their bedrolls long before first light, and that was one morning they had no trouble rousing the younger ones, for every man was as impatient as the others to get back up the mountain to examine the strike. Breakfast was half over before the clouds in the eastern sky were showing any brightness. They had awakened to a morning of drizzling cold rain, which, while it might be dampening their clothes, was having no effect on their spirits. A general feeling of optimism smoothed over the bumps of grumpiness and early-morning ill-humour that might otherwise have retarded preparations for the climb on that day of unusually early rising. As soon as it was light enough for them to make their way, they started up the slopes, carrying a small ration of grub and all the tools necessary for an examination of the site. Well before mid-morning they were on the ground where the boys had lain kicking their heels in frustration the day before. Winslow Hall sent Narcisse and Dauney on a double errand: to find the horses and bag a deer so that the party could begin the homeward journey, perhaps that very afternoon.

As the two full-bloods left on their search, the remainder of the company set about the task of assessing the strike. They were working under some difficulty; the cold rain of the valley had become snow at this elevation, and a good three inches covered everything. At least there was none still falling. The men went about their work in an orderly manner, the youngsters obeying orders while Winslow Hall, his brother Osner, and the other elders discussed and conferred, using the wisdom of their experience and the knowledge, scant as it was in those days, they had garnered throughout their lives in the craft of prospecting.

As prospectors, these men were now engaged in making one of the most important decisions of their lives. Looking back at them from an age when prospecting, like everything else, has become as much a science as modern technology can make it, it is hard for us to imagine the degree of uncertainty within which they operated. It was only in the '30s of the present century that mineral detection became scientific rather than merely descriptive. In early days, it is safe to say, the great majority of prospectors were ignorant of all but the most rudimentary theory, and based their work on rules of conduct and simple tests like the knife-scratch the boys had used the day before, usually making important decisions with the aid of what appears to us as pure intuition. And yet, they discovered rich sites, many of which still support towns and cities. Most of them failed to find the riches they thought they wanted, and after spending lives of hardship and strenuous outdoor labour retired to shacks or cabins to be watched over by kind neighbours. And who can say that their lives were not as happy and worthy as any other? The few who became rich often remained so for only a short time, being ill-equipped to handle their money wisely. They have our respect as the vanguard of civilization—the rough-and-ready folk opening up new territory for the benefit of developers and money-handlers who comfortably followed them.

Here on the site, Winslow Hall and the other decision-makers of the company had first to decide whether or not their discovery was important enough to warrant their further efforts. The samples they were holding in their hands were certainly rich enough, but they were still unproven by assaying, and there were also other factors to consider. Was the outcropping of any reasonable extent? In what direction did it run? How far did it extend downward? To find at least partial answers to these and other questions, the party began stripping the overburden off large areas of out-

139

crop and digging test pits here and there to reach bedrock, moving farther and farther from their starting point. Only nine years before, Dana's *Handbook of Mineralogy*, a book famous in the mining business and still used in an updated edition, had been published. We wonder whether or not the company carried that book as a guide. However that may be, the results of their efforts were very pleasing, encouraging enough, in fact, that Winslow decided to order some trenching through one or two small veins and along the length of some well-defined larger ones. This laborious work took a few hours. Early in the proceedings they heard a single shot and wondered if the hunters had bagged a deer. The elders were finally satisfied that the strike was a very rich one and called a halt to the work.

Soon afterward, as the company were congratulating themselves on their good fortune, Narcisse and Dauney appeared, leading the horses. Tied to the back of one of them was the prepared carcass of a deer. The horses, like the boys on the previous day, had wandered along the clearings until they too felt themselves moving downward. Unlike the boys, who had turned eastward at that point, they had remained on the easier route until, only a short distance farther, they came up against a thickly forested area. There they had stayed until discovered by the two full-bloods, whom they were glad enough to see.

The mood of the company suddenly changed from jubilation to apprehension. Who has not felt that rush of anxiety which comes on the discovery of some treasure, that fear of losing it to someone else before we can secure it for ourselves—a patch of huckleberries, perhaps, so close to the highway that we must immediately change our plans and fill our sweaters, not daring to return home for buckets; an antique chair, the very one we have had in mind for that space in the hallway, sitting all too exposed in the window of a second-hand store, necessitating that we enter at once and use most of our pocket money for a deposit on it? Such a feeling now seized the members of the company as they stood looking at the telltale havoc they had worked on the landscape. Anyone chancing on that scene—and they were well aware that theirs was not the only party to come prospecting into Canada that year—could not fail to know what had been going on, and, examining the site more carefully, might well get to the recording office first and rob them of their strike. It was certainly too late in the season now to make the long journey over to Wildhorse Creek; and anyway, perhaps the Canadians had moved their recording office to another place, now that the new railway had been pushed through. No, the only thing to do now was to hide their diggings as well as they could and get back home. Then, early in the spring—*very* early, because once a strike was made there was no hiding it from the hordes of other prospectors, who seemed to have a sixth sense that allowed them to ferret out a new strike however secret it was kept—*very* early in the spring they would be back to guard their treasure. Accordingly, they all got busy filling in test holes and trenches, and replacing overburden to make the site as nearly as possible as it had been before their arrival. That done, they lost their sense of anxiety and once again enjoyed the elation proper to their good luck.

Looking back as they were setting off down the mountain— happily in possession of the lost horses and a supply of fresh meat—Winslow Hall remarked, "Well, boys, that looks purty good. Prob'ly nobody's gonna be up here this late in the season, anyways. Ever'body's headed back home fer sure by now. An' let's hope it snows real hard real soon."

After one more night in the camp at the base of the mountain—this time they hobbled the horses—the company set out for home, retracing its steps down the lovely Salmon valley. There is a story that, as they were camping near the border a few days later, a canoe frantically paddled by a lone Indian suddenly appeared round a bend in the river. One of the full-bloods called out to him in the native language, whereupon he stopped, observed that the company was largely Indian, and paddled ashore. On being questioned, he admitted that his haste was due to the fact that he had shortly before robbed a white man's camp and was now afraid he was being pursued. "Did you get any grub?" "Yes." "Have you got it with you?" "Yeah." The Indian prepared to paddle away. "Hey, wait a minute!" shouted Will Miller. "I'll give you thirty-five bucks for that grub!" Glad to rid himself of the incriminating evidence, the man accepted. A few minutes later the company, their new supply of food staples packed on the backs of the horses, were on their way back up the trail for a couple of days' further exploration and staking on the site. Whether that story is true or merely another of time's inventions it is now too late to tell.

The source books do not let us know whether the company remained together and followed the Tiger Pass trail home, or split into two, some of them cutting across to the Columbia where the boats were stashed. It seems likely that they would have wanted to retrieve their boats. It also seems likely that, remembering their unguarded treasure on a mountaintop up in Kootenay, they would have wanted to slip into Colville quietly, not wishing to draw attention to the route they had used for the trip. We will assume, then, that they did just that.

# CHAPTER 15

*Which tells, following a brief look at the people of Colville, Washington, what the Hall party did on returning to their claims in the spring of '87; but also containing an account of the naming of Toad Mountain, a discourse on the relationship of the Silver King mine to the city of Nelson, the final occurrence in the story of Robert Sproule, and sundry other matters.*

DURING THE LONG MONTHS of waiting out the winter in Colville valley, members of the company remained close-mouthed about their secret. But no one could suppress the news of how rich the ore samples were, once they got into the hands of the assayer. For weeks, speculation about the whereabouts of the ore strike was the main topic of conversation around the potbelly stove in Uncle Billie Brown's little store at Marcus. Like hounds at the scent of a rabbit, the seasoned prospectors felt their blood stirring with more than the warmth of the stove when they thought of that bonanza awaiting exploitation up in Canada. Uncle Billie Brown—stepfather of Will Miller—kept his ears open to the talk. Soon he had information of a plot to follow the Halls back to the site in the spring, and was pleased to pass the news on to the company.

But the strands of conversation that wove themselves among the spittoons around the stove concerned other topics, too. The murder of Hammill up at Big Ledge and the subsequent tribulations of Robert Sproule were still major topics. One of the first questions asked by members of the company on their return had been, "What has happened to Sproule?" and the answer had been that, after a last tormenting eleventh hour reprieve on October 1st, he was finally hanged in Victoria Gaol on the morning of October 29th, 1886. To the end, he had declared that he was innocent. As if to torture him further, fate had decreed that on the very day before his execution he should receive notice that he had been awarded fifty thousand dollars in litigation he was involved in on the east coast. Around Uncle Billie's potbelly stove there was endless discussion about whether he was guilty or innocent. The case dragged on for months as a news item. Sproule's brother Frank was petitioning the Supreme Court of Canada for permission to sue the government. All in all, the hanging had caused much ill-feeling between the Canadian and American governments.

We can be sure that the people of Colville valley kept their eyes and ears open to other mining news from Canada, too. They kept abreast of events up at Big Ledge—now being called "Hendryx Camp"—and must certainly have been aware of Dr. Hendryx's activities in logging, road building, and steamboating, as he worked out his plans for development on Kootenay Lake. We can imagine the spittoons twanging frequently as conversation became animated regarding job possibilities and staking prospects at Ainsworth's Hot Springs or Hendryx Camp.

While plots were hatching and preparations being made to discover the whereabouts of the much-discussed orebody by trailing the Hall party to its site when spring came, the company, thanks to Uncle Billie Brown's information, was hatching plots of its own for evading its would-be followers. They would simply lay scent on a false trail and then depart in comfort from a concealed starting place. Meanwhile, there were other things to think about—mainly preparing a plan of action for raising money and developing the site. Luckily for them, they had a neighbour, one John McDonald, rumoured as "well-connected" in the Old Country and known locally as "Sir John." He was ambitious, and shrewd enough to guess that the Halls, able prospectors and woodsmen though they were, had little of the business sense required to raise capital or develop a mine and were probably at a loss for what to do next. He approached them with that bluntness generally accredited to persons of his homeland, pointing out their need and his ability to help them. In return for a partnership as business manager in the company, he would undertake to raise capital and "make money for all of us." Wisely, the Halls accepted his offer. Sir John's first official act was to appoint another partner as chemist. Then, warming to the business ethic, he sought to reduce the company, now numbering seventeen, to its original roster of fifteen names. He chose to eliminate Narcisse Downey and Dauney Williams on the grounds that they had been hired for pay on the trip and were therefore not to be considered as partners. Disappointed, but seeing no way to dispute the decision, the full-bloods accepted the two hundred and fifty dollars bonus offered them and withdrew.

Early next spring, in keeping with their plan, the party made a show of loading a couple of big boats borrowed from Uncle Billie Brown with supplies for the journey northward. Leaving Marcus—well observed by the community—they began to row as fast as they could up the Columbia, knowing that after a safe interval their followers would also be on the river. At Little Dalles narrows they cached the boats and cargo in the bush on the east shore and hid themselves in a position from which they could see anyone passing on the water. As soon as they saw their followers going by in hot pursuit upstream, they loaded their supplies onto horses which had been waiting for them there, and sneaked back toward Colville. Soon they were on the trail over Tiger Pass, heading north. By that ruse, they got back to their strike in Kootenay country in time to explore the site more carefully and locate the choice claims.

They worked hard all that summer of '87, developing their group of claims into the *Silver King* mine, famous even in that first year because it immediately drew the attention of mining people and financiers all over America—and famous now, when its visible remains have all but disappeared except in photographs, because the people whom it drew into the area camped on the south shore of the west arm just where it becomes the lower Kootenay River and began to build there the shacktown that grew into the city of Nelson. The *Silver King*, for all the rich promise of its early years, was not destined for longevity. The city it engendered would long outlive it, gradually effacing all traces of its existence, until a century later only a few street names remain to remind unknowing generations that gentle Nelson was once a rough-and-ready smelter town. But during the years of its ascendancy the *Silver King* made the very character of the little community, its sprawling, busy smelter dominating the landscape while its working needs dominated the thinking of the townfolk. Indeed, the city owes even its continuing existence in the present day to the mine that failed so soon after creating it. If the ore discoveries at present-day Rossland, Ymir, and other places nearby had come before those of the *Silver King*, one of them would likely have replaced Nelson as "Queen City of the Kootenays," and Nelson would have gone the ghostly way of other towns when its mine failed and its smelter closed. But before Rossland and Ymir were even born, Nelson had defeated them as rivals by establishing itself as an important distributing centre above and beyond its ties to the *Silver King*, with an elite of business and professional persons and government officials already putting down roots. And Nelson had even closer rivals—its sister communities on Kootenay Lake itself. The community that became present-day Ainsworth was, as readers of this tale already know, well established before Nelson came on the scene, and could easily have become the "capital" city of the lake. Kaslo and Balfour also vied for premier status in early days. Indeed, the site of Balfour, not that of Nelson, was the proposed terminus of the railway John C. Ainsworth almost persuaded the British Columbia government to let him build along the lower Kootenay River from the Columbia to Kootenay Lake. Balfour was also the site favoured by yet another figure of Nelson's folklore, soon to appear in our tale. But for a few critical years the *Silver King* eclipsed the mines of Ainsworth's Hot Spring and Hendryx Camp, drawing the eyes of the mining world away from those two earlier settlements. And so, by the time John C. Ainsworth's railway was finally built by someone else, its destination was not Balfour but Nelson.

Whether the *Silver King* was destined for longevity or not, the Hall party didn't know or waste time thinking about. They worked all that summer of '87 with the fervour of hope. And the mine *was* destined to make them all much richer than they had been before. There was going to be a lot of trouble, but in the end they would win out, at least to their own satisfaction. The first item on their agenda was to get the claims recorded, and that was not easy. On January 5th of this very year (1887) the British Columbia government, attempting to keep abreast of the rapid developments on Kootenay Lake, had divided Kootenay into districts. Our old acquaintance Gilbert Malcolm Sproat had been appointed Gold Commissioner of the North Kootenay District, with headquarters at the new railway town of Revelstoke (or Farwell, as some still called it). Kootenay Lake was not included in his district, but he observed it and reported on it. All these changes meant for the Hall company was that they still had to journey to Fort Steele to record their claims. (They did not know that the Gold Commissioner over there, Mr. Vowell, had been moved to nearby Donald, a CPR town on the east arm of the Big Bend.) This being a time of rapid growth and departmental change, the source books are contradictory and confused. However, it appears that the first recording of the *Silver King* was made by one A. D. Wheeler, a man famous in the annals of early Ainsworth. He made an on-the-site recording, acting under an old "election right" he had been granted back in '84 at the Big Ledge and Ainsworth Camps. In the summer of '87 he was at the *Silver King* site, staking a few locations for himself. Hearing of the Hall company's need, he offered his services. After recording with him, however, the Halls had second thoughts. As Wheeler tells us in a memoir published in the *Nelson Daily News* of June 10th, 1914, they became worried that their recording with him might not be quite genuine and sent someone over to Fort Steele to record it there also. Commissioner Vowell—at Donald—immediately recognized the date of Wheeler's recording as the legal one.

The Hall party's claims were safely filed and their ownership of the *Silver King* was apparently secure, but we must not make the mistake of assuming that production followed closely on the heels of possession. The bringing of a mine to production is an enormous task even today, and was certainly much more challenging in the year 1887. The quantities of ore that the company believed to be underground had to await the proof of actual mining, and that couldn't even be started without a permanent presence on the site. Hence the first and indeed the *only* problem for the remainder of that summer was to prepare for a long winter on the mountaintop. Let "Sir John" McDonald travel or do whatever else was necessary to raise capital for the development of the ore body, but the rest of the company, including even the chemist, would have to be on the site, clearing land, whipsawing lumber, building log cabins and animal sheds, constructing fireplaces, cutting cordwood and roofing-shakes, making trails, toting supplies up from Colville, all the while hunting and cooking meals to keep themselves alive for the labour, and in general living the rough life of an outdoor camp in the wilderness. For the coming winter, shelter would have to be rudimentary. If the mine prospered, amenities could be added as the community grew. Meanwhile, the summer advanced and winter came nearer.

Word of the new strike in Kootenay moved with the steamers and stagecoaches up and down rivers and wagon roads, clicked along steel through mountain passes to railway towns as far away as the coast and down into the States. Prospectors began arriving—"hordes" of them, as always. On the mountain the *Silver King* claims became surrounded by others, and the air was filled with the noise of men at work. On July 27th, the mountain received its name. Two men, Charlie Townsend and Ben Thomas, unknown to history except for this one incident which materializes them for a brief moment from the formless murk of time, were staking a claim called the *Jim Crow*, also saved from total oblivion only by this incident. Townsend was seated on a log about one and a half miles from the *Silver King* writing the location notice of their claim. He had stopped after the words "situate on," wondering what to put. Suddenly a big warty toad jumped from under the log and plopped ponderously at his feet. Immediately Townsend wrote

"Toad Mountain." And to this very day the mountain goes by that name. (This incident bears the earmark of legend. It is too neatly constructed: the toad jumping out at just the right moment. And it is hard to believe that, if true, such an obscure incident occurring to two such obscure men should be remembered. More likely, someone once asked "How did this mountain get to be called Toad Mountain?" and someone else made up a story to explain why. Later, names were attached to the story, perhaps by the very men named in it. Even that exact date is suspicious—July 27th, 1887. Who can remember the dates for an event whose significance becomes apparent only much later? The story comes from a very early source, written only ten or eleven years after the event; we are therefore tempted to accept it as true. Even if it is a legend, it is "true" in the sense that it is a real part of the history whose events, actual or legendary, are unfolding before us.)

Down on the shoreline of the west arm, five as-the-crow-flies miles from all the activity on Toad Mountain, the tent-town continued to grow steadily around Arthur Bunting's log cabin, so steadily in fact that Arthur (typical of their time, the source books do not let us know whether his wife was with him or not) conceived the idea of making some money by obtaining land for a townsite. Accordingly, as '87 grew into its autumn he filed for pre-emption rights, unaware that G.M. Sproat had reserved the site in '83.

Winter came that year to a land that was no longer empty of people. Busy communities of men at the Ainsworth, Hendryx, and *Silver King* camps worked late into the final month. One little steamboat, Dr. Hendryx's *Surprise,* plied the waters of Kootenay Lake. (*Midge* was moored at Rykert's on the border as B-G and his men were busy building a community at Canal Flat.) On the shoreline where the west arm narrows to become the river, tents, shacks, and a log cabin or two gave notice of a future town. Only when the snow deepened in late December and men retired into their snug homes did some semblance of winter's customary primeval silence reappear. Up in Revelstoke Gilbert Malcolm Sproat wrote his report to the Minister of Mines and dated it Farwell, December 24th, 1887. In it he included a letter written to him on the 6th

December by C.H. Montgomery, a well-known storekeeper of Colville. With a part of that letter we will end this chapter.

Those mines were discovered late in autumn of 1886 by Winslow, Hall & Co. Nothing was done until spring of 1887, after the discovery had become known. I outfitted two men who went to the mines with about ten others, and all made locations, working them during the summer. I myself went there in September last, to look at the mines and see what my men were doing. I found about thirty men in camp, and more coming every day – the mines the best ever discovered on the Pacific Coast, – ledges there running from ten to thirty feet in width, and all looking well.

Mr. Cobaugh, who went in there with his assay office with Messrs. Hall & Co., made assays from the rock of the different ledges as high as 1,600 ounces in silver. The average assay of ore at the time I was there ran a little over $300, and without a doubt this will be one of the best camps in British Columbia.

At the time I left this camp, the last of September, there were about thirty claims located, and men working on about eighteen of them. Experts were coming in from all parts of the country examining the mines. I am informed there have been about twenty-five more locations since I left.

Montana and country south, as well as our own, are all excitement now over these mines, and there is no doubt but that as early as they can get there in the spring there will be 1,000 or 1,500 men in that camp. The only drawback there now is an outlet.

The only easy way to go to this camp now is by Northern Pacific Railway (Kootenay Station), 40 miles land travel to Bonner's Ferry, from which excellent water navigation, down Kootenay River and through Big Kootenay Lake to the western outlet, six or seven miles from the mines.

If we had a waggon road from mouth of the Kootenay River running up the river say twenty miles, thence six to the camp, we could have an easy outlet for our ores by Columbia to C. P. R. at Revelstoke, thence to Victoria or wherever we wished to go, and goods and people could get to the mines easily that way.

There is one thing we need in that camp very much, and that is a recorder, as there are several parties there who have done work and are unable to record it, the season of the year preventing them going either to Revelstoke of Wild Horse Creek, which works a hardship, for, as a general thing, prospectors do not have an overplus of money, &c.

(Signed)  C. H. MONTGOMERY.

# CHAPTER 16

*A sprawling, unruly chapter, bursting at the seams in its attempt to encompass events which were occurring on the west arm of Kootenay Lake at a rapidly accelerating pace in 1888; and containing, amid various digressions and diversions, not only the important account of Nelson's birth under the able midwifery of Malcolm Sproat, but also accounts of further activity on the part of our old friend Harry Anderson, the arrival by boat of one Charles Busk, and the adventures of Robert Yuill, a typical denizen of the Kootenays in those early times.*

THE BRITISH COLUMBIA government had been doing a lot of thinking about Kootenay. The reservation placed on the lands around the lake for John C. Ainsworth's proposed railway in 1883 was under consideration again. We recall that there had been a public outcry against the foolishness of giving the Ainsworth Syndicate so much land merely for building a short rail line between the Columbia River and Kootenay Lake. We also remember that, in Chapter 9, Malcolm Sproat had marked out a site for the town that might someday become the "capital" of west Kootenay. That site was, of course, a part of the lands reserved for the Ainsworth Syndicate. The time period for the Syndicate to begin work on the railway had now passed without its having done anything. The government, taking the recent developments on Kootenay Lake to indicate that the townsite Sproat had marked out in '83 might soon be needed, decided to cancel the Ainsworth Syndicate's land reservation, thereby freeing the townsite for its own use. Accordingly, the following notice appeared on page 36 of the *British Columbia Gazette* of January 26th, 1888.

> LANDS AND WORKS DEPARTMENT,
> VICTORIA, B. C., January 25th, 1888.
> Notice is hereby given that the reservation placed upon certain lands in Kootenay district, in consideration of the provisions of the "Columbia & Kootenay Railway and Transportation Company Act, 1883," notice of which was published in the British Columbia Gazette and dated 23rd May, 1883, has been cancelled, and that the lands referred to will be open to sale and pre-emption one month from the date hereof.
> F. G. VERNON.
> Chief Commissioner of Lands & Works. [21]

Another notice announcing that the Sproat reservation and three others of '83 were in effect appeared on the same page:

> LANDS AND WORKS DEPARTMENT
> VICTORIA, B. C., January 26th, 1888.
> Notice is hereby given that the following described blocks of land have been reserved from sale or settlement until further notice, viz:
> 1st. Commencing at the head of the West Arm of Kootenay lake, on the south bank of the outlet, thence south two miles, thence west two miles, thence north two miles more or less to the Kootenay river, thence following the windings of said river to the point of commencement.
> 2nd. Commencing at the mouth of Bear creek, opposite Fort Sheppard, thence northerly along the Columbia river 10 chains, thence east 20 chains, thence south 20 chains, thence west 20 chains more or less to the Columbia river, thence following the bank of the said river to the point of commencement.
> 3rd. Beginning at the northeast corner of the Hudson's Bay Company's land at Fort Sheppard, thence west one mile, thence north two miles, thence east one mile more or less to the Columbia river, thence south along the bank of the said river to the place of commencement.
> 4th. A square block of forty acres fronting on the east side of the Columbia river, on the flat about two miles north of the mouth of Kootenay river, known as "Sproat's Landing." F. G. VERNON.
> Chief Commissioner of Lands & Works. [21]

The first description is meant to be of the site Sproat had reserved in '83; however, by a mistake either of Sproat himself or some other government official it is actually describing a block of land a little to the west of the reservation.

The fourth description is of a site near where present-day Robson is situated, upstream a couple of miles from "Sproat's Landing," so-called because a brother of Malcolm Sproat had pre-empted land and settled there. (He was one of several pre-emptors who had acquired land along the Columbia River south of Revelstoke as soon as the trans-Canada railway came through.) The government, thinking the location might one day be important, set part of it aside as a townsite reservation. And, of course, it did indeed become a town a few years later, when the railway was built from the Columbia River to the west arm of Kootenay Lake.

The government also had other changes for Kootenay. The 1887 division into North and South districts was not proving satisfactory, and on March 14th, 1888 Kootenay was again officially divided—this time into the East and West districts still in force today. Malcolm Sproat remained in Revelstoke as Gold Commissioner—he also held other official positions—but now Kootenay Lake was under his direct jurisdiction. His immediate concerns this year were to get a mining recorder on the west arm; to decide on suitable headquarters for the new West Kootenay district; to get a trail made from the *Silver King* to the Columbia River so that ore could be taken by boat up to the railway at Revelstoke; and to look into the business of creating a town on his '83 land reserve.

Getting a mining recorder on the west arm was a simple matter. He knew Harry Anderson, the constable who pursued and captured Robert Sproule in Chapter 12, and recommended him for the job. Anderson's appointment was announced in the *Gazette* of April 6th, 1888.

In Sproat's opinion, the long, narrow district of West Kootenay could not be well served by headquarters at Revelstoke. That town was too far north, and transportation from it to the busy mines on Kootenay Lake far from adequate. Sproat still felt the same as he had in '83 when we observed him staking out the reserve in Chapter 9. The feeling that this site was the better one for a "capital" of West Kootenay made him eager to develop it. Perhaps, he thought, an even better possibility was for Revelstoke and this new town to share the administration of the district.

As always, the government's chief concerns were to prevent profits from British Columbia resources flowing southward into the States, and to assist Victoria merchants to reap profits as the infrastructure for the Kootenay mines developed. Now, acting through its Kootenay agent Malcolm Sproat, it was determined to do all it could to transport *Silver King* ore in British territory as long as possible even if all the nearby smelters were in the States. Sproat was instructed to connect Toad Mountain with the Columbia River. This would necessitate the building of a trail thirty or so miles long, as well as the maintenance of ferries over the Kootenay and Slocan Rivers. Sproat's private opinion was that ore could not be drawn "Canadianwards" without a railway to the Columbia. However, he obeyed instructions and the trail was begun. It was to lead down the mountain from the *Silver King* mine to Kootenay River, then down the south side for about fourteen miles to a ferry, thence down the north side, across the Slocan River, and on to Sproat's Landing.

It is likely that Sproat made more than one journey that spring from Revelstoke to view in person all the activity on the west arm. It would be a journey involving effort and discomfort—steamboat or canoe from Revelstoke to Sproat's Landing, and Indian trail up the Kootenay River to the west arm. He most certainly was on the scene during the summer months, actively pursuing his aim of developing the townsite. The conflict with Arthur Bunting was not yet settled. The error in gazetting, already mentioned near the beginning of this chapter, made it difficult for Sproat to lay claim to the land he had wanted. Meanwhile Harry Anderson, on the lake in pursuance of his new job, had the same idea as Arthur Bunting—to make a little money on land speculation. He applied for pre-emption rights on a block of land (present-day Fairview) along the shore just to the east of Bunting's and had it surveyed during the summer. He constructed a cabin at the eastern end of his pre-emption—in fact, just east of one of the two mouths of the creek that now bears his name, the very creek that Richard and Justine Fry had panned unsuccessfully back in Chapter 5. In this cabin he set up his recorder's office. As he needed a recording location when filling out forms, he used "Salisbury," intending that the settlement that would develop on his pre-emption should go by that name. He built a long trail from the tent-town around Arthur Bunting's cabin to this office. It went up over the bluff which at the present day divides Nelson neatly into two parts.

When he heard that the government was disallowing Bunting's pre-emption he made an attempt to acquire that land also. But by this time—mid-summer—Malcolm Sproat was on the scene, determined, in spite of the error in gazetting, to get the land he wanted for the government. Bunting's claim was negated on a technicality, and Anderson withdrew; however, there was bitter feeling for a long time over the ease with which the government, acting through Malcolm Sproat, had ousted Arthur Bunting. The bitterness is manifested as late as 1897, in an article called "History What is History" by one Tom Collins, which appeared in the *Tribune* of September 25th, 1897.

Arthur Bunting's cabin was near the mouth of the small creek beside which Dick and Justine Fry had camped in the summer of '82, and Sproat and Farwell in '84. Also there were the two cabins of Dick Fry's sons-in-law. Around these three cabins the tent-town of the Toad Mountain prospectors had grown. Amazingly, there were already—such was the optimistic belief in the importance of the Toad Mountain claims!—three businesses being conducted in tents. These were a hotel run by Josephine and John Ward, a blacksmith shop operated by Frank Hanna, and a supply store owned by William Dennee and Sandy Devine. These people were hoping to purchase property so that they could remain in more permanent quarters throughout the winter.

Malcolm Sproat was eager to accommodate these business persons in their desire to remain over the winter, and also to make the governmental claim to ownership of the townsite clearly visible. To that end, on September 3rd, 1888 he prepared a memorandum to the government indicating his plans for the site. With the memorandum he enclosed a map he had drawn earlier in the summer. That sketch map is one of those priceless documents which delight historians, a primary source of truly unassailable

Sproat's Sketch Map

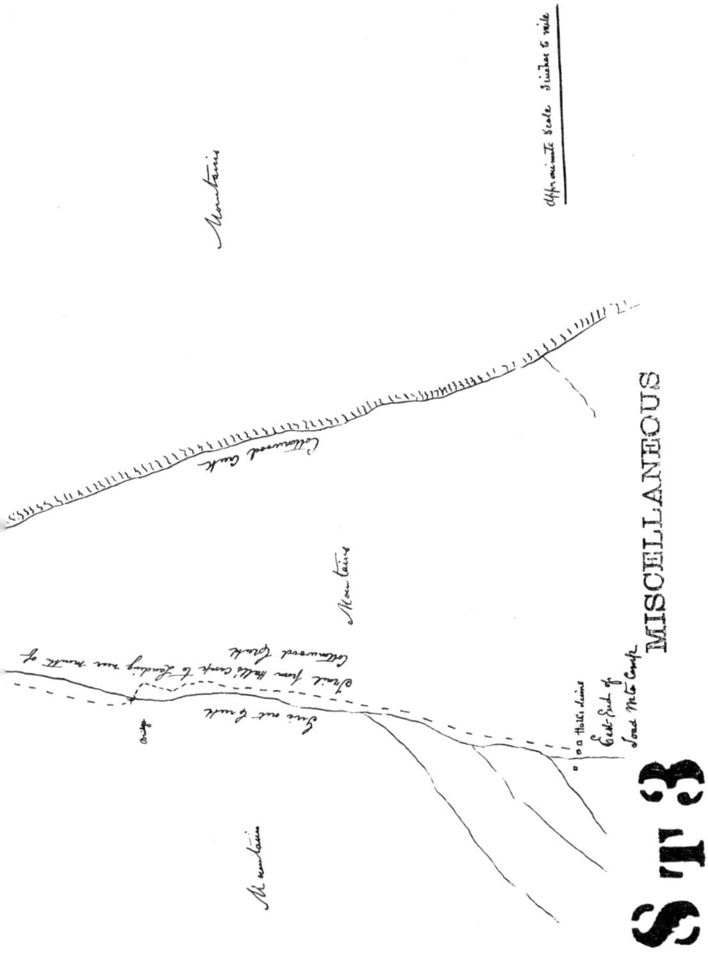


Office of the Surveyor General, Ministry of the Environment, Lands and Parks, Province of British Columbia

integrity. More than that, however, it is one of those gratifying flashes of light which, acting like rays of sunshine through a rift in thick clouds, give sudden moments of warmth among the dusty cold notations of government record books or the murk of secondary sources. For a moment as we study it we can feel the presence of the man Malcolm Sproat, seated—where? in a tent on the shore near the cabin of Arthur Bunting, a shore now buried under yards of fill? on a rock on the strip of benchland that will become Vernon Street?—drawing this annotated sketch map, in the very manner we ourselves might do, of a region still recognizable despite the century and more of change that intervenes between us and him. His map is a precious document that dismisses all need of speculation and allows us to sit in as witnesses at the moment of Nelson's birth. As such, it must be reproduced here so that we can examine it in loving detail.

At the top we see the west arm of Kootenay Lake just where it narrows to become the lower Kootenay River. Stretching from the bottom and emptying into the west arm is Cottonwood Creek, the very creek that Dick Fry and Justine followed up to the tiny mountain lake in Chapter 5. (The lake is just outside the boundary of this map.) The present historian, for all the times this creek has appeared in his story, has never given it a name, in the belief that it did not have one until much later. Now, here is Malcolm Sproat already calling it Cottonwood Creek on his 1888 sketch map, that irrefutable primary source—forcing the writer's hand (both figuratively and literally) and necessitating that he tell the story behind that name much earlier than called for in his original plan. Here, then, is the story. Dick Fry for a short time maintained his trapline in partnership with a man called "Cottonwood" Smith. As Dick's other interests took more of his time, the trapline along the creek became associated more and more in people's minds with Cottonwood Smith. Gradually the Creek came to be known as Cottonwood Smith's Creek, and finally, simply Cottonwood Creek. We observe that Malcolm Sproat has indicated by stippling that it flows in a narrow valley between steep mountains. We see "Hall's claims" indicated in the lower left-hand corner. We can imagine, somewhere between that point and the Creek, the view-point where the boys had their panoramic sight in Chapter 13.

Along the shoreline to the right (east) of the mouth of Cotton-wood Creek, a much smaller creek enters the lake, on a stretch of beach we are already familiar with. This creek is not yet named and, indeed, will not long outlive its naming. Near the creek, to the east, we see the tiny squares which denote Arthur Bunting's cabin and those of Dick Fry's sons-in-law, as well as some of the tents and other cabins that cluster around them. The square de-noting Bunting's cabin represents Nelson's first "house," which was finally torn down in 1897 to make room for the railway. Its logs lay around for some time, but, alas, the busy folk engaged in making the town grow had no time to think of reassembling them in the interests of history. From the cabins—which are situated at the best landing place for boats—we see the dotted line which indicates the trail leading from the tent-town across the flats and slopes of the future city, and up the long steep climb to the top of Toad Mountain. Just east of the cabins we observe how Sproat indicated by more stippling the bluff at the end of the mountain spur that so neatly divides present-day Fairview from "uptown."

We can surmise that the map must have been drawn in late summer, because it indicates that Harry Anderson (who, as we know, only got his job as mining recorder in the spring) has al-ready had time to file for pre-emption of his land and build his cabin at its eastern end. We see the cabin on the map—at the far right of the shoreline. It is situated near one of the two mouths of the creek that will one day bear Anderson's name, somewhere, it seems to this historian, at the western end of present-day Lakeside Park. Today, that branch of the stream has long been filled in, its course no longer traceable under the houses of Fairview. The map does not show the trail that led to Anderson's cabin. It started at the tent-town and crossed over the mountain spur, probably in the same place as the road that runs just below present-day Gyro Park, and then found its way down to the flats again. Just east of the bluffs, Sproat has indicated by a cross on the shoreline the approxi-mate position of the northwest post of Anderson's pre-emption.

A little below Bunting's cabin on the map we see a large rectangle. In it are the words: Proposed Portion of Town Site. Sproat's whole reserve comprised 160 acres and was recorded as District Lot 95 Group 1, Kootenay District. This rectangle represents a small part of that reserve, four complete city blocks and the halves of four others, surveyed immediately by Malcolm Sproat so that merchants and others could buy lots and remain throughout the winter of '88-'89. Those city blocks exist today as he created them. They had to be resurveyed later, of course, because Malcolm Sproat, although a knowledgeable man with many abilities (as befitted an official in pioneer territory), was not a recognized surveyor whose work could be entered into record books. The survey map he produced, however, since it differs only in small ways from its appearance today, can be reproduced here for our fond examination. It represents the newborn infant whose birth we have witnessed and whose adult stature we know today.

## Sproat's Survey[22]

Nelson Land Use Plan Based on Sproat's Map

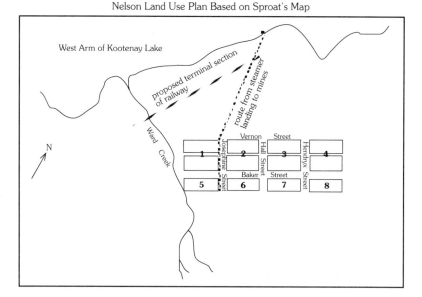

Looking carefully at the survey we observe that Sproat put his first street, Vernon, quite a distance from the lakeshore. The map does not indicate that Vernon Street is on a bench much higher than the land between it and the lake. In fact, in several places the bank is very steep and a present-day observer on Vernon Street looks down on the roofs of buildings below. Sproat intended that the flat land along the lake should be used for industrial purposes. He has even included the terminal section of the railway that he believed must eventually be built from Sproat's Landing on the Columbia to his townsite. We observe that small creek—very soon to be called Ward Creek—near whose mouth was the tent-town. Sproat thought of Vernon Street—width 100 feet—as the principal commercial thoroughfare. Blocks 1, 2, 3, and 4, which were intended for businesses are divided into larger lots than blocks 5, 6, 7, and 8, all, with the exception of block 5, intended for the homes of miners. Block 5 was reserved for government buildings. The map shows us that Sproat—even at this very early date in the town's history—had already named the streets: Vernon and Baker after government officials (F. W. Vernon was at that time Land Commissioner, and James Baker, the eventual founder of Cranbrook B.C., at that time the Member of the Legislative Assembly for Kootenay); Hall after Winslow and Osner Hall; Hendryx after our old acquaintance Dr. Wilbur Hendryx, who changed Big Ledge into Hendryx Camp; Josephine after John Ward's wife, the first woman in the developing town, and much more energetic than her husband who, some of our sources indicate, liked to take things easy. The unnamed street along the creek is still only a deep gully which will not be completely filled in for several decades. Like the creek, it will come to bear the name Ward, after Josephine's husband. The creek, of course, is intended to supply water to the townsite from its upper reaches, while carrying away sewage in its lower. Part of Sproat's proposal was that the railway would have its terminus at the boat landing. From there a "route"—a wagon road probably—would pass along the flats, up Josephine Street and on to the mines on Toad Mountain. It is evident from all the foregoing that the birth of Nelson was a very orderly one. Malcolm

Sproat is often called "the father of Nelson," but he was also its self-assured and highly competent midwife.

In the first pages of this important chapter it was stated that Harry Anderson had his pre-emption surveyed. We must now pause and take note in a paragraph or two of the surveyor he hired, for he, like Anderson himself, is one of those characters who move, half-remembered, as legendary figures in the earliest pages of Nelson's history. Some of them—Dick Fry, Grohman, Sproule, Woodbury, Ainsworth, Hendryx—have prominent creeks, towns, or streets named after them. Anderson too has his creek, and Sproat, a peak near Revelstoke. Busk—that is the surveyor's name—has only a minor feeder-creek unknown to most people. Busk, once a prominent landowner, businessman, maker of events, and moreover the first of those Britons whose actions determined that the bias of Nelson's social structure should be toward the English rather than the American, has gradually had all memory of his name effaced, so that now only the older generations, in driving along the north Shore from Nelson to Balfour, know when they are passing places that once evoked his memory in everyone.

Charles Westly Busk was born on November 13th, 1852 in Greenwich, Kent. His father's position as a well-known merchant and importer insured that his son should enjoy the life-style of the upper middle class, able, during that period of the British Empire's full flowering, to move freely throughout most of the world. Young Charles, having spent his boyhood in Cape Town, South Africa, graduated from Trinity College, Cambridge in the year 1876, the very year that Dick Fry sent the letter to his brother Martin asking him to come to the Bonners Ferry trading post. This was the period when science, under the aegis of men like Thomas Henry Huxley, was making inroads into the classical curriculum of England's universities. Charles Busk graduated as a civil engineer in the first class at Cambridge to specialize in applied science. In the late '70s he emigrated to Canada and got a job with the engineers at work on the Canadian Pacific Railway Company's new transcontinental line. In '84 he left the CPR to open a civil engineering office on Bastion Square in Victoria, enjoying life as a member of the establishment in that city. An unpleasant and financially disastrous experience with a business partner caused him to leave Victoria with bitter feelings. Travelling through the States, first by the Northern Pacific Railroad and then by stagecoach, he reached Bonners Ferry, where, discovering that a new steamer, the *Galena*, was about to leave for Kootenay Lake on its maiden voyage, he elected to get aboard. Thus it was that Dr. Wilbur Hendryx's decision to put another boat on the lake for the furtherance of his operation there came just in time to provide Charles Busk with transportation to the scene of Nelson's birth. On July 11th, the *Galena* deposited Busk on the boat landing near Arthur Bunting's cabin. Very soon after being deposited there, he met Harry Anderson and entered our history by accepting the job of surveying Anderson's pre-emption.

Malcolm Sproat had been right in thinking that a trail from Toad Mountain to Sproat's Landing wouldn't really do much to keep *Silver King* ore in Canada. Even as that trail was being constructed, the Hall brothers' company had decided that their ore would leave Kootenay through Bonners Ferry and make its way down to a smelter in Butte, Montana. To that end they had decided to ask help from the one man in the whole region who had the capability of realizing their wishes—Dick Fry. Down in Bonners Ferry he had the pack horses and their feed, the trading post that could provide workers with food, and, above all, the reputation that made the Halls feel he could surmount all the difficulties inherent in the operation—even to the obtaining of a boat for carrying ore from the tent-town on the west arm, along the length of Kootenay Lake, and up the river to Bonners Ferry, whence it could be packed to the smelter in southwestern Montana. Dick Fry was glad to accept the challenge. He got on his saddle horse and trotted down to Sandpoint to see if he could buy a little steamer, the *Idaho*, which had been lying idle on Pend d'Oreille Lake since the completion of the Northern Pacific Railway along the lakeshore had made it unneeded as a workhorse in railway construction. Finding its owner willing to sell, Dick bought the *Idaho* and had it hauled on wheels to Bonners Ferry.

By the time it got there, a barge had been built and loaded with mules and supplies, all ready to be towed up into Canada to the tent-town on the west arm of Kootenay Lake. By mid-summer the *Idaho* had nosed onto the beach in front of the tent-town, and the mules were on their way up the trail to the *Silver King* mine. We can see the trail ending at the water's edge on Malcolm Sproat's sketch map, and we can read his words "Landing now used" to indicate where the *Idaho, Galena,* and—let us not forget them— the *Midge* and the *Surprise* could dock. Incidentally, we need no longer talk about the "tent-town." As well as immediately providing his first streets with their names, Malcolm Sproat had made the suggestion to government officials that the townsite itself be called "Stanley" (after the Governor General of Canada), but, he added, if that name proved unacceptable "Nelson" (after the Lieutenant-Governor of British Columbia) would be equally suitable. (In his article of October 9th in the *Tribune*, Sproat tells us that "ever since I was thrashed at school for misspelling Constantinople, I have been fond of short words. Most of my own towns, you may observe, have two syllable names.") For the first few months of its existence the infant town did go by the name "Stanley." Soon, however, government officials, observing that there was already a "Stanley" in the Cariboo district of British Columbia, decided on "Nelson." For a time there was some confusion about what the town's correct name was, and this was added to by the desire of Harry Anderson to name his adjacent pre-emption "Salisbury." Ever since then, many secondary source books have stated that early Nelson had three names.

It was a busy lake that summer of 1888, and this chapter must grow much longer to accommodate the tale. We are ignoring all the activity those two arch entrepreneurs John C. Ainsworth and Dr. Wilbur Hendryx have brought about at their respective camps up on the main lake, while we concentrate our attention on the lower end of the west arm where Nelson is being born. But we must not forget that Ainsworth and Hendryx Camp are going concerns and have drawn many prospectors and other developers into their spheres of activity. While the little town of Stanley grows apace, these two older communities are also adding to their stature. Indeed, Dr. Hendryx, unmindful yet of any poetic Shadow that might intervene between his idea and its realization, has very big plans which we will examine in due course as his abundant drive to succeed makes them happen. Meanwhile, four steamers are present on the lake to facilitate movement between the centres of activity—little *Midge*, put there by B-G, whom we have not forgotten although he is well off-stage for the time being; *Surprise*, Wilbur Hendryx's first boat; *Galena*, his third (we omit his second, a short-lived one); and *Idaho*, the boat that Dick Fry has brought to barge ore from the *Silver King* down into the States.

This whole business of carrying ore over such a very long distance from a mine to a smelter is financially a very risky one, and the first shipment from the *Silver King* is really a trial run, to see if the operation is economically feasible. Only high grade ore, hand-picked to fill the sacks, has been toted by ponies down the long trail from Toad Mountain to the boat-landing. When it has been concentrated and separated into its component elements far away in southern Montana, only then can the financial experts associated with the Hall company decide whether or not the mine should continue to operate. But everyone is exceedingly hopeful, not only the financial backers in England, but also every prospector and small business person on the site at Stanley.

While all the aforementioned mining and land pre-empting activities were going on at Stanley during that spring and summer of '88, there was a fellow up in Big Bend country—in fact, at the Illecillewaet River, which enters the Columbia about five miles below Revelstoke—by the name of Bob Yuill. (We know something about him because in 1918 he wrote a so-called diary of some of his adventures. Years later—sometime between 1918 and 1935—a woman at an old hotel in Nelson, the *Kootenay*, was cleaning out some forgotten trunks and other trash, and had built a bonfire to burn up the mess. Happening to be there at the time, a man named D.A. Acton—this one event perpetuates his name—picked the diary from the flames. It eventually fell into the hands of one R.G. Joy, who happened to be the historian of the Nelson

Association of Old Timers, and he used it in a talk he gave at the Old Timers' banquet on May 29th, 1935. The diary was then printed in the *Nelson Daily News* of Monday morning, June 10th.) Anyway, one day in June '88, Bob Yuill was asked by Gus B. Wright—builder of the Cariboo Wagon Road, husband of George Ainsworth's sister, and chief representative of the Ainsworth Syndicate in the Kootenays—to go to Revelstoke to help one James Delaney pack up the goods in his store there and transport them to Ainsworth. Delaney was going to Ainsworth (Yuill called it Warm Springs in his diary) to become the manager of a store being built for Wright and his partner, Joseph Fletcher.

During the first days of August, the goods—13,000 pounds of them—were packed in small bundles (for carrying by ponies), loaded onto a catamaran[23], and floated down the Columbia River to Sproat's Landing. Here Yuill and his men found a tiny settlement with a store run by a man called R.E. Lemon. Lemon had seen a business opportunity when government crews started building the trail that was to connect the *Silver King* to Sproat's Landing, and his store was now making life easier for the gangs of workmen cutting brush up to the Slocan River. Bob Yuill and his crew had to wait at Sproat's for two weeks for the Indians who were bringing ponies up from Little Dalles in Washington, a long overland haul. Bob, who liked to enjoy himself in drinking bouts—he speaks of them in his diary—didn't mind the wait at all. A fellow called Tom Ward was already operating one of the ferries needed on the trail—the one across the Kootenay. At the hotel he maintained on the site—only a short walk of fourteen miles or so from Sproat's—he kept a good supply of booze.

The Indians finally arrived, and Bob was able to get them organized for the trip to Stanley. They had with them "all kinds of stock, colts, horses, old mares, squaws and kids, all colors and sizes." They had come up on the west side of the Columbia from Dalles and consequently had to cross over to the east side. Bob was amused at the sight of the large party crossing the river, still quite high from the spring floods. While the animals swam across, the Indians paddled alongside downstream to see that none drifted down with the current. After they all got across, the Indians made camp. In due time, Bob's party began the trek up the north side of Kootenay River. Soon they came to the Slocan River, which they crossed on the new ferry only recently put into operation by "a red-haired chap named Fitzgerald." To pay Fitzgerald for the ride, Bob tells us that he used cash instead of the "government vouchers good as gold" that he had been given by Wright. A little later, after crossing the flat where the community of Shoreacres stands today, they came to Tom Ward's ferry and were carried across to the south side of the Kootenay. Tom Ward refused to accept payment, saying he knew G.B. Wright and would collect from him when he came through. (Tom never did get paid his hundred dollars or so, for Wright, who was in Victoria, came to Ainsworth the American way, up through Bonners Ferry.) Above Tom Ward's ferry, the river became full of rapids, and the trail passed several waterfalls. This was the stretch of the lower Kootenay that prevented any possibility of water transport from Stanley to Sproat's Landing, and that formed the boundary between the territories of the Kootenay and Lake Indians. At Forty-nine Creek the government trail headed away from the river, up toward the top of Toad Mountain. If they continued to follow it, they would end up at the *Silver King* mine and would then have to descend to Stanley from there. To avoid doing that, Bob sent a crew ahead to cut a makeshift trail along the river, a much more direct route to their destination. Following after them, the main party finally crossed over Cottonwood Creek at about the position of present-day Latimer Street, and went down into Stanley. There, we may be sure, the white men of the party enjoyed the hospitality offered at hard-working Josephine Ward's hotel-in-a-tent, while the Indians camped near the shoreline. The time of their arrival was about the middle of July.

At Stanley they and the 13,000 pounds of stock from Delaney's store were still a long way from Ainsworth. Bob Yuill had to figure out some means of getting them onto the lake for the last leg of the journey. The large party of Indians were, of course, paid and sent back home, but several white men and 13,000 pounds of goods were still a formidable load. The *Idaho* "came along one day," but its captain would not carry them as his vessel was "an American bottom" and could not legally do so. A few days later the *Galena* appeared at the boat-landing, but its captain, while admitting he was going up to Ainsworth's Camp, also refused the commission. Undaunted, Bob Yuill began searching for rowboats. A fellow called Mike Doyle was willing to lend him a "sort of box"; another small boat came from Dr. David LaBau, of whom we will hear more later; Dick Fry provided a good-size rowing vessel, the *Lady-of-the-Lake*, which had once been the property of John C. Ainsworth. Difficult as it may be for us denizens of a motorized age to imagine, Bob Yuill and his crew then began transporting those 13,000 pounds of goods from Stanley to Ainsworth by rowboat. They had to make several trips, all but one of which were made in the weeks of late August and early September. Then, leaving the last load stored in a tent on the beach at Stanley under the care of "an old cook," they remained in Ainsworth, building the store for Wright and Fletcher and cutting trails up to some of the mines back of the town. It was only in November that Bob and three other men finally went back to Stanley in two borrowed boats to bring up the remaining load. On the way back to Ainsworth, when the two heavily laden boats, each occupied by two men, were just off the mouth of the creek that would one day be named Coffee, a disaster occurred. One of the borrowed vessels, the *Tacoma*, being rowed with or without the aid of a sail—it is impossible to determine whether a phrase in the diary, "with all sail set," is to be taken literally or metaphorically—by Bob Yuill and his companion, suddenly began shipping water and sank within five minutes, leaving the two men and most of the packaged goods free-floating in the lake. The other boat, about two miles ahead and close in, pulled ashore, unloaded, and set out to the rescue. But a third boat got there first, and effected the rescue; not, however, until Bob had had to save his friend from drowning (he does not say how). The drenched men were taken as fast as possible through the chill November air to the beach at Coffee Creek, where they were able to dry their clothes around a fire before going on to Ainsworth. That night about ten o'clock "along came the *Idaho*" with G.B. Wright aboard bringing supplies for opening one of the mines. Next day, Bob Yuill, his brush with death on the previous day forgotten, was up on the mountain high above Ainsworth, working at that mine—helping to build a cookhouse, bunkhouse, and assay office. We will leave him there—a fine example of that race of courageous, uncomplaining, hard-working and hard-drinking men who appeared at the time they were needed to perform the brute labour of pioneer days. Perhaps our present-day nostalgia for their era, our sometimes imperative desire to fill our leisure time with activities which palely suggest theirs—our hunting, our summer-holiday camping, trekking, boating, fishing from cars at roadside streams, around which a whole industry has arisen to insure that we experience only the barest minimum of the discomfort needed to sustain the illusion that we are "roughing it," perhaps all this is a manifestation of our unconscious envy of the "realness" of their experiences. As our lives become more hedged-in with concerns over security, safety, longevity, and comfort, perhaps the increasing "acting-out" quality of our arts and entertainments, and, indeed, of our world in general, is a deep-rooted reaction to our lack of some much-needed kind of experiential "reality" they had and we have lost. Be that as it may, Bob Yuill, besides epitomizing the pioneer type for us, has served a useful purpose in our history, adding colour and a sense of actuality to our account of the year 1888. Although he stayed around Kootenay Lake for much of the remainder of his life, married and raised a family, it is unlikely, in the press of other names and events, that we will find time to give any account of more than one or two of his further adventures.

During the weeks of Bob's labours on the lake, Malcolm Sproat had not been idle concerning the development of his townsite. He was eager for a sale of lots to take place during early autumn so that the merchants and miners could begin building business locations or homes and remain in Stanley over the coming winter. In September he finally got permission from his superiors to arrange for the sale, but when the auction took place in October, only one person outside of Kootenay—a Mr. Green of Victoria—bought a lot, and as if to reinforce his faith in the town he bought two. John Ward and some others on the site bought a few, but the outside investors were all from either Revelstoke or Donald and had bought their lots on speculation, since those towns were suffering a serious financial decline after the completion of the Canadian Pacific Railway. Although 55 out of the 88 lots were bought, Malcolm Sproat was unhappy with the result of the auction and complained that he had written, previous to the sale, "hundreds of letters to persons throughout British Columbia and Washington territory, descanting on the future glories of the capital of southern Kootenay." The difficulty, to use Sproat's own words, was "that neither the government nor the people down there [i.e., south of the border] had any faith" in the undertaking. In the British Columbia government's eyes, once the *Silver King* began shipping its ore through Bonners Ferry, there was no more need for Stanley. The logical place for a town would be on the main lake. Ainsworth, already a growing community, now, this very summer, had its first store—a real one, not just one in a tent. Revelstoke and Donald may indeed have experienced a decline, but when merchants there contemplated moving, the reasonable place in their eyes to go was not Stanley, still largely a town in the imagination of Malcolm Sproat, but the relatively long-established townsite of Ainsworth. Other business persons from Revelstoke and the Big Bend country—one of them very important to our history—were contemplating a move to Kootenay Lake, but the time was still a couple of years or more away when they would consider Stanley. No, we must admit that Malcolm Sproat's baby, though it had an orderly birth, was at the beginning a slow-grower.

Meanwhile, traffic on the Columbia River was steadily increasing. More and more boats were coming from Revelstoke to Sproat's Landing, all of them loaded with people curious about the *Silver King* mine and the rumoured new town on the west arm of Kootenay Lake. More and more parties walked the trail and used the ferries. And all the while, survey posts for a railway stood unnoticed part way along the same route—the railway that John C. Ainsworth's Syndicate had proposed from Sproat's Landing to the site of present-day Balfour. The survey had stopped along the river just west of Stanley, the Syndicate having lost interest because of all the impediments the government had placed in its way.

# CHAPTER 17

*In which we first examine an error in* Henderson's
British Columbia Gazetteer and Directory *of 1889
and then abandon Robert Yuill on the west arm of
Kootenay Lake so that the author may indulge himself
in a short but important digression.*

Readers of *Henderson's British Columbia Gazetteer and
Directory—1889* (published sometime in the winter of '88—'89)
observed the following notice in the "S" pages of the section listing towns and settlements.

> Stanley—a mining town in the Toad Mountain district, 26
> miles from Sproat's Landing.
> Nearest railway Ashcroft, distance 275 miles.
> Dodd, W.W.—drugs.
> Fletcher, Anderson—general store.
> Peebles, John—blacksmith and general store.

Merely casual readers—perhaps browsing through *Henderson's* pages in the search for idle amusement over their breakfast
coffee—found themselves unable to form any clear mental image
of where Stanley might be, since two of its referents were unknown to them, and quickly passed on to the next item. Investors
with money to spend, prospectors looking for somewhere to go,
and other serious readers leafed further among the "S" pages, then
the "Ts,"—and perhaps even among the "Ls" and "Ms"—only to
become more puzzled, there being no listing for "Sproat's Land-

ing" or "Toad Mountain." They had to be content with the speculation that "Stanley," considering the location of Ashcroft, must be somewhere in Cariboo country. *Henderson's* had made an error, confusing the new town on the outlet of Kootenay Lake's west arm with another "Stanley" which was indeed in the Cariboo. Messrs. Dodd, Fletcher, and Peebles had probably never been near Sproat's Landing or even heard of it. They would no doubt have become posthumously famous as pioneer merchants of *their* town had that Cariboo "Stanley" survived for more than a few years; however, it had not, and their fate has been to take form but briefly on this page—the unwanted and short-lived personages of a mistake.

It is easy to imagine the mistake being made: down in New Westminster the office of *Henderson's* is chaotic as publication deadline looms close. "Only at the 'Ss'," wails a harassed clerk, clutching his furrowed brow where the few remaining hairs of his head lie plastered in sweat, "and yet another one—or is it *two?*— of these damnable mushroom towns that appear in the bush every year, only to disappear in the next! Surely there can't be *two* Stanleys! Put all the info together and let's get on with the job!"

But the Stanley 26 miles from Sproat's Landing really *was* there, and already had a lot of people living in it (not one of them named Dodd, Fletcher, or Peebles). Behind the terse wording of *Henderson's* garbled notice there was indeed a flesh-and-blood reality alive and kicking on the south shore of the west arm. We even know what the people there did on New Year's Day of the year '89.

On the last day of the year 1888, Bob Yuill noticed a bad smell outside the door of his cabin at Ainsworth Camp and decided that the ham and sourbelly he had stored there were a little too far gone for healthful consumption. The smell set him to thinking. His bacon supply was finished, and other staples were low, too. There wasn't much doing around Ainsworth. The store didn't have much of anything just now. Most folks had left till spring, and the rest were pretty well in hibernation. For days now it had been rain-ing—one of the mildest winters for a long time. There had been a few snowfalls, but little remained of them. Today, low cloud hung drearily over the lake. Well below halfway on the mountains, a white line showed under the cloud, where the rain was turning to snow. Four miles across the water, the shoreline at Hendryx Camp looked remote and lonely in the dim light. For some reason the sight raised memories in Bob of cheerful kitchens and the kind of food and warmth that only a woman could give. Tomorrow would be New Year's Day, and that thought made his memories more poignant. There were people over at Hendryx Camp, including a woman, for the Dr. and his wife were staying the winter. But a trip across four miles of water at this season, even to see them, wasn't to be undertaken too hastily. And he'd have to row in a small boat: *Surprise* and *Galena* were not in use; they were tied up over there for the winter, no good to anybody. Bob's loneliness took shape as a yearning, vague and unnamed, but unyielding in its demand for action. He looked over to Hendryx's again. It was even less visible now in the failing late-afternoon light. So close and yet so far over that forbidding stretch of water . . . it was be-yond reach. But Stanley . . . Stanley, for all its thirty-mile distance, wasn't—not if you kept the shore close all the way. A warm win-ter, no wind, no sign of much change in the weather . . . there was little risk, none at all! The thought relieved the yearning that was tormenting him. He would row to Stanley the very next morning to get the supplies he needed from Dennee & Devine's store! Sud-denly happy, he ran down toward the shoreline to inspect the heavy rowboat he intended to use.

Winter still brings us days like that one, and we who live around beautiful Kootenay Lake all know how Bob was feeling on that New Year's Eve so long ago. Nowadays, though, we have a multiplicity of palliative gadgets and diversions on hand, and do not need to make the massive effort that he is about to make in driving back that mid-winter melancholy.

Early on New Year's morning, very early, well before it was light, Bob set out on the journey from Ainsworth Camp to Nelson, retracing the route followed by B-G and Darby & Joan back in '82. They had paddled a light Indian canoe; he rowed a heavy freight-boat, large enough, he tells us in his diary, to carry a load of one ton. The cloud cover had lifted, leaving the snowy mountains visible, and there was a feeling of colder weather in the air. After reaching the west arm, Bob had the current to help him. Hour after hour he floated alone toward Stanley through the silence of that winter morning, resting in the narrows where the current was strong and rowing hard through the wide lagoons. He knew, as we also know, how short the days are around the winter solstice and that made him anxious to get to his destination. We cannot guess how much of the poet Bob had in him, or if he took time to savour the mood of that sombre day. Perhaps, like B-G in the summer of '82, Bob was too busy thinking about commonplaces to be aware of his surroundings. Certainly the mountains and the water on that winter day had the same painterly beauty they had had when B-G first saw them—the same, but not the same, for then they had been an exultation of green and blue and sunny gold, and the slopes had been lush with trees. Now, a series of forest fires having burned through the area in the intervening years, those slopes were bare; nevertheless, there was an intense, sad beauty in the stark shapes of the black, grey, and white landscape that Bob was slipping silently through, charred skeletons of dead trees grotesque against freshly-fallen snow on the hillsides, and the slatey water quiet beneath his gliding boat. It was a scene to delight the heart of a painter. We hope Bob enjoyed it, too.

Enjoying the scenery or not, he had made good time. Difficult as it might be for us to imagine, he was now in sight of Stanley, and it was still only late morning, a good half-hour before noon. As we know, Bob was no stranger to hard labour, and he had made this journey many times before. In the distance he could see the peak near which the *Silver King* mine and camp lay, and the long shoreline where the few buildings and tents of Stanley were not yet visible, still too far away for even the landing-place to be distinguished.

Weary and bored with his solitary labours, anxious to see the friends he had not seen for months, Bob had reached that stage of his long journey where, if we can judge by our own experience, impatience and eagerness to get the job done set in. It is a state of tension that grows steadily as the minutes go by and is relieved only when the destination is reached, in Bob's case when he runs the prow of his boat onto the gravel and mud of Stanley's shoreline. Used to privation and perhaps less in need of immediate gratification, more stoic than we are, he probably did not experience that tension as demandingly as we would, but undoubtedly he felt it to some degree. It is not a state that any compassionate author would allow his characters, real or fictional, to endure for too long. Nevertheless, we are going to suspend the action and compel Bob to wait—impatient and weary as he might be—while the author makes a point or two about his manner of writing this history, a manner that thoughtful readers may already have been evaluating for themselves.

It is evident that the purpose of this work has been, not to present the facts of Nelson's past in the form of an academic history, but rather to infuse those facts with the breath of life, to make us "be there" as we are when we read a story; for the history of Nelson *is* a story, a saga, worthy in its humble way to be sung as was Homer's epic of Troy. The heroes, the immortals, of *our* saga are the people of the first days of West Kootenay country, and the landscape in which they perform their deeds is our lake enfolded by its mountains, not some far-away pebbly beach on the shorelines of the eastern Mediterranean. But already the past they inhabit is in many ways as inaccessible and mysterious as that remoter past of the *Iliad's* heroes. Already their lives have acquired something of the uncertain and legendary aura that surrounds the fighters of the Trojan War. It is fitting, then, that we employ the narrative mode to evoke the time they lived in. Furthermore, the author need make no apology for this, though it flies in the teeth of those purists who demand that history consist of bare facts ungarnished by imagination, no matter how carefully introduced. After all, what *is* history? One of the sciences, as some insist?

Surely not. It is a construction of the human mind, just as inescapably as the sciences themselves are; and its understanding demands the full mind and spirit—the total *humanity*—of the seeker after knowledge, exactly as does understanding of the sciences if we are to make meaning of them above and beyond their mere usefulness in all kinds of gadgetry. Napoleon was defeated at the battle of Waterloo on the 18th day of June in the year 1815. This is a bare fact, soon forgotten by every school child who is forced to remember it until exams are over. Historian A will assign various motivations—economic, political, religious, etc.—as his explanation of how time produced that bare fact. Historian B will pursue *her* interests by exploring the psychopathology that formed Napoleon and the millions who willingly followed him. Thackeray, in one of his novels, choosing to take his readers to a ball held in a nearby town on the eve of the battle, illuminates the bare fact in yet another way by engaging his readers sympathetically, even empathetically, in the emotions of his characters. It seems that all three of these approaches, and many others too, are necessary for the "complete" knowledge of history.

Bob has waited long enough. Let's put the oars once again in his hands and advance our tale by getting him to Nelson.

# CHAPTER 18

*Which is mainly an account of Nelson's first New Year's Day.*

SHORTLY AFTER NOON of New Year's Day, 1889, Robert Yuill arrived at the shoreline of Stanley and landed, either by rowing the prow of his boat onto the mud and rocks of the beach or by easing alongside the jetty that had been built there (probably by Dick Fry and workmen from the *Silver King*) to facilitate the loading of ore onto the *Idaho*. We must remember, of course, that in those earliest days the shoreline was very close to the present-day railway bed—not a hundred yards or so farther out into the lake, where decades of filling and other tampering have since placed it. However, the day of his arrival being in the middle of winter when the water level was at its lowest, Bob undoubtedly had to leave his boat a good distance from the summertime shoreline and walk over many yards of oozy mud, gravel, and rotting vegetation until he found the trail—or perhaps one of several that left the beach—leading up the steep, low bank onto firmer ground. Malcolm Sproat has clearly indicated on his 1888 sketch map how far out the shoreline reached at low water.

We should take a moment, now, to relocate that invaluable map, for it will help us imagine the route Bob followed when he came ashore. On it we can see the dotted line indicating the trail that leads from the boat-landing to the *Silver King* mine, six miles away high on the mountain. The lower end of that trail is what Bob followed to get to the settlement. On the shore we see the tiny squares indicating the three huts of Arthur Bunting and Martin

Fry's sons-in-law, as well as a double square probably representing a supply house owned by the sons-in-law. Scattered along the trail, we see other squares, indicating tents or log cabins, built in the best spots their owners could find on the rough, uneven ground. All or most of them appear empty to Bob, since there are very few of Stanley's inhabitants who have not left to spend the winter in more amenable surroundings. We also observe the large rectangle denoting the four blocks that Malcolm Sproat surveyed.

For our convenience we will enlarge this section of Sproat's map and reproduce it here, first deleting the words "Proposed portion of townsite" that Malcolm wrote inside the rectangle. Also we will add something that was not on the map when Malcolm Sproat drew it: a blackened square denoting the log store of Hume & Lemon. We must place this square precisely—as precisely as a sketch map permits—because it represents the only building on the map that has actually been put on a bonafide lot of Sproat's townsite. All the other squares denote structures that were erected

## Sproat's Map

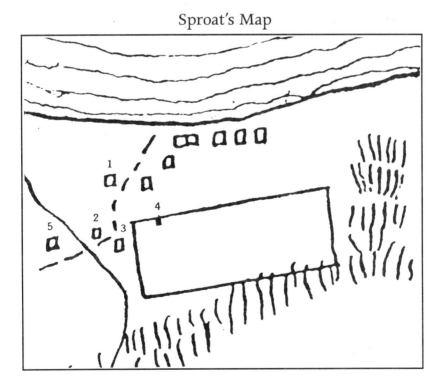

wherever their builders decided to put them; they are, in fact, the homes of squatters. Hume & Lemon, however, have obtained one of Malcolm Sproat's surveyed lots, hence their log store sits on a perfectly legal site, just east of the middle of the first block in the rectangle and faces the street which Malcolm Sproat named "Vernon" after the Provincial Land Commissioner. The building is not quite finished. It is being put up by none other than the Fry brothers—Dick, omnipresent, ultraversatile, and as indefatigable as B-G's "Joan"; and Martin, the younger one, also a go-getter. They brought it to a livable state before Christmas, and will return to finish the job after the holiday season is over. No doubt they are with their families in Bonners Ferry at the present moment of our story; also no doubt, they journeyed south in the *Idaho*, there being no need for that boat at Stanley, since the *Silver King* is stockpiling its ore—perhaps up at the mine, but more probably down at the lakeshore (it can more easily be transported down the mountain by rawhiding in winter)—to be shipped out to Bonners Ferry in the spring.

The log store, then, faces out onto Vernon Street, which is, of course, only a street in Malcolm Sproat's mind: the reality is merely a mess of logs and stumps on an open swathe, more or less in a straight line, where trees were cut down to facilitate the survey. From the small front windows of the store there is an unobstructed view across the "street" to the steep bank, and, below that, to the flatland and the lake beyond; for, contrary to what has been said previously about "cabins hidden among trees," it is more likely than not that most of the forest in this area has already been cut or burned off. Early settlers had no time to think of anything except pushing the wilderness back to get themselves a little breathing space as fast as possible. As a matter of fact, probably the best way to imagine the site is as a small collection of log cabins and tents (the latter, of course, having most likely been taken down and stored for the winter unless they are being lived in) standing amid a devastated forest of charred tree trunks.

Clearly, there are contradictions and hesitations in the last few sentences, and they indicate that the writer is at a loss regarding the scene as it really was. That being the case, no further reference to the landscape will be made; readers must for the remainder of the chapter supply external details themselves from the rich storehouses of their own imaginations, always remembering, of course, to avoid sedulously the danger of unconsciously picturing the terrain of a century ago as being in any way what it is now.

So, Robert Yuill left his rowboat on the shore that first New Year's Day, about one o'clock in the afternoon, and made his way up the trail toward the cabins of Nelson, then called "Stanley." He was heading for Dennee & Devine's general store (#1 on the map). This was a shack made of poles and cedar shakes. Their original store had been a tent on the flats closer to Cottonwood Creek, but they had moved to this location when it became apparent where most of the traffic to the *Silver King* was going to be. In his diary, written in 1918, Bob tells us that it was situated "where the Grand Central Hotel now stands," meaning the northeast corner of Ward and Vernon, which at the time of *this* writing is the site of the Nelson & District Credit Union. Other source books, more correctly perhaps, place it just in front of the old Provincial Gaol site, which in today's terms is the lawn of the white Provincial Building, and that is where we have designated it on our map. Whichever of the two sites it really was, when he reached it he saw only the empty shack, already in disrepair. Dennee & Devine had sold out to Hume & Lemon who had soon after dispensed with the shack and erected the new log store (the black square) on the lot that Dennee & Devine had previously bought from Sproat. Unperturbed at finding the store closed, Bob continued along the path, certain that he would find people up at John and Josephine Ward's hotel-in-a-tent (#2 on the map; in modern-day reckoning, perhaps where the old stone horse-trough now stands in front of the Heritage Inn). Arriving there, he began to feel some misgiving, for it too was missing—only a patch of bare earth showing where the big three-room tent had stood the last time he was here. Was Stanley deserted? Had he made his long trip for nothing? Then, hoping to find John and Josephine in their home, he turned eastward. No smoke was coming from the chimney of their log cabin (#3), only fifty yards or so away through the charred tree trunks. Just beyond, however, there *was* smoke—the faint, almost invisible smoke of a well-established fire—from the chimney of a larger, brand-new cabin (#4). If Wards weren't at home, then there certainly must be somebody next door. No one answered his knock at the door of the Ward home. A minute later, after peering through a window which showed him the dim and friendly light of a candle on the back wall of a large room, he stood knocking at the door of the new cabin. It was opened by a stranger, but when Bob walked in a big smile lit up his face. The room was full of men, and among them were several whom he recognized as the pals and companions of former exploits—Nick Moon, Tom Collins, Dr. Labau, Ike Naile, Charley Mally, Ike Lougheed, Jim Commorford, who had been one of his companions when they moved the store for Gus Wright from Revelstoke to Ainsworth last summer, and, best of all, Cy Johns, down from the *Silver King*. Even Old Bart Henderson was there, the fellow who had guarded the goods on the beach all last summer. These men hailed Bob boisterously as a well-liked friend, and hurried forward to welcome him into the room.

"Look what the breeze blew in!"

"Bob Yuill! How'd *you* get here, you ol' bastard?"

"Can't you stand Ainsworth any more, Bob?"

"Thought you had drowned last summer!"

Answering their friendly jibes in kind, Bob shook hands with each in turn, and was then introduced to the remainder of the company. Counting himself, there were fourteen men in the room. Four of them—Dr. Labau, Charley Ewen, Tom Collins, and Nick Moon—were the only miners who had remained in town for the winter. They were working a site up on the hill behind the town (where the present-day cemetery is). The man who had opened the door for Bob was a newcomer, Colonel E.S. Topping, managing the store for Hume & Lemon, both of whom were probably in Revelstoke at this moment. Ike Naile and P.J. McDougall were in town only for the day, to have a holiday and to see if anybody had brought them mail. They were working at the *Poorman*, a claim that was giving good showing in gold. (It was part of the goldbelt that was the source of the nuggets that had caused the rush on Forty-nine Creek back in the 60s.) Five other men—Ike Lougheed, Ben Thomas, Charley Mally, Cy Johns, and Jim Commorford—were down from the *Silver King* to see what "town" had to offer on New Year's Day. And, of course, not to be forgotten, Old Bart Henderson, adding one more to the number of men who had chosen to winter-over in Stanley, had left his snug shack and joined the gathering too.

Much of the room was lined with shelves on which were displayed all kinds of goods: tools, articles of clothing, candles, food staples, and anything else a sensible storekeeper would know was needed by miners and prospectors. Wooden boxes and barrels stood in various places, mostly shoved back into corners and against walls to accommodate the present crowd. On parts of the floor whipsawed planks had been laid; other areas showed only bare, well-packed earth. Between the centre of the room and the back wall stood a big potbelly stove with two or three benches around it, the latter consisting of planks resting on short logs. The chimney pipe ran straight up to pass through the roof near its apex. Seven or eight feet above the heads of the crowd, several widely spaced log wall-ties ran across from one side-wall to the other. Here and there along the walls, a few of those steel candleholders that miners use while drilling at the rock face had been hammered into the logs. The candles they held—well away from the moss chinking between the logs—along with a coal-oil lamp or two standing on barrel tops, provided a little light in addition to that coming through the small windows. Of these, only some had glass panes; others were covered with oiled paper. Near the door through which Bob had entered, a rectangular table—on regular business days the counter over which sales were transacted, but today pushed well back out the way—stood almost invisible under a load of varied objects (small kegs of nails, etc.) that had been piled on it to make more space in the room. Much of the room's central area was taken up with a large and obviously temporary table made of several floor planks that had not yet found their proper vocation, all these resting on uprights made of short cedar logs, from some of which shreds of bark were hanging. Along both sides of this structure was an assortment of makeshift chairs and benches composed of whatever logs, bark, or pieces of plank had come to hand. Two or three real chairs were scattered among them. When Bob arrived, most of the company had been seated around this table having a smoke or a chew. A few lingering pots, bowls, and platters gave evidence that they had eaten a meal there not long before.

Introductions over, Bob was escorted by several of his special buddies over to the benches and spittoons around the potbelly, where they began to catch up on the news. Colonel Topping, interested in hearing what the new arrival might have to say, came along too. Old Bart Henderson was already there, warming himself out of the drafts. Bob was as eager to learn all about the goings-on at Stanley and the Toad Mountain camps as his cronies were to hear about Ainsworth. They talked about those things for a while, then Bob expressed a desire to learn where Wards and most of the other denizens of town had gone.

"Well, most all of 'em took off outa here 'bout early November, er . . . maybe late October, just when it started to get a little cool," said Nick Moon. "John Ward jus' folded up the hotel, lock, stock an' barrel, and stuck it in their cabin, an' him an' Josephine hot-footed it down ta Spokane. All the guys stayin' at the hotel went with em'. We ain't gonna see any a *them* till spring!"

"Mosta the cabins are empty," put in Ike Naile." All them guys jus' drifted off—down ta the States mos'ly."

"Is Harry Anderson around?" asked Bob.

"I dunno," said Nick Moon. "I ain't seen 'm for months. He could be up there in 'is office, but . . ."

"He ain't there," broke in Charley Ewen. "Looks like Salisbury don't have its owner present jus' now. Somebody rowed up to the Landing just the other day to see him. . . Who was it, now . . ."

"Tom Collins," offered Old Bart Henderson.

"Yeah, Tom Collins," continued Charley. "He couldn't find Harry anywheres around. His office was locked up. The cabin part was open but it didn't look like anybody'd been there fer a while."

"Well, Harry Anderson was here at Christmas. I know that for sure," interjected Dr. LaBau, who was keeping an ear cocked at the conversation around the stove while he conversed with P.J. McDougall and a couple of others at the table. "He was at the dinner party Mrs. Hanna gave in her cabin on Christmas Day. You were there, Ike."[24]

"Yeah, sure," said Ike Naile. "But he might have left by . . . "

"That whole bunch's gone to Victoria fer the holidays," said somebody. "All them bigshots—Anderson, Malcolm Sproat, . . . eh . . . what's that new guy's name? That English guy that did the survey for Harry Anderson?

"Oh, you mean Busk." said Jim Commorford.

"Ya, that's the one."

"Busk!" exclaimed Bob. "I know that bloke. He was up at Ainsworth last fall, lookin' to buy land. He asked me about that stretch I own up at the mouth of Eleven-mile Creek."

"Ya mean you own that big delta up the arm at Eleven-mile Narrows?"

"Well, not the actual delta, but just back of it—on the flat and up onto the hill."

"Yeah, Busk, an' Anderson, an' Sproat . . . ," resumed the previous speaker, who wanted to complete the thread he had begun, " . . . you wouldn't catch *them* stayin' around here fer the winter! I bet they're all in Victoria right now, eatin' out every night in those big houses where the sassiety ladies have Chinamen cooks in their kitchens . . . "

"An' goin' to Navy balls an' all that gover'ment stuff," added Jim Commorford.

"Well," put in Cy Johns," they ain't got nothin' over us. Them pigtail cooks couldn't put out a better meal than the one we got today from Mrs. Hanna, an' we didn't have to get all dressed up to eat it, either."

Amid the general expressions of agreement that followed Cy's statement, Bob suddenly piped up, "Speakin' a grub, where can I get somethin' ta eat around here? I'm hungry as a bear, an' I ain't been sittin' around all day like yous guys."

185

"Well, Bob, if you'd gotten here a bit earlier, you could've had New Year's dinner with us, courtesy of Jane Hanna," said the Colonel. "You shoulda rowed a wee bit faster."

"Maybe she'd be willing to give Bob some leftovers right now," Cy Johns suggested. "Where's Frank Hanna? He can take you over there an' ask his wife."

"Frank's up at the shop," Colonel Topping replied. "He's sharpening a big order of drills for the *Silver King*. Do you know him, Bob?"

"Oh, yeah, he did some blacksmithin' fer me last summer. But I've never met Mrs. Hanna."

"Well, don't worry about that, Bob. She's a real kind lady. I'll take you over there. She won't mind a bit."

"Well, okay. Let's go before you all hafta carry me over." Bob rose to his feet. "But wait, I can't let a woman see me till I've spruced up a bit. Hold on till I run some water over my face. Anybody got a comb?" Taking one of several that were laughingly offered, Bob enquired where the water barrel was and then disappeared through a door in the back wall.

A few minutes later, he and the Colonel were on their way over to the small log cabin (#5 on our map) that was the home of Frank and Jane Hanna, situated, in present-day terms, just behind the City Parkade, perhaps in the middle of the alley or at the back of the Royal Bank building. It was not far from Hume & Lemon's store and it seems hardly worthwhile for us to expend much imaginative effort in picturing the two men walking there. But on the map there is a thin, wavy line representing Ward Creek between the store and Hanna's house. That line puts a heavy burden on our imaginations, for it indicates not only the small creek itself but also the very large gully it runs through. It is a v-shaped gully, as much as twenty or more yards across and nine yards or more deep. The two men cannot cross over the gully, there being no bridge, but must walk or slide down one side, cross the creek at the bottom on stones or logs, and climb up the other. Today there is not the slightest remaining trace of that gully; it has been filled in for many decades.

On New Year's Day of 1889, however, Ward Creek gully ran—in present-day terms—from the flats at the shoreline up the sloping bank under the old Land Registry Building—the handsome brick edifice that now houses the Ministry of Mines—across Vernon Street at an angle, under a corner of the Heritage Inn, across Baker Street at Walter Wait's News Stand, up the middle of Ward Street to Victoria Street, through the site of the old Opera House on the southeast corner of Ward and Victoria, and on up through the residential area to the mountain. Undoubtedly we could trace the history of its gradual filling-in and final disappearance by using ancient record books of the city, but there would be little point in doing that. Suffice it to say: there is a story, easily confirmable, that if you stand in a certain place in the basement of the present-day Heritage Inn and remain silent, there will gradually impinge upon your senses the ghostly voice of that imprisoned stream, still gurgling as it did when it was a laughing brook reflecting the dappled light of a forest, gurgling through the culvert or whatever else it was they confined it in. You can stand there in the Heritage Inn, at the bottom level of that vanished gully, and hear old Ward Creek running through the darkness, still singing of past days.[25] But enough. We will assume that Bob and the Colonel have crossed the gully and are now standing in front of the Hanna cottage.

We should take a paragraph or so, just before the Colonel knocks, to think about Robert Yuill, a young man on the brink of being introduced to a young woman he has never before seen and receiving a New Year's Day meal from her. As he stands in front of that door, his thoughts and feelings as an individual are perhaps not of great importance to our tale. But Bob is more than an individual. He represents for us a whole class of men flourishing at that time—the itinerant prospectors and miners who, after the fur traders and explorers, were the pioneers of our land. Surely, all of us who wonder about those early days must inevitably want to understand to the best of our ability their attitudes, their thoughts and feelings. In our eyes, they are the embodiment of a great deal of romance. We spend much time reading about them, restoring the towns they pioneered, reliving in a pale, sanitized manner, their trekking and camping exploits, and in general nourishing a feeling of nostalgia about them. Probably we don't very often think about them more deeply than that.

They must have been a mixed lot—men from most of the European nations, from the States, and from Canada itself, all with the dream of striking it rich. Most of them probably had little formal education beyond a few years of grade-school. Occasionally other types could be found among them, more educated men who had for one reason or another chosen the rough, free life of the wilderness camps—Dr. LaBau, for example, a physician from the States. As prospectors and miners, they were a humble class, on the bottom rung of the social ladder. Of those who took up the life as young men, only a few made it rich with a lucky strike; others, abandoning the prospecting trade, grew old as miners, carrying their bedding from camp to camp, sleeping in roughly constructed bunkhouses, eating from tin plates and drinking from tin cups, working at hard labour ten hours a day for three dollars and fifty cents. The Dr. LaBaus among them had the option of removing themselves from the ranks when they wished; many others finally achieved permanent jobs in the settlements and married; an equal number lived out a humble old-age as bachelors in shacks on the edges of towns, helped out in their declining years by kind neighbours.

Respectable women—we are tempted to say "virtuous women," so readily do the old-fashioned phrases come to the tongue when speaking of those times—respectable women were not too often in social contact with the earliest prospectors and miners. Mrs. Hanna will be the first that Bob has seen for some time, since he hasn't been over to Hendryx Camp in a long while. Because he is young, and because his loneliness has made him wonder when, if ever, he will take the step to become a married man, he is anticipating this meeting with a degree of excitement and curiosity. He is prepared—or rather has been prepared by the circumstances of his life—to feel awkward and deficient in social graces while in the presence of Mrs. Hanna. It will not occur to him to call her "Jane." To him, she will remain "Mrs. Hanna," no matter how soon he may begin calling her husband "Frank." (We have already heard Colonel Topping calling her "Jane," but he, a man fifty-six years of age, has a particular status in that family, as we will learn later.) That formal address is one of the outward signs of the special way men thought of women—"respectable" ones—in those days.[26] But now, let us return to Bob, who, standing at Mrs. Hanna's door, has probably never given a thought to any of these things and is merely preparing to act in the normal fashion of a man in his time and place. The Colonel knocks, Mrs. Hanna answers, and the two men enter her house.

She gives Bob the meal he needs. There was never any doubt that she would, this woman "small and dark and much loved for her kindness," as she was described in the Trail *Times* many years later. And, sensing at once Bob's uneasiness, she also took pains to cajole him into feeling comfortable. The food she set before him consisted mainly of wild ducks, left over from the New Year's dinner the others had enjoyed earlier in Hume & Lemon's store. "They were well cooked," Bob tells us in his 1918 diary. "I never enjoyed any meal better as I was quite hungry after rowing . . ." We can be sure there were other reasons for his pleasure: he must have basked in the domesticity of that neat cabin, its feminine touches— curtains on the windows, tablecloth under the plates, here and there a display of china. Mrs. Hanna's four small children were there—(where else would they be on a dull winter's day in the wilderness?)—and Bob must have felt envy for the life that Frank Hanna had already made for himself. The meal passed quickly while conversation, eased by the presence of a woman, flowed freely among the three adults. As the men were leaving amid a profusion of "thank yous" and "come agains," we wonder if Bob wasn't, for a brief second at least, aware that now his vague longing of yesterday at Ainsworth Camp had been satisfied. He must have left Mrs. Hanna's cabin elated by a sense that before much more time passed there would be other homes here, by a sure hope that soon, very soon, other women would arrive and he and his friends might take the step that Frank Hanna had already taken toward a more responsible and felicitous life.

Already, as they made their way back toward the store, the afternoon was darkening, arousing in human beings and all other creatures that familiar sense of urgency for preparation against nightfall. Bob reminded himself it was time to buy the supplies he needed and load the boat in readiness for an early morning take-off. Accordingly, he began talking to the Colonel about flour, bacon, sourbelly, and other matters of a similar nature. Back at the store, they found the company grumbling about finding some better way of celebrating New Year's Day than sitting around talking. The Colonel, who had certain information they hadn't yet heard, told them to hang on for a while longer, while he and Bob did business. Soon Bob, as he tells us so laconically in his diary, purchased "most all the eatables they had." There was no shortage of manpower to help him carry his purchases down the trail to the shoreline. What would have cost one man many long trips was accomplished by many in one. While they were all loading up the boat, Cy Johns, who had been quietly gazing up the west arm, suddenly remarked to Bob, "How'd ya like a companion ta spell ya off on the long row?"

"Sure, who ya thinkin' of?"

"Me. I got a hankerin' ta see what's doin' up in yer territory. There's nothin' to keep me up at the *Silver King* jus' now, an' Ben, er Charley, er one o' the others can tell the boss where I've gone."

"Fine!" exclaimed Bob, who was delighted at the prospect of a visit with his old friend. He didn't have to ask what Cy would do for bedding; he knew that, in the easy-going way of miners, Cy would already have his blankets with him, he and the others having intended to spend the night in Stanley. Bob made sure the men loaded the boat in a manner that would leave room for another person. Then, everything battened down for the night, they all returned to Hume & Lemon's.

Up at the store they found a discussion in progress. " . . . an' if there's any in town I think we oughta use it."

"Me too. John Ward won't give a damn. He's sittin' purty in Spokane right now, so how's he gonna care?"

"He won't even remember he had it." General sounds of agreement followed that statement. The men were so intent on their subject they hardly acknowledged the entry of Bob and his helpers.

"Well, I dunno." Frank Hanna, who had returned from his blacksmith shop, paused to give Bob a brief nod and a smile before going on. "I'm not even sure it's there. All I know is, there was a few bottles left, and he didn't take 'em with 'm. I know that fer sure 'cause I helped 'm load fer the trip."

"Well, okay! Let's find the stuff an' use it."

"All right boys!" Colonel Topping raised his voice as if he had come to a decision. "Tell ya what I'll do. I got the key to John Ward's house. A couple a you guys go over there an' see what you can find. If it's there at all, I know 'xactly where it'll be—there's a little closet in the corner—southwest corner—at the back. You go in there 'n' see what there is, 'n' tote it back here so we can see what we got."

This suggestion met with complete agreement and was followed by much talk about who should perform the errand. Finally they all chose Cy Johns, Frank Hanna, and Bob—Cy and Bob because they were both well liked by John (and might even be absent when he returned in the spring), and Frank Hanna because, besides being himself a good friend of John's, his wife was on intimate terms with Mrs. Ward. And anyway, no one really thought easy-going John Ward would be angry just because his friends and neighbours had taken the liberty of borrowing a little booze for a New Year's party. The consensus was that, if anything, he would be pleased. After all, he almost owed it to them for the relief of his guilt at spending the long winter amid the comforts of Spokane while they stuck it out here at Stanley. Furthermore, how could he begrudge a few bottles when he'd be bringing lots more back from Spokane in the spring? No, there was no problem at all. Clearly the New Year's party could proceed. The three men entrusted with obtaining the wherewithal were hurried on their mission, exhorted by the Colonel as they went out the door to "be sure to lock up the cabin on your way back." They had good luck: there were a few loose bottles of gin and rum in the cupboard as well as an unopened case of Canadian whisky. The loose bottles they left untouched, perhaps thinking that John Ward would be more understanding when he found they had not taken everything. But they laid hands on the whisky with alacrity, knowing that a hero's welcome awaited them when they returned with it to the crowd at Hume & Lemon's store.

The hero's welcome they indeed received; then, knowing how rough things might become when the drink started flowing, the company, with admirable foresight, appointed Old Bart Henderson—the eldest and presumably the most sensible among them by far—as Comptroller of Refreshment. Always grateful to be accepted among the younger men, Old Bart agreed to take charge. The party began, an all-male party, for we can be sure that Mrs. Hanna and her children remained well out of the way.

Our source book—Bob Yuill's 1918 "diary"—is offhand about the party, reducing what must have been several hours' activity into a few spare sentences. It merely states: " . . . Old Bart Henderson took charge of it, and we helped ourselves. McDougall was getting strong and commenced firing the kegs of nails and heavy ware around. Ike Naile put out for the *Poorman*. He was afraid of McDougall and thought he would kill someone." We need not enlarge upon the scene. Knowing how an excessive intake of alcohol acts upon different personalities, we can imagine the inevitable progress of the party. The sharing of a case of whisky among only fifteen participants, all unrestrained and in full holiday mood, must lead unavoidably to behaviour highly unlike that seen at an afternoon tea. We can imagine the evening's relatively sedate initiatory moments, the eager opening of the bottles and the first quaffings of neat whisky, the general aura of determination to be festive; we can follow those first moments into the second phase—in which alcohol loosens the tongues of even those normally hesitant of speech and the room becomes a babble of still coherent though all too loudly proclaimed remarks underlined by excessive laughter; and we can move on to the behaviour typical of phase three. Here the checks and balances of normalcy have disappeared; freed by drunkenness, the variously constituted personalties of the celebrants reveal themselves unrestrainedly. The boisterous become more boisterous; the gregarious push their gregariousness to an alarming degree, leering too close for comfort into the faces of those nearby; the abusive begin to abuse their neighbours about hitherto forgotten slights and grievances; the bellicose brandish clenched fists and dare others to make a false move, while the introverted retreat to corners and sink into torpor. It is at this point, two hours or so after the opening of the first bottle, that P.J. McDougall begins to hurl kegs of nails about the room and alarmed Ike Naile leaves for the *Poorman*. (We are glad we don't have to accompany him, for it is now dark.) Old Bart Henderson has given up all pretence of controlling the refreshment and, himself among the inebriated, sits dozing quietly beside the stove. Colonel Topping, having decided that he must keep his wits about him, if only to save Hume & Lemon's store from excessive damage or even total destruction by fire, has stopped drinking and sobered up considerably. The party finally reaches its logical conclusion: those still able to do so find their bedrolls and bunk down in corners of the room or nearby cabins, leaving others already asleep wherever they have fallen. We can imagine the shoutings and cursings as men stumble about outside in the dark looking for the cabins. Frank Hanna and the Colonel douse the candles, check the fire, close the door, and make their somewhat erratic way across the gully of Ward Creek to the Hanna cabin. The historic men's party of New Year's day '89—which will no doubt be talked about for years to come—has ended. The variously constituted personalities of its participants have passed beyond the strife and hilarity that drink brought them and are peacefully united in the profound slumber of satiety.

Very early next morning, though perhaps a little later than they had intended, Robert Yuill and Cy Johns leave the sleeping community and begin their long row up the west arm to Ainsworth Camp.

# CHAPTER 19

*Which is devoted entirely to the examination of a photograph taken in 1889.*

THE HOLIDAY SEASON went by and was soon followed into the past by winter itself. As spring freed the trails and waterways for travel, those who had gone to Spokane and other points south straggled back to Kootenay Country. Likewise, Busk, Anderson, Sproat, and others of their kind returned from the social scene in Victoria to take up residence again. Interest in the *Silver King* and its neighbouring mines on Toad Mountain continued to draw more and more prospectors and speculators to the region. Among the many visitors that summer of '89 was one called George Mercer Dawson, the man after whom Dawson City in the Yukon is named. Since 1875 Mr. Dawson had been working with the Geological Survey of Canada, exploring the virtually uncharted wilderness of British Columbia. In '87 he surveyed the Alaska boundary in the vicinity of the Yukon River. In '92 he was appointed British Commissioner on the Bering Sea Natural Resources Commission. In between those two dates he passed through Stanley for reasons unknown to this historian.[27]

On a hot afternoon in early summer—we know the date exactly: July 2nd—he took a photograph, perhaps the earliest we have of Nelson. No historian can look at this picture without feeling a glow of warmth toward George Mercer Dawson; we couldn't have asked him to set up his camera in a better position if we had been there with him. His photograph shows us precisely what we want to see—the first of the four and a half city blocks laid out by

George Mercer Dawson's View of Stanley, July 2nd, 1889. G. Dawson, photographer NAC PA 38003

Malcolm Sproat in his initial survey, and, furthermore, the development that occurred on its lots during the first year. And, as if that wasn't enough, we can even look up the path along which Robert Yuill walked to get from the lake to Hume & Lemon's store on that memorable New Year's Day.

In present-day terms, the row of tents and buildings to the left of centre is the 500 block of Vernon Street, between Ward and Josephine. The camera appears to have been positioned in what is now the small triangular block formed where Lake and Front Streets meet Ward.

The photograph reminds us of Gilbert Malcolm Sproat contemplating his future townsite in Chapter 9, for this, minus the buildings, is the landscape he was looking at then—a sloping plain leading from Kootenay Lake toward the wide valley of the south-flowing Salmon River. At that time, however, it would have been forested.

Perhaps the first thing to notice as we look at the photograph is that it dispels our previous doubts about the landscape. There are certainly no "cabins hidden among trees"; the site is indeed "a small collection of log cabins and tents . . . standing amid a devastated forest of charred tree trunks." The devastation is too extensive to be man-made, and is undoubtedly due to a forest fire which had swept through the valley only a few years before the photograph was taken. The forest has begun to grow back, but so far only in the form of bushes and other small plants. We can identify thimbleberry in the immediate foreground. The mountains that we observe stretching away southward to the Salmon River valley cannot be seen from this site at ground level today. They are, however, the ones all Nelsonites know: Morning, looming massively at the right; Toad, bearing patches of fire on its flank; and the others that we pass one by one when we drive toward Salmo. Toad, more than 6,000 feet high, is much bigger than it appears in the picture. What we see is merely its bulging lower flank. Out of sight above and beyond that bulge is the *Silver King,* producing the ore that caused this settlement to be born and will keep it growing. Nearly ten years from the time of this picture must pass before a tramline is built to carry the ore down to the town, the tramline which for decades will be a familiar sight to Nelson-ites but is at the present day hardly traceable on the mountainside.

The fires burning on Toad are undoubtedly an indication that hordes of prospectors are now swarming over all the mountains in the vicinity.

In the middle distance, just above the big tent that is shaped like a truncated pyramid, there is a rocky hump stretching over to the right edge of the picture. That granitic formation is present-day Rosemont. In front of it, separating it from the foreground, lies the valley of Cottonwood Creek, unseen in the picture from this angle, but indicated by a line beginning at the tip of the truncated pyramid and moving toward the right margin. Above the big log building at the right end of the row there is another prominence—the high sloping plateau which is today the South Nelson area. As Nelsonites know, present-day houses on its edge look across the valley of Cottonwood Creek to those of Rosemont. Higher up beyond that prominence—about at the edge of the mountain coming from the left—lies the present-day cemetery.

The photograph has immortalized, though anonymously, two, possibly three, human beings. The first of these—we see him on the path between the tent and the cabin—has been caught in mid-step, and he alone, along with the veils of smoke in the distant background, gives animation to this otherwise curiously static scene. He is so tantalizingly distinct we can almost see how he is dressed as he walks quietly up the path. Indeed, given the few clues we are able to observe, many of us have perhaps already imagined his clothes, even to the type and colour of his hat. Observing his build and his stance, we may, some of us at least, have gone so far as to imagine what kind of man he is. His head is tilted downward. He is thinking about something important to himself. The path starting at our feet invites us to follow him as he walks past the tent and along to the row of buildings—to follow him, but not closely enough to disturb his thought. If only we could know what he is thinking, all the things he is aware of, how much we could learn about that day.

At the far end of the path, near the big building at the right end of the row—the corner of Ward and Vernon in our day—another human being is standing. Too distant to be seen distinctly, he is revealed as a man only by his shape. He tapers to a point on the ground. The voluminous skirts worn by women of that time would not do so. Half an inch to his right, there is another shape which could be that of a person setting off down the path. It would be pleasant to think of this as a woman. Jane Hanna and Josephine Ward are certainly on the scene, and others of their sex may have arrived by now. Jane and Josephine, however, would probably at this hour of a summer's day be on some outing with their children. Is there a connection between these two persons at the top end of the path and the man walking toward them? Are they all three part of a forgotten scene which some imaginative viewer could fancifully reconstruct? We must, of course, resist the temptation to pursue such unhistoriographic speculation.

By piecing together evidence derived from various primary sources such as letters, reports, diaries, and old histories, researchers have been able to determine with a high degree of certainty who occupied all the buildings in the row, except one.[28]

We recall from Chapter 9, how Malcolm Sproat in the year 1888, anxious to get his townsite established before winter, sent a memorandum dated September 3rd along with his sketch map to the government. Anyone taking time to read that memorandum will find him fussing like an intelligent and devoted mother hen to ensure that his tiny brood of pioneers—a hotel-keeper and his family, two storekeeping partners, and a few prospectors—are housed all snug and warm for the winter. Building a reasonable argument in support of his actions over the space of a few pages, he reveals, almost apologetically, that he has bent the rules and sold lots—even before the government has approved his survey—to the hotel-keeper and the storekeeping partners as deserving persons who are "holding the fort" and "have stayed with the place." To keep things as right as possible, he has held an auction (at which hardly anyone was present). Messrs. Dennee and Devine, the storekeepers, have acquired two lots for their business—6 and

7 of block 1 at a cost of $75 per lot. John and Josephine Ward have been sold the first two lots of the same block on which to build a log hotel (they already had their log house on the site). For the corner lot they have paid $100 and for the second one $75. Now, a few months later, the two large log buildings in the row are the result of those transactions.

At the end of the row we see the big new log hotel that the Wards have built. The first real hotel in Nelson, it stands on what will one day be the corner of Ward and Vernon Streets. It is going to be named the "Lakeview Hotel" but it is still too newly built for the sign to have been placed above the door. It is probably not big enough to hold anything other than the eighteen beds that John and Josephine brought up from Spokane, where the former spent what Malcolm Sproat calls "all his means" to begin the Canadian hotel venture. Hotel guests and indeed most of the male population of the district are fed their meals in the big white tent that has already been described as a truncated pyramid. It is an enormous tent, rather like those used for circuses, and is the Wards' former hotel-in-a-tent, now used as a kitchen and dining hall. The hotel-in-a-tent has, we might say, become a restaurant-in-a-tent.

We should take a moment to think about how important hotels and public eating-establishments are to a community. Eating an early-morning breakfast in one of Nelson's present-day hotels or coffee shops, for example, we find ourselves, not among a company of overnighters and travelling salesmen, but surrounded by business persons, work crews, and office workers, all of whom have elected to leave their homes to meet their friends and fellow workers for breakfast, cajoled and coaxed to wakefulness by a waitress who is familiar with their every culinary need. It is a jolly time, and cheering to any lonely traveller who witnesses the scene. Coffee breaks and lunch repeat the pleasure. If this is the case at the present day, how much greater must have been the need for such places in pioneer time. No one had an established home then. Travellers were in the majority. The "hordes" of prospectors lived in cabins and tents or more make-do accommodations, all lonely and in need of a good meal. We recall how Hume & Lemon's store had to serve as the site for the New Year's party. And what a blessing Jane Hanna must have seemed on that occasion! We can be sure that John and Josephine Ward were taking very little business risk in opening their hotel.

The second log building, the one near the other end of the block on lot 6 or 7 (or perhaps partly on both), is already familiar to us. Soon after Dennee & Devine bought these lots they sold them to Hume & Lemon, who then built their log store on the property they had acquired. It was, of course, the scene of the all-male party which Robert Yuill attended on New Year's Day, and was built several months before the Wards put up their new hotel. Neither Hume nor Lemon is in attendance at the store; Hume is in Revelstoke, where he is still involved in at least two businesses, and Lemon is probably at Sproats Landing, where he has retained his general store. No doubt their manager is inside the building, or perhaps seated outside, behind the filled sacks or other goods which appear to be stacked in front of the door. Or perhaps, with other business persons, he is inside the big tent having an afternoon cup of coffee.

The third wooden building in the row is the small shack just to the left and slightly to the rear of the Lakeview Hotel. It is made of cedar shakes, and is on the same lot as the hotel. Formerly it was the makeshift office of Gilbert Malcolm Sproat—perhaps he sat in there to draw his famous map—but now it is occupied by one Terrence Giffin. In the absence of Sproat, who has resigned from the government employ and is at present in business in Revelstoke, Giffin has been appointed mining recorder, constable, government agent, and whatever else might be needed in a new camp. For the time being, he has made this conveniently vacant shack his business headquarters. We can surmise that he is living at Ward's Hotel, entertaining friends and acquaintances during the long evenings with tales of his adventurous younger days in the California and Cariboo gold rushes of the '40s and '50s.

When we last saw Colonel Topping he was busy in his role as Hume & Lemon's deputy manager, dousing the lights of the store at the conclusion of the New Year's Day stag party. Since that time his life has changed considerably. He had taken the job of store manager almost as a favour to Hume and Lemon during their absence. His real desire was to get rich, and he was using most of his spare time in prospecting. One spring day, a couple of months after the party, he stooped to get a drink from a creek and accidently discharged his gun, wounding himself severely in the wrist. Thus disabled, he had to find something to do less strenuous than prospecting. Observing that Terrence Giffin was being stretched thin by the demands of his several offices, he suggested that a Deputy Mining Recorder could be of assistance. Terrence Giffin thought so, too. The Colonel began proceedings with distant Victoria to obtain Canadian citizenship and was given the job. Now, at the time of this picture, he has set up deputy headquarters for himself as a bonafide government employee in the small tent immediately to the right of Hume & Lemon's store, thereby leaving a more relaxed Terrence Giffin to pursue the duties of his other jobs in the nearby shake shack. We observe, then, that Stanley, soon to be called Nelson, has already received, on its very first surveyed block and in only its second year as a real settlement, a tiny governmental hierarchy comprised of two men invested with the powers of several offices, the nucleus of what will one day become a large body of officialdom that administers the whole district and makes Nelson Queen of the Kootenays. The Colonel's new job in the tiny hierarchy does not appear to be one that will bring him the riches he desires, but life is full of surprises. Perhaps an opportunity will present itself.

Tucked between the two government offices is another tent, its flaps pulled far back to make an inviting entrance. It is a small general store, rival to Hume & Lemon's big one two doors away. Its half-owner, J. A. Gilker, has been in Stanley only about a month and came as the result of a chance meeting. Jim Gilker had come to Kootenay country from Campbellton, New Brunswick only six years before, working, like so many others in our story, on the building of the CPR's transcontinental line. By the summer of '85 he was part of a gang stringing telegraph lines along the CPR right-of-way before the rails had been laid. After the driving of the last spike at Craigellachie, he remained working on the railroad at Revelstoke. As an investment for his earnings, he decided to put money into a business venture and became the partner of one Frank Wells in a general store in Revelstoke. Mr. Wells ran the store while Jim continued working at his railway job.

One day in the fall of '88 the west-bound train was standing in the Revelstoke station while Jim was busy on the platform. A small white dog ran up to him and, in the manner of friendly dogs, began sniffing at the legs of his overalls. Jim bent down to pat him and then, responding to the dog's mood, began to romp with him. Pleased, as dog owners always are when they see someone taking an interest in their pets, its master struck up a conversation with Jim. It turned out that the master was M.S. Davys, an English engineer who was to become an important figure in mining circles in the Kootenay's early days. Monty had just paid his first visit to Stanley and the Toad Mountain mines and was now on his way back to the coast, having minutes before completed the second leg of his journey up the Columbia on a steamer from Sproat's Landing. He greatly impressed Jim with his praise of the Toad Mountain mines, assuring him that Stanley was certain to grow into a sizeable town. There, Jim thought, is an opportunity for me to escape from this dead-end railway job and strike out in business for myself. As fall darkened into winter, the idea became more and more compelling. He talked Frank Wells into agreeing that they open another Gilker & Wells store in Stanley, and then arranged for a six-month leave of absence from the CPR. In due time he set up the tent we see in George Mercer Dawson's photograph. It houses the small stock of goods that will give Gilker & Wells a footing in the commerce of growing Stanley.

Jim Gilker never returned to Revelstoke. After a few months he moved the store to Baker Street. A few years later his partnership with Wells dissolved. Wells remained in Revelstoke while Jim took full possession of the store in Stanley, which was by then, of course, renamed Nelson. He decided to deal only in men's wear. Gilker's Men's Wear became a fixture of Nelson until well into the

'50s of the next century, and the Gilker family an established part of Nelson's life.

At the time of this picture—and for months to come—the movement of mail in and out of Stanley was very irregular. A box in Hume & Lemon's store was used for the mailing and receiving of letters. American postage stamps were mainly in use. Dr. Hendryx undertook to carry mail to and from Bonners Ferry in the *Galena* without remuneration for his services. From Bonners Ferry the mail went to Sandpoint, then east or west on American railways. Either Hume & Lemon or their manager must have tired of the arrangement, for Jim Gilker, on returning one day from fishing, found the box in his store on Baker Street. He accepted the *fait accompli* without complaint and improved the situation by replacing the old box with a new one from, he tells us, "the saloon." This box, a gin box, was neatly divided into compartments to prevent the bottles from breaking. These compartments made excellent alphabetical letter holders. Later, the Canadian government having established a proper postal service, Jim Gilker became Nelson's first official Postmaster, a position he held for twelve years.

Only one edifice in the row—the large white tent at the left end—remains to be discussed. There is, however, nothing much to say about it; no one knows its purpose or who owned it. It appears to be out of line with the others, as if it had been put up at the edge of the bank on the near side of the "street."

Readers remembering the events of the previous chapter will be looking for the home of Frank and Jane Hanna. It must certainly be the long house with the porch, in the middle distance just to the right of the restaurant-in-a-tent. We recall that, to reach it from Hume & Lemon's store, Bob Yuill and the Colonel had to descend into the gully of Ward Creek and climb back up the other side. The gully, not visible of course, runs in its lower reaches from a point just to the right of the Lakeview Hotel, passes at some distance behind the restaurant-in-a-tent and the big cabin, not yet identified, and moves down to the lake beyond the picture's right-hand edge. We see the Hanna house perched above its far bank.

In present-day terms this house is perhaps in the alley behind the City Parkade, the basement of which is in the bank of the gully.

Two edifices in the photograph remain unidentified. They are both wooden structures and lie along the path Robert Yuill followed on New Year's Day. The bigger might well be the one he expected to find Dennee & Devine's store in. Beyond that speculation, there is nothing much to say about them.

And now, our examination of the photograph completed, we know Nelson as it was in the second year of its life, when it was still called Stanley: eleven tents and shacks, perhaps along with one or two others that are hidden from our view, set in both an orderly and a disorderly fashion amid the rocks and stumps of a burned landscape. Our thanks to George Mercer Dawson for leaving us this most perfect primary source.

# CHAPTER 20

*Whose single purpose is to chronicle the arrival at Nelson of one John "Truth" Houston in the year 1890.*

A PERFECT PRIMARY SOURCE it may have been, but George Mercer Dawson's photograph failed in one respect: it didn't give us the feeling of how busy a settlement Stanley was in '89. At the time he took the picture, the bustling hordes of prospectors we know were there must have been temporarily somewhere else—up at their claims on Toad Mountain, no doubt, making all that smoke. Perhaps some of them were constructing trails. However deserted the town looks, we know from a remark made by Jim Gilker that it was a lively place. Many Indians with packtrains were up from Colville, hired by the prospectors to move goods to and from the claims. And other kinds of men—speculators, businessmen, mining promoters drawn to the strike as inevitably as the miners—are on the scene in that picture. It is the guess of this historian that Baker Street, out of range of the camera, is a much more active location than Vernon. We can safely bet that there are tents up there, housing men who have purchased lots— for, contrary to Sproat's intention that Vernon Street should be the business centre, Baker Street is where most early development took place—with the purpose of erecting hotels and stores. Baker Street, in the block corresponding to the one we see on Vernon, must be noisy with the clamour of digging, hammering, and sawing as sites are cleared for the laying of foundations.

Developments up at the Toad mountain mines were continuing to be very promising, and down at the townsite optimism was strong. Seventy tons of ore grading 269 ounces of silver and 20 percent copper came down from the *Silver King* in 1889 and were towed by barge up the lake and river as far as Bonners Ferry, finally to reach a smelter in Butte, Montana. For a year or so after that, work at the mine was directed principally toward development rather than production, but the Halls were very pleased with what they were finding.

The spring of 1890 saw the arrival in town of the man who was to dominate Nelson for nearly two decades and become one of the few of its citizens to whom a monument has been erected. His monument—placed in front of the Hume Hotel, now the Heritage Inn—for many decades comprised, with the old stone horse-trough and the cenotaph, a landmark as familiar to Nelsonites as their own backyards. The cenotaph at present graces the courtyard of the new Provincial Government Building. But the monument to John Houston—backed by the horse-trough, which now holds bedding plants in the summer—remains where it was first put, shaded in late afternoon by the giant chestnut trees which make that block one of Nelson's finest and must have been planted near the time the monument was erected in 1915.

Secondary sources, not to mention tertiary ones, have left us conflicting reports of the route taken by John Houston to effect his arrival onto the pages of our tale. This historian, however, chooses to think that, being in New Westminster at the time, Houston would have travelled to Revelstoke by train, down the Columbia by boat to Sproat's Landing, thence on foot over the trail to Nelson.

In accordance with that choice, it is here stated that on a day in mid-March, soon after the waterways and trails had cleared themselves of most of winter's blockage, three men were to be seen disembarking from the catamaran *Dispatch* at Sproat's Landing. One of them was encumbered by several large, heavy crates which the *Dispatch's* crew had to help him unload. That was John Houston, publisher of frontier newspapers, and the crates were full of type and parts of a dismantled printing press. The other two men were W. Gessner Allen and Charlie Ink, printer. It was the intention of John Houston, along with his two friends, to publish a newspaper in the rising pioneer town of Nelson.

John Houston liked publishing newspapers in pioneer towns. His earlier years of wandering throughout the American West had taught him to enjoy the excitement of the frontier. Born in Ontario, he left home at the age of 15 to stay with relatives in Chicago and became apprenticed to a printer. From there he headed south to spend a few years working on newspapers in Missouri and Texas. Finally, after a stint of newspaper work in New York, he came west to Montana and Idaho. Restless, he wandered back to Texas and took charge of a big printing business in Dallas. From there he tramped westward again, this time along a southern route to Los Angeles. Besides a natural desire to roam, he seems to have been coping with too strong a penchant for alcohol. Finally, in 1886, he turned up in western Canada to work for *The Calgary Herald*. Then, following the CPR into British Columbia, he came to Donald on the east arm of the Big Bend. There he established his own newspaper, *The Truth*, printed one page at a time on what he called a "nutcracker" press, using "a handful or two of very old type, borrowed from the *Calgary Herald* . . . " The paper gained a reputation, but, dissatisfied with Donald because he saw it as showing no potential for growth, Houston moved farther along the railway line to New Westminster, where he re-established *The Truth* on September 5th, 1889. Still restlessly searching for the right place and attracted by what he was hearing about rugged Kootenay Country, he developed a yearning to see Nelson. There is some evidence—at least inferential—that he paid the town a visit in the spring of '89, perhaps to see what it had to offer him. Be that as it may, he was certainly there in spring of 1890 and, having already decided he came by way of Revelstoke, we have chosen to intercept him on his journey, just as he disembarked from *Dispatch* at Sproat's Landing.

Sproat's was beautifully situated on the low land at the mouth of Pass Creek, a few hundred yards upstream from the junction of the Kootenay with the Columbia. Gilbert Malcolm Sproat's brother, one of the earliest settlers along the Columbia after the CPR transcontinental reached Revelstoke in '86, had filed a claim for 320 acres of land there in May 28th, 1888. Traces of his homestead still remained. But now, the main features of the place were R.E. Lemon's general store and the sawmill of the Genelle brothers. A few other small businesses and a hotel of sorts completed the town. Not to forget, of course, a most necessary feature—the livery stable of Joe Wilson's pack train. Joe did an increasingly thriving business providing transportation along the trail between Sproat's and Stanley; not for long, however, for the railway to connect the two places was at last under construction. (We recall that John Ainsworth had first proposed it back in '82.)

We cannot guess what time of day John Houston and his two friends arrived at Sproat's. Whatever schedule the catamaran *Dispatch* and its running-partner the steamer *Marion* attempted to keep, they hardly ever succeeded. The long wilderness run from Revelstoke down to Little Dalles in the States was beset with problems, not the least of which was maintaining a steady supply of dry cordwood at the various fuel stops. Whatever their time of arrival, however, unless it was in the dead of night, the three men's first act must have been to seek out Joe Wilson and arrange for horses, good strong ones, to carry all that printing equipment.

Aided by Joe Wilson, they were soon on the trail to Stanley, the very trail we followed with Robert Yuill in Chapter 16. But there was a difference now: the trail—or large sections of it—was in the process of being converted into a railway bed. Yes, the railway proposed by John Ainsworth away back in '82 was at long last being built, but not by him. The government had rescinded his option after years of inaction, and the Canadian Pacific Railway Company, wishing to cut off any prospective rival, had begun the railway itself and already had work crews along the route. The work in progress had probably not progressed far enough to be a hindrance to the travellers, but no doubt there was enough blasting taking place—especially in the canyon where the Brilliant dam is today—to make them take special care. Once across Tom Ward's ferry and heading toward Forty-nine Creek on the south side they were free of construction because the railway was continuing along toward Stanley on the north side.

The journey from Sproat's to Nelson could easily be made in a couple of days by travellers unburdened with too much luggage; even one, if you were young and in a hurry. But John Houston, considering the heavy printing press his horses were toting and the fact that he was a newspaper man on the lookout for copy, may well have taken longer. He would have wanted to gain all the knowledge of the country he could, and of the CPR construction along the route. We can imagine the men stopping to give their horses a rest whenever an opportunity presented itself for conversation with construction workers or bosses. And he certainly would want to linger a bit at both ferries, probably overnight at Tom Ward's, where there was a hotel with a bar. Finally, however, they reached a point on the flank of Morning Mountain from which they could look down on the tents, the hotels, and the houses of the growing town called Stanley or Nelson.

It is not recorded that any earthquakes or thunder storms, or even squalls of wind, marked the occasion, but it *was* a momentous one, this meeting of John Houston and the town finally interesting enough to check his obsessive wandering and lay claim to his restless soul. Leading his pack horses down through the burned landscape into the heart of the busy settlement, the future city's first mayor may or may not have had some presentiment that here, just eight months before his fortieth birthday, he had come home at last; that here he had found the stage on which his complex, idiosyncratic, obstinate, impetuous, obstreperous, combative, unyielding, compassionate, and highly aggressive nature could act out its tormented destiny.

# CHAPTER 21

*Which, after telling us what John Houston, Gessner
Allen, and Charlie Ink did after they arrived in Nelson, presents another photograph for our examination.*

THE THREE NEW ARRIVALS wasted no time getting settled in. According to the *Nelson Daily News*, reminiscing on October 5th, 1910, young Charlie Ink made it *his* first work in town
to construct a log cabin for himself on a convenient plot of land
near the bluff at the east end of Baker Street. Perhaps the two older
men took lodging in one of the hotels—the Lakeview on Vernon
(now under new ownership) or the more opulent Nelson on one
of Malcolm Sproat's original lots on Baker Street. In truth, however, it was more probably the Lakeview, since the Nelson may
not have been quite ready to open for business yet, the supply of
lumber in town having been a little unsteady. George Owen
Buchanan, the first lumber supplier on the lake, had had his sawmill in operation for almost a year now. But he was kept running
to supply both Hendryx and Ainsworth Camps as well as booming Nelson. Owen had wisely obtained, as early as the spring of
'89, a timber limit along the west arm (where Harrop is today) and
got into business with a portable sawmill just when whip-sawyers
up at the *Silver King* and other Toad Mountain mines were becoming hard pressed to keep up with the demand for mine timbers
and planks, while down in Nelson lot-buyers were eager to begin
construction. Buchanan was having a hard time to keep everybody
happy, but even as Houston, Allen, and Ink arrived in town, two
new lumber businesses were preparing for operation. The Say-

ward-Davies Lumber Co. of Victoria was opening a mill at Pilot Bay on the main lake, and—even better for Nelson—Monty Davys and his partner J. H. Tolson were putting together a third portable mill to be called the Nelson Sawmill a mile or so south of town on Cottonwood Creek. Monty Davys was the M.S. Davys whose friendly little dog had approached Jim Gilker up in Revelstoke (two chapters ago). He was also the chief engineer up at the *Silver King*. In a place like Nelson in 1890, there was no end of opportunity for imaginative individuals with some money to deploy the forces of their energy in several directions.

Houston, Allen, and Ink began immediately to deploy *their* forces in more than one direction. Preparations for beginning the newspaper did not use up all their energies. They soon had a company formed and launched into the real estate business. Complex John Houston, though generally taking the side of the common man against capitalists, was not adverse to a bit of land speculation himself. Travelling about to conduct auctions of lots he had purchased—up the Slocan valley in one recorded instance—fit right in with his desire as a newspaper man to know the area intimately. For both businesses a building was required, and since lumber and manpower were becoming available at an increasing rate, it would be no problem to build one, at least serviceable enough for the summer months. Later, during the long autumn, it could be made winter-ready. So, as he went about his businesses, John's head was filled with plans for his office building. How we wish we knew where that building was and what it looked like. As yet, time has yielded up no picture of it. One of our sources, however, remarks in passing that it stood on Baker Street just to the east of George Bigelow's general store, and if we want to see where *that* was we must look at a photograph.

A most satisfactory primary source this picture certainly is, but not a perfect one for the simple reason that its date is unknown and must be inferred. We know that the International Hotel was constructed in 1891, and it is there, looking quite complete, over on what is now the corner of Vernon and Stanley Streets (A). We know that the Tremont Hotel (B) was also constructed in 1891, and

Nelson, B.C. *circa* 1890. KMAHS 61.4.2

there *it* is, still under construction, on Baker Street, in the middle of what is today the 600 Block between Josephine and Hall Streets. And now, since we have this photograph before us, we should continue to examine it, not forgetting that our purpose in bringing it out was to determine the possible location of John Houston's newspaper and real estate office in 1890. We will do that in a moment or two but, first, leaving John suspended in the space-time of '90, let us explore the '91 picture. It will save a thousand words.

As all Nelsonites will discern at once, the photographer stood his camera about halfway up the bluff near the east end of Baker Street, at a point approximately in line with the alley between Baker and Victoria Streets. The centrepoint of the picture is the cluster of buildings around what today would be the junction of Baker and Ward Streets, the heart of Nelson. It is clear that Baker and Vernon have extended westward over Ward Creek gully, which means that Sproat's original survey has been extended in that direction. To the right we see the west arm of Kootenay Lake flowing around the western tip of Elephant Mountain. Just out of our sight the water will change its placid character and become the lower Kootenay River, moving in a series of rapids and waterfalls to the Columbia about thirty miles westward. (Also just out of our sight behind the end of Elephant Mountain is the sandy point where the Lake and Kootenay Indians held their 1867 rendezvous in Chapter 2.) In the far distance of the picture we can make out fragments of a straight line running along the burned-off flank of Morning Mountain until, losing itself amid vegetation and rocky prominence, it moves out of the picture along with the river it is following. That is the Forty-nine Creek Trail. Closer in to Nelson, we can see it very distinctly—near the left edge of the picture—angling out of a patch of smoke up onto the mountain. We recall from Chapter 16 how Robert Yuill stopped at '49 Creek on his way up to Stanley from Sproat's Landing and sent a crew ahead to cut trail, because he did not want to follow the regular route up the creek to the *Silver King* mine. The line we see in this photograph is the trail Bob's crew opened up. It has since been walked by dozens of travellers, including John Houston and his friends, as we saw in the previous chapter. Long-time residents of Nelson will observe that it takes more or less the same route as the present-day old highway to Taghum, now known as the Granite Road. In about the same position, but closer to the left edge, we can see a smaller white line making a curve to the left. That is the wagon road to the Silver King Mine. It has wended up through town and crossed the canyon of Cottonwood Creek over a bridge (on present-day Latimer Street) just before we observe it. Our friend Bob Yuill was in charge of the work gang who put in the bridges and culverts for the road.

If we look very closely at the photograph we can see a third line running along Morning Mountain, but right down at the water's edge. It is a railway bed and is especially visible where it cuts through rock bluffs. Just before it disappears behind Elephant Mountain there is a trestle showing black beside the white rocks of the shoreline. We can pick out the line again in the middle distance. Having made a curve around the shoreline toward Nelson, it emerges into view once more in front of the forest of trees silhouetted against the water, and ends at a wharf (or rather a cribbing filled with rock ballast) which juts beyond our sight into the lake. Incidentally, that forest of cottonwood trees so charmingly showing in silhouette will, forty years after the taking of this photograph, come to be known as the "CPR jungle," temporary home to an ever-changing population of men of all ages who are riding the rails back and forth across Canada, looking for jobs in the Hungry Thirties. Nowadays nothing remains of those trees or the high-water swamps that bred them.

The railway, of course, is the one we saw under construction in the previous chapter; now, a year later in this picture, it is being completed into the Nelson Yards. (All the smoke tells us that crews are still at work.) John Ainsworth proposed it away back in '83; the Canadian Pacific Railway has finally built it. Nelson has become a CPR town. From now on its destiny is linked to that of the railway, which has been granted ownership of its whole waterfront and much property—entire blocks—in the town itself.

From now on the town's whole growth—its size, its shape, its character, the very tenor of its ways—will occur only within the bounds set by its intimate association with the CPR. For long years after the *Silver King* has become only a memory, generations of Nelsonites will be telling the time by the coming and going of trains, will have learned to love the sound that linked them to all other Canadians from sea to sea—that lovely, gentle, comforting, sad wail of the steam-whistle, dopplering into their hearts as the train approached, passed, and disappeared down the tracks.

Returning to the photograph, we can find, even at this early date, some buildings which survived almost unchanged into times within living memory, others which survive today much changed, and one or two that still exist in recognizable form. Both Baker and Vernon Streets are clearly indicated by the rows of buildings lining them. Along Vernon all the buildings are on the south side facing the lake. In the middle distance, marking the western end of the row, is the already-mentioned International Hotel (A). In present-day terms, it is on the southwest corner of Vernon and Stanley Streets, in the 300 Block. At the near end of the row is the Grand Hotel (C) in the middle of the present-day 600 Block. The International is going to burn to the ground in 1894, but the Grand lives on today as the Lord Nelson Hotel. The building we see in this photograph was torn down in 1913 and rebuilt in stone and brick. That second building still exists, and if you look up at the top of its false front you can see the name Grand Hotel carved in stone. Years later, an addition was added in the direction of Hall Street and the whole renamed New Grand. Still later it went through further name changes: New Grand to Nelson and finally Lord Nelson.

We notice in our photograph that the original building has two outhouses in its backyard, undoubtedly the "Ladies" and "Gents" facilities. We can even tell which is which, for an anonymous man has been immortalized about to enter one of them.

In between the International and the Grand lie the 400 Block—on the west side of Ward Creek gully and still almost empty—and the 500 Block—the one that George Mercer Dawson so tele-cooperatively photographed for us back in '89. It has completely changed; not one of its original edifices remains. The partnership of Hume & Lemon has been dissolved, and the old log store has disappeared. Hume has built himself a new store in the same block (D), while Lemon has built a much bigger one in the 600 Block, on the southeast corner of Vernon and Josephine (E). This building stood a long time, and many living Nelsonites can still remember it as the Ark, a second-hand store. The building marked (F) is a rooming house built by John Ward to replace the old log Lakeview Hotel, which he sold and then repurchased. It, as we already know, is on the southeast corner of Vernon and Ward.

Both Hume and Lemon probably wish they were up on Baker Street, for that, as the picture suggests, is where commercial development is mainly occurring, not on Vernon as Malcolm Sproat intended and they anticipated. Lemon has even had a huge sign R.E. LEMON painted on the west slope of his roof (there is already a professional sign-painter in town) to attract the crowds on Baker Street down to Vernon.

On Baker we can see the heart of the future city developing around an unlikely spot—Ward Creek gully. (Unlikely from our point of view but not from theirs, for they would naturally want to be near a water supply.) Crossing the gully is a bridge (G), built in the summer of 1890 by a crew of men under Owen Buchanan, with timbers and planks from his mill up the west arm. It is exactly at the intersection of Baker and Ward Streets, although Ward Street is not there yet, because, as we have observed before, much cribbing and filling will have to be in place before that street can be built.

Like Vernon, Baker Street seems to be developing faster along its south side. Perhaps businesses like to face the lake. Only two commercial buildings—though perhaps the oldest and certainly among the biggest—have been put up on the north side. In present-day terms they are a little to the west of middle in the 500 Block. (It is difficult, often impossible, to locate the exact lots on which these old buildings were situated, since they disappeared

216

before plumbing and other records were kept). In the picture we can see that there is quite a large space between them and the gully over which Ward Street will take shape. The further of the two is the Nelson Hotel. We can clearly see the big cornice topping its false front. This false front is so large it seems that the hotel is a mere attachment on *it*. The Nelson's owner clearly believed in the false front as a valid means of impressing potential customers and was determined to have the biggest one in town, even though all anyone had to do was walk to the side of the building to see through the whole deception. However, either because of the false front or in spite of it, the Nelson did indeed have an impressive reputation for a long time as one of the town's best hotels. The building on the near side of the Nelson is George Bigelow's general store, the reference to which was the cause of our viewing this photograph in the first place. It has a huge sign painted on the side facing us, but for some reason it fails to show up in this picture. (Perhaps that busy sign-painter has not quite yet had time to do it.)

Appearing to face the Nelson across Baker Street, but actually a few lots closer to the bridge, is Hugh Madden's first Madden Hotel (H), more modestly false fronted than the Nelson. Beyond it, out of our view on the edge of the gully is Hugh's restaurant, the English Kitchen. In a year Hugh will pull the English Kitchen down and erect—out of stone and brick—his second hotel, the Madden Block. A charming building, it will grace the heart of Nelson for nearly six decades until in the 1950s—sadly only a short time before the value of such buildings becomes recognized—it will in its turn be razed.

Moving westward across the gully, we see the roof and false front, with its peaked cornice, of the Silver King Hotel. One more building beyond it, and Baker Street loses itself in unsurveyed open country. Out there, just where the land slopes down to Cottonwood Creek flats (at the crossing of present-day Baker and Falls Streets) lies the grave of old Bart Henderson. When he died a few months after the New Year's party—about the time John Houston arrived in town—they buried him out there, thinking it a remote and quiet place. In a few years, however, his bones, and those of some others who died after him, will have to be moved, first to the site of the present-day City Tourist Park on High Street and then in 1898 to the present-day cemetery, this second removal being accomplished by one Thomas Jerome, the city powder-man, who used for the job a conveyance aptly named the Resurrection Wagon.

Moving back to the near end of Baker Street, we come to the already-mentioned Tremont Hotel (B), still under construction and so new that it doesn't have its false front attached yet. Only five years from the time of this photograph it will be torn down and resurrected in stone and brick as the Tremont Block, its facade elaborately decorated with pilasters, urns, a bracketed cornice, a course of dentils, and a corbel table—the proud construction of Nelson's earliest firm of architects, Ewart & Carrie. Today, one of the Tremont Block's three sections remains—looking much as it did then in the middle of the 600 Block.

At the extreme near end of Baker—probably between what will be Hall and Hendryx Streets—we observe three small buildings with peaked roofs, and these we must speculate about. The middle building has a cloth sign stretched between two poles set well out into the road to catch the attention of people closer to the centre of town. We see it from behind very clearly in the picture. In another photograph we can actually discern the letters on that sign because they show through the cloth. They read ƎOHƧ . Is this building really a shoe store (it seems unlikely to the present historian that there would be a specialty shop at this stage of the town's growth) or is the sign an evasive way of advertising another kind of business? The town is steadily filling up with people who are mostly men—prospectors, miners, mining promoters. Closely following on their heels are other men, business persons of all kinds—storekeepers, sign-painters, labourers, clerks, etc.—all bent on contributing to the town's growth by catering to the needs of the population while making a living for themselves. Inevitably, as had happened in all the towns which sprang up along the railway as it came across the continent, certain business*women* have as quickly arrived with the same purpose. In short, the three buildings at this end of Baker Street may be brothels. We know for a fact that, a few years hence, the east end of Baker Street will draw the attention of the town's growing forces of respectability, which—shocked by the uninhibited behaviour and loud piano-playing going on in houses there—will demand that the inmates of certain of them be removed to a more remote location.

At the left edge of the picture another grouping of houses indicates Victoria Street, but on the way over there we should stop to take notice of two buildings under construction. The first of these (I) is a residence—the *Nelson Daily News* of January 7th, 1911 will refer to it as "the old Red House"—well set back from the street on the northeast corner of Victoria and Stanley Streets. We see its uncovered studs supporting its pyramidal roof. Two blocks nearer us is half of the unfinished Scroggs Block (J), its roof also supported by uncovered studs. Its lower end is at the alley between Baker and Victoria Streets. Its entrance—on the side facing away from us—opens onto Josephine Street. As soon as this half is complete, Mr. Scroggs is going to continue on up to Victoria Street with the second half. We can see the roof-boards projecting from the upper end of the first half waiting to be fitted onto the roof of the second. The Scroggs block will endure until 1921, when it will be torn down and replaced by the long stone building that is there now.

Victoria Street is defined for us by two houses; one (K) has endured until the present day and is at the time of this writing undergoing extensive alterations. The other (L) is probably in the 300 Block. The houses in between (in the 400 Block) are out of line because they—like their successors today—are set much farther back on the lots and must be climbed up to by long flights of stairs. One of the houses, perhaps (M), in the 400 Block is of great interest to us. It is on the southeast corner of Victoria and Stanley Street, and is the new home of the Drs. Arthur. It will remain where we see it until 1911, when it will be towed away to 515 Silica Street (where it is today) to make way for the big brick YMCA building which is still there at the present time. Strictly speaking, at the time of this picture (M) should not be called the home of the Drs. Arthur. It holds as yet only one doctor—Dr. Edward Charles Arthur. His wife will not become Dr. Isabel Arthur for a few years yet.

Now, a quick look at the group of buildings (N) at the right-hand edge and our perusal of the photograph is complete. These buildings seem to be placed haphazardly. Perhaps that section of the land has not been surveyed yet. In front of them we see a wide white strip. That must be the trail up which Robert Yuill walked in Chapter 18, now upgraded to a wagon road. It follows more or less the same curve that modern-day Ward Street takes as it merges into Front.

We have completed our examination of this 1891 photograph without, alas, answering the question that began it, and must still ask, "Where is the building that houses John Houston's newspaper and real estate business?" There seems to be no building at all "on Baker Street just to the east of George Bigelow's store." The little shack with the tent beside it is too small to consider and the tiny log house with the washing behind it and the path leading up to it may well be the cabin young Charlie Ink built for himself, but it most certainly isn't a newspaper office.

We will accept defeat and return at once to 1890 and John Houston planning his office, *wherever* it is going to be. But for that, we must begin a new chapter, this one having been filled up already.

Side view of the Nelson Hotel (Photo Courtesy Bob Emory)

This photograph was taken by Neelands Bros. Photographers, from a position at or just south of the present-day intersection of Stanley and Victoria Streets (perhaps from the roof of Edward and Isabel Arthur's house). It shows the rock bluff (much different from its present-day form) which marks the edge of Nelson proper. Beyond is Harry Anderson's pre-emption, the one he called Salisbury and which today we know as Fairview.

The picture centres on Baker Street where it crosses over Ward Creek gully on the bridge built by Owen Buchanan, the heart of Nelson then and still so today when the bridge is gone and Ward Street runs up the filled-in gully.

We see only the east and west ends of the bridge, most of which is hidden by the Silver King Hotel, facing the lake from about the middle of the present-day 400 block.

Across the gully, facing away from the lake somewhere near the middle of the present-day 500 block, is the Nelson Hotel, attached like an afterthought to its enormous false front. Indication of Nelson's booming economy are the additions tacked on the backs of both hotels.

Facing the Nelson across Baker is Hugh Madden's big hotel. Beside it, shored up from falling into Ward Creek gully by log cribbing, we see Hugh's English Kitchen.

Poles, giving evidence of Nelson's telephone system, can be seen along Baker Street and elsewhere.

Someone living in one of the houses away down by the lakeshore has hung a nice white wash out to dry.

# CHAPTER 22

*In which, returning to find John Houston, we come upon him, not where we left him in the spring of 1890 proposing to build an office, but already—time having continued to flow by while we examined the photograph—seated in that elusive office in late December of the same year.[29]*

OUTSIDE, IT WAS A DARK, sombre afternoon with a wind blowing down the lake, islands of steaming horse dung dotted here and there along the expanse of newly whitened streets, and a foreboding in the air of more snow to come; inside, John Houston, seated on the swivel chair at his desk, was feeling warm and contented, pleased with the world, and more than just a little self-congratulatory. It had been a good year. More and more these days he was thinking how right he had been in following his hunch about coming to Nelson.

John was alone in the office. Saturday was the day *The Miner* came out every week, and after two or three days of pretty hectic work in the printing and composing room both Charlie Ink and Gessner Allen had taken the day off as usual. Charles Dake was gone too, out somewhere delivering the papers to stores, hotels, and other distribution points. John looked over to the table near the door where, earlier in the afternoon, there had been several piles of today's edition. Now only two or three single copies were lying there; Charles Dake probably wouldn't be returning to the office. And, thank God, the "ram pasture" was empty today. (The big room upstairs had acquired that name because—owing to

Gessner Allen's reputation as the only person in town capable of helping the wounded and physically impaired—it often had so many miners and prospectors lying about in it with sprained ankles, bruised thighs, oversize cuts, and other medical afflictions that it looked like a dormitory up at one of the mines.) John sighed. This afternoon his office actually felt like a real newspaper office, not a hospital and two or three stores all rolled into one. He glanced at the boxes of crockery and bales of retail goods that were standing about on the floor, the result of his having given in to storekeepers who continually begged for storage space "for just a few days."

Saturday, the 27th of December, the last Saturday of the year . . . John's mind flew back to June 21st—the day when no. 1 of *The Miner* had come out . . . and now, twenty-seven Saturdays later, no. 28. Amazing how much had happened in those twenty-seven weeks . . . Suddenly feeling a little melancholy—though not enough to dispel his mood of contentment—he glanced at the clock above the desk and got up to lift the coal-oil lamp from its wall bracket. Trimming its wick, he began to think of the events of those twenty-seven weeks. He set the lamp on the desk, lit it, and replaced the glass chimney . . . only four o'clock and getting dark . . . but, don't forget, each of the last six days had been a tiny bit longer than the previous one. He tipped a few pieces of coal from the scuttle into the fire, opened the damper on the stovepipe, and reseated himself at the desk.

In front of him, *The Miner's* complete output—all twenty-eight numbers, neatly folded—was stacked against the wall. Choosing one at random, he eased it out of the pile, opened it, and laid it down on the desk. It had opened at page 8, and he began scanning the "Small Nuggets of News" column. A block of four news items caught his eye:

---

From 4 services held at Ainsworth, conducted by W. J. Small, a Presbyterian missionary, $31.70 was raised by passing round the "plate." Pretty liberal people at Hot Springs.

---

223

> Mr. and mrs. E. L. Weeks of Sand Point, Idaho, and mrs. J. C. Rykert of the custom-house made a first trip to Nelson last week; but they only saw the city by electric light, as the Galena did not arrive until 10 at night and departed the next morning at 4.
>
> Customs collector Rykert has put up some of the finest hay ever stacked on Kootenay river. He will have no trouble in selling it, as the demand will be large this fall, both at Nelson and Ainsworth.
>
> Dr. D. LaBau came down from Hot Springs in a row-boat, arriving at Nelson at 1 o'clock Wednesday morning. He was accompanied by H. Anderson, mining recorder at Ainsworth. Dr. LaBau was called to attend R. D. Atkins, one of the owners of the Hall mines, who is suffering from a serious attack of pneumonia and intermittent fever.

The first one caused him to smile—he couldn't remember now whether his comment about the "pretty liberal people" was meant to be serious or sarcastic—but he had a real laugh at the second as he imagined the ever-increasing discomfiture of the three tourists when it became more and more apparent that *Galena*—hours late—was not going to reach its destination until after dark. He could imagine the late-night scene as the captain, feeling strongly at fault, solicitously sought to ease their disappointment, however slightly, by playing *Galena's* electric searchlight over the sleeping town.

He turned the pages idly, going backward, and stopped on the sixth. Ah! Here was something interesting—a long letter from that ridiculous Baillie-Grohman fellow about that asinine scheme of his to prevent flooding on the flatlands at the south end of the lake! John smiled as he remembered when he first heard of the scheme, back in his days at Donald. The whole East Kootenay country, he recalled, had followed with unflagging interest the goings-on at Canal Flat, where Baillie-Grohman had actually built a canal from the Kootenay River over to Columbia Lake, using shovels and wheelbarrows in the hands of hundreds of Chinamen to remove the earth. As a newspaper man, John had obtained statistics and still remembered some of them: the canal was 6,700 feet long and 45 feet wide, and there was a difference of 11 vertical feet between the Kootenay River and Columbia Lake. Baillie-Grohman had had nothing but trouble over the whole undertaking. Four years of endless negotiations with the provincial government were followed by one problem after another as the work began. First the residents of Golden and the farms along the upper Columbia had petitioned against the canal, arguing that the increased flow of water from the Kootenay would flood their farmlands. Then it was discovered that the federal government, not the provincial, had jurisdiction over waterways. After much negotiation, the canal was permitted, but only if a lock was built in it to prevent continuous water flow. That, of course, negated the whole reason for the canal's being built. Nevertheless, the plan had gone ahead. To obtain lumber for construction of the lock and buildings, the company of which Baillie-Grohman was now the general manager shipped a small steam-driven sawmill by rail from Brantford, Ontario to Golden, thence by improvised barge upstream to Columbia Lake. Dozens of times, particularly on the salmon spawning-beds at the headwaters, the barge ran aground and had to be unloaded, refloated, reloaded, and set going again. It had taken twenty-three days to reach Canal Flat from Golden. Anybody else would have had the sense to give up, thought John, but not Baillie-Grohman. Maybe there were some people who thought Baillie-Grohman and his scheme made sense, "but I'm not among them," said John to himself. A small settlement had grown up around the works at Canal Flat—a store, a post office, a hotel (of sorts, thought John, who had spent a night in it once), the sawmill, and a few other buildings. He smiled sardonically as he thought of B-G's satisfaction when the town became known as Grohman. Finally, in the summer of '89—John remembered the exact date: July 29—the canal was completed. Only two boats ever passed through the lock, and the canal—now of no consequence to Baillie-Grohman's scheme—had begun slowly to fill in.

And now—John shook his head in disbelief—the damned fool had transferred his attentions to Nelson, where he had hired Harold Selous—an up-and-coming contractor; John respected him highly—to dredge out the river downstream a mile or so—at *Grohman* Creek, plague take him! The scheme *might* have worked with the canal at Canal Flat, but now that that was no longer an active component, anybody who wasn't blinded by his own conceit would see that digging some gravel out of the river couldn't help a dammed bit. And yet, Baillie-Grohman, now the general manager of yet another company, had been in town during August to oversee the dredging. Thinking with satisfaction of the hard time he had given Baillie-Grohman editorially over the year, John made a mental note to ask Harold Selous what *he*

> "The Stanley of the Kootenay Lake country," as W. A. Baillie-Grohman so dearly likes to be called, will be at the scene of his dredging operations, 2 miles below Nelson, within a couple of weeks. He will be accompanied by mrs. Grohman and the children.
> *The Miner.* August 2, 1890. P.8.

thought about the whole business. Work had stopped down at the creek-mouth for the winter, but Harold was living in town, and he might even be at The English Kitchen for supper tonight. . . . Come to think of it, there were a few other things he wanted to talk to Harold about. Maybe some of the other go-getters in town would be at the Kitchen tonight, too, and they could have a real planning session. One thing for sure was needed very soon and that was a system for fire-fighting . . . all those new wooden buildings going up everywhere with no regulations . . . and something would have to be done soon about water and electricity, and sewage too. Ward Creek was getting pretty foul down there in the gully . . . Maybe the town should start making noises about getting incorporated. That would make dealings with the government easier, and affairs within the town too . . . Only the other day Jim Gilker had been going on about the state of Her Majesty's mail . . . and a wharf was needed badly—before that bunch that now owned Harry Anderson's pre-emption built one up there and stole business from Nelson. . . . More streets were needed. Perhaps there should be a petition to the government for an extended survey . . . my God, that damn Busk fellow—John began heating up as new threats to Nelson's continued development presented themselves—was already trying to get a settlement going up where the west arm joined the main lake. If he succeeded with that the CPR might extend beyond Nelson and make its terminus up *there*. . . .

His mood of contentment somewhat ruffled by these thoughts, and even more so by having reminded himself of the CPR, John grumpily folded the newspaper in front of him, pushed it aside, and reached for another. This time he knew what he was looking for—an article in one of the very early numbers, the second or third he was sure. He even knew the page—page 1, because he remembered he had wanted to give it prominence. Easing no. 3 out of the pile, he unfolded it and looked at the first page. Ah yes! Here it was: "A Great Mogul Visits Us." His sarcasm, he noted with satisfaction, had been apparent even in the headline. Scanning through the article, he felt his mood changing for the better. Yes, he had given Mr. W.C. Van Horne, president of the Canadian Pacific Railway, his due as one of the most prominent railway men on the continent, and the big-shots in his entourage too. Just enough over-praise to admit a touch of ambiguity, a little hint of irony. How condescending the great man had been! Making it clear he thought the thirty-mile stretch of railway a useless piece of nonsense—almost beneath his notice. And all the time playing politics—not revealing to the people of Nelson whether the company was intending to end the railway here and give the town the importance of being the terminus, or extend it up to the main lake and make Nelson a mere siding. Keep everybody scared—John remembered how real estate sales had declined recently—so that the company, land-hungry as always, could wring concessions from the town! That was all tied in with what the Chief Commissioner of Land and Works down in Victoria had done only a month before Van Horne's visit—reserved a four-mile-square block around the whole townsite, which meant that the town couldn't expand because its borders were surrounded by a solid block of land reserved for CPR use. Already folks were angry, and wondering if the town wasn't doomed. You just watch—John was muttering to himself indignantly—they'll rescind that land reservation only if we grant a lot of *our* land in return. Glancing again at the article, he smiled as he read its ending words: " . . . after presenting a Siwash with a cigar, Mr. Van Horne led the way down the river bank, leaving our people in an anxious sweat as to whether Nelson was to be a railroad town or a siding." That would show Van Horne—if he ever read it—that we were on to his game. What a good touch the part about the cigar was—the great Mogul distributing largesse to his subjects by presenting an Indian bystander with a cigar! Laughing at his own irony, John was thinking that if Van Horne hadn't made that ridiculous gesture, he'd have had to invent it himself.

Contemplating his editorial battles with the CPR over the last few months, John felt his mood changing for the better again. His record as a newspaper man had been good. He hadn't let them get away with anything. His readers had heard all about their successful blocking of would-be rivals wanting to build railways into Kootenay country from the States, and he had consistently taken the side of the labouring man against the company. That business, for example, about all the white men quitting work and young Doc Arthur being scared to go out on calls. Let's see, that had taken place in mid-summer and he had written a good piece about it in no. . . . let's see, no. 6? He pulled the July 26th number from the pile, and there it was on page 1 under the heading "Contractors And Men Dissatisfied." He began scanning the article.

# CONTRACTORS AND MEN DISSATISFIED.

Conflicting reports come from the railroad camps between Nelson and Sproat . . . . . . . . . . . . . . . . . .
. . . . . . . . . . . . . . . . . . . . . . . . . . . . . . . . . . . the men are dissatisfied at the low wages paid, and that they are leaving in large numbers daily. One report is that Whitehead, McLean & McKay have lost all their white men and now have no laborers on the work except Italians and Chinese. . . . . . . . . . . . . . . . . .
. . . . . . . . . . . . . . . . . . . . .the railroad company will still be the gainers, for they collect fare from every laborer brought on the work, and the more men leaving the more fares collected, and the larger the earnings of the company . . . . . . . . . . . . . . . . . . . . . . . . . .
. . .the railroad company should be indicted for swindling and obtaining money under false pretences. A case in point: Seventy-five cents a month is deducted from the pay of every man on the work for hospital fees. This amount is not, as many of the men believe, deducted by the contractors, but by the railroad company. The company hires a doctor, paying him about $100 a month, and until recently has furnished him with no medicines. For a time the men were so enraged at the treatment that they threatened to ill-use the doctor on sight, and he was afraid to go among them when called on. In this way they collect $600 or $700 a month and pay out less than $200. Another case: The fares of the men from the point at which they start are deducted from their first earnings and not only the fare in, but the company has the gall to deduct the steamboat fare back to Revelstoke. Of course, the officials of the company know full well that the men, being ignorant of the true facts, will vent their feelings on the contractors, and not on them . . .
. . . . . . . . . . . . . . . . . . . . . . . . . . . . . . . . . . . . .
. . . . . . . . . . . . . . . . The road when completed will be one of the worst constructed in Canada, and if the Dominion government should inspect it, pointers might be obtained to use in the arbitration suit now pending between it and the Canadian Pacific Railway Company.

About 2 miles of steel are laid east from Sproat.

Thinking about Dr. Arthur made John forget for a moment his on-going battle with the CPR. The town needed a doctor badly. There were minor accidents at the mines and in town every day, and serious illnesses too. Atkins up at the *Silver King* in June was a case in point, and that Lewis fellow being killed in November by a rock-blast down at Baillie-Grohman's works, and—in the same week—Mrs. Foster, the only launderer, midwife, and nurse in town, hit on the head with a rock. Harold Selous, as justice of peace, had punished the culprit with a $29.25 fine, but what if she'd been badly enough hurt to need a doctor? No, it clearly wasn't good enough just to have Drs. LaBau and Hendryx around. They were both up on the main lake and engaged in mining. Some day there'd be a real disaster and those two wouldn't be where they could help. The town—and the whole district—needed a resident licensed doctor. And there he was—that young fellow already hired by the CPR in the early summer, but five miles down the river at the bridge-construction site where he'd set up headquarters in the camp there. A nice young fellow—John had met him two or three times, one of them when he'd gone down there on a fact-gathering foray. He had, John knew, left his bride of a year back home in Ontario, pregnant of course, when he accepted this job in the wilderness. Now, if he were to move into Nelson—where he could serve both the townspeople and the CPR workers—he could bring her out here and set up a home. Yes, thought John, it would be very nice to have young Doc Arthur as the town physician, and no doubt his young wife would ornament the social scene very gracefully. He would bring the subject up at the Kitchen tonight and the boys could start working on Doc to make the decision. Come to think of it, though, maybe he'd already *made* the decision. He had promised—John had reported it only two weeks ago in no. 26—to open a drugstore in the spring. Maybe that was an indication that he intended to move into town himself. Well anyway, John decided, the boys and he would encourage him all they could.

Suddenly he was aware that it had become totally dark outside and that only the lamp was keeping the darkness from the small part of the room he was in. He turned to look behind him and saw the huge outline of his shadow on the wall, which was itself only a lesser darkness. To his right, the absolute blackness of the other room was faintly outlined by reflected light from the door frame. Deep shadows extended from corners and, beneath the desk, his feet were non-existent in blackness. All at once the room seemed colder, but, reassuring through the bright squares of isinglass on the stove's door, the burning coals of the fire gave him a sensation of increased warmth. He glanced at the clock, its round face looming from the semi-darkness of the wall, and said aloud, "It's time to go."

Carefully folding the newspapers and returning each to its correct location in the piles, he groped under the desk for the pair of heavy snow boots he kept there and proceeded to put them on his feet, then took time to place the indoor shoes he had just taken off where the others had been. He then walked over to the street door and got a lantern which was hanging on one of the hooks of the coat rack standing there. Bringing it back to the desk, he opened its glass door, turned up the wick, lit it, and closed the door. He returned the lamp on his desk to the wall bracket, turned it off, closed the damper on the stove (he would come back later to stoke the fire for the night), and, picking up the lantern, was ready to leave. At the door he put on his hat and coat and emerged into the winter night. He locked the door, dropping the key into his coat pocket.

Snow had been falling heavily for the last hour and a half, and now the flakes were coming thickly enough to cover even the freshest piles of horse dung within minutes. Not that any horses had been by recently. It was supper-time and Baker Street was lifeless; not a wheel-mark nor a hoof-print disturbed the even white blanket. John knew that most of the stores—certainly Hume's and Lemon's on Vernon Street, George Bigelow's and Joe Wilson's meat market on Baker—were still open and would remain so until quite late. The town—even with this heavy snowstorm—would liven up considerably in an hour or two when miners, driven by loneliness, came down the wagon roads and trails to make a few purchases and visit the girls farther east on Baker. And the barrooms at the hotels would be busy. Labourers downstream would think nothing of walking the five or so miles from the railway camp at the bridge-site. Maybe even young Doc Arthur would hike in for a meal at the Kitchen, if he hadn't gone home to Ontario for Christmas. Right now, though, there was no sign of life on the street, not a ray of light nor the tiniest echo of a sound as the falling snow shut him off from everything outside himself. He could be alone in the universe. Light from the lantern he was carrying penetrated only two or three yards around him before its last diminished rays were reflected back by the relentless flakes. Beyond that the blackness was impenetrable.

Turning toward the restaurant (near Ward Creek bridge, a block or more along the street) he began walking carefully, almost feeling his way. He knew that there were several small buildings along the street, all of them in a straight line fronting the sidewalk that was going to be there someday. Keeping these buildings within reach on his left and being careful not to stray into the gaps between them, he would reach his destination easily. Leaving his own building behind, he soon got beyond the space between that and its nearest neighbour. There, he paused to look in the window. It was a commercial building, untenanted as yet, but only a few days ago occupied, he knew, by a newcomer to town. Peering into the empty front room he could see, through an open doorway, the faint glow of a lamp or candle in a room at the back. He smiled to himself, thinking of some unknown person having an evening meal there, perhaps reading today's *Miner*. All over town most of the population—and three hundred people had eaten Christmas dinner in Nelson this year as opposed to the twelve in Mrs. Hanna's house in '88—were probably doing the same, all happy that their little settlement was flourishing and would continue to grow . . . reading his *Miner*. . . . Suddenly John saw himself as one of the developers and guardians of the town, at this very moment on his way to discuss possibilities for its future with some of the community's important men . . . a newspaper man, one who informed, gave public voice to ideas and opinions. Someone a few weeks ago had accused him of "trying to run this community." Well, why not? Somebody had to run it. Why not the editor of the local newspaper? Come to think of it, maybe that's why he liked being the editor of a frontier town newspaper. Hell, anybody could report the news, but for him, this job meant he was at the centre of things, put him right into the middle of the fray. He *liked* giving opinions, exposing hypocrisy, taking on the big boys, fighting for the common man . . . and, looking back at the record of *The Miner's* first year, he could feel proud of himself. He hadn't been afraid to take on even the government. Maybe he *wanted* to run this community. The end of the year was a good time to make a few decisions, settle a few questions. . . . He was now a part of this town, had come to feel it was his. Maybe it was time to marry . . . and maybe he ought to think about being on his own in the newspaper business. Having partners was a bit restraining for him. . . .

He found himself at the sidewalk in front of Hugh Madden's hotel. There was only a thin layer of snow on it and the step up to it. Hugh, as befitted the owner of a first-rate hotel, was keeping it swept. The windows of the Madden House were well illuminated, and light streamed out onto the sidewalk. Ignoring their invitation, John passed by the entrance and down the step at the other end. Here, the path was swept too, and warm yellow light poured through the steamy windows on either side of the doorway of The English Kitchen. He put his face close to the misted glass of the first one and peered into the crowded room. Against the far wall, two or three figures—he couldn't make out who they were—were already seated at the big table that Hugh kept reserved for them there. John took a moment to knock his hat against the door post, shake the snow off his shoulders, and stamp his feet. Then, after turning down the wick of his lantern, he opened the door and went in.

# CHAPTER 23

*A small chapter whose purpose is to reveal what life*
*had in store for three persons we first met in Chapter 18.*[30]

ON THE EIGHTH PAGE of *The Miner* no. 9, dated Saturday, August 16th, 1890, John Houston printed the following news article.

---

**Encouraging Reports from Trail Creek.**

If the Trail creek excitement keeps a-growing, Nelson will soon be as "dead" as Revelstoke or Sproat or Colville. On Thursday mr. and mrs. Hanna and their 4 children, E. S. Topping, M. A. McDougal, J. H. Hope, John Buchanan, and others left the rustle and bustle of this camp for the noisy whirl of life at the camp on the headwaters of Trail, Sheep, and Stony creeks. On Tuesday R. E. Lemon came in from the new camp, and reports about 40 men scattered among the hills over there, all of them being from this section. There is a good restaurant at the mouth of the creek, some 8 miles from the mines, and no lack of supplies. Mr Lemon brought in a sample of ore from the Josie, one of his claims; also a sample from the Center Star, a claim belonging to Joe Bourgois . . . . . . . . . . . . . . . . .
. . . . . . . . . . . . . . . . . . . . . . . . . . . . . . . . . . . . . . . . . . .
. . . . . . . . . . . . . . . . . .

---

All present-day inhabitants of West Kootenay country will recognize at once that the claims mentioned are among those that brought about the birth of Trail and Rossland. The article, even in its second half which has been omitted here, makes no mention of the *LeRoi* claim, richest of them all and the one central to the story being told in this chapter.

We recall that "Colonel" E.S. Topping, unable to do heavy work after injuring himself with an accidental gunshot only a few months following the '89 stag party, had obtained the governmental position of Deputy Mining Recorder and set himself up in one of the tents shown in George Mercer Dawson's photograph, thus abandoning his dreams of wealth and prestige for a secure job. Fate, however, had its own plans for the Colonel.

With the discovery of ore at Ainsworth, Big Ledge, and Toad Mountain, hordes of prospectors were now roaming the hills all over West Kootenay country. Two of these, Joe Moris and Joe Bourgeois, were working a claim, the *Lily May*, in high country near the source of the little creek that the east-bound Dewdney Trail followed for six miles or so down to the Columbia River. Bored with the poor showing at the *Lily May*, the two Joes set out one day to investigate a big red outcropping on a hill across the valley from them. Reaching it hours later, they became very glad to have made the effort. They staked four claims, which they named *War Eagle, Centre Star, Virginia,* and *Idaho.* Then they staked an extension, calling it *LeWise.* Wanting to legalize their discovery as soon as possible, they decided to set out for the Recorder's Office in Nelson immediately. Accordingly, they returned to the *Lily May*, packed a few things for travelling, and set off down the old Dewdney Trail along Trail Creek. Rather than walk along the new trail up the Columbia to Robson (the new railway terminus a mile or so above Sproat's Landing), they decided to camp on the flats at the mouth of Trail Creek until one of the river boats came along. The wait would not be a long one—three or four days at the most. That summer the Columbia & Kootenay Steam Navigation Company of Revelstoke (C&KSN) had three vessels in operation on the Columbia: their original one, the catamaran *Dispatch* on whose maiden voyage Robert Yuill, we recall, had brought his supplies from Revelstoke in August of '88; the *Kootenai*, the

American sternwheeler that Harry Anderson had flagged down when taking Robert Sproule to prison back in Chapter 12, now refurbished by the C&KSN after lying on a sandbar at Little Dalles for several years because the completion of the CPR transcontinental had put it out of business in '86; and the new sternwheeler *Lytton,* built by the Company at Revelstoke and launched on its maiden voyage on July 2nd, 1890. The *Marion* may have been making runs too.

We will not venture to guess which one of the four came along first, but, whichever it was, it carried the two Joes in a few hours up to Sproat's Landing. From there it was an easy walk along the combination trail and railway bed to Nelson. And so it was that on a hot July afternoon of the year 1890 Colonel E.S. Topping looked up from his desk in the little tent and set in motion the process by means of which he would receive the gift that the two unwitting messengers of fate standing in the entrance had come to give him.

Joe Moris and Joe Bourgeois stated their business, and E.S. Topping duly recorded the *War Eagle, Centre Star, Virginia,* and *Idaho* in his book under their names, then paused to await their wishes concerning the *LeWise.* The two prospectors had already formed a plan to save themselves some money before they entered the tent. Knowing that four claims between two men were lawful but the fifth was not, they had decided to offer the recorder the extension with the proviso that he pay the fee for recording all five. Making a decision that altered his life, the Colonel agreed to the proposal, paid the required twelve dollars and fifty cents, and entered the extension as his own, first changing its name from *LeWise* to *LeRoi.* On hearing that name *LeRoi,* anyone familiar with West Kootenay mining history knows without being told that Colonel Topping had suddenly and unknowingly become a rich man.

A few days later he decided to visit his *LeRoi* claim and easily persuaded his friend Frank Hanna to accompany him. When the two men reached the flats at the mouth of Trail Creek, they set up their tent and got into conversation with some fellows who were already camping there. From them they learned the shortest route

236

to the claims at the top of the creek. Early next morning they set off up the old Dewdney Trail to find the Colonel's *LeRoi*. A few hours later they were on the site and talking to the two Joes. On examining the claims, both Frank and the Colonel became enthusiastic. The location gave all indications of being a rich one. Taking some samples for assaying, they returned to the flats in time for a late supper in the tent restaurant that some enterprising fellow had already set up there.

While waiting for the boat next morning they took a good look at the Trail Creek flats. His active mind thinking well beyond the development of his own claim, the Colonel couldn't help but notice what a perfect place for a townsite the flats were. His enthusiasm was contagious, and soon Frank Hanna too was eagerly discussing business possibilities. If the mines up at the top of the creek developed into something big—both men felt sure they would—there was steamboat transportation right on the spot, with easy access to railways both north and south. It was inevitable that a town should develop here. They kept their excited discussion well out of earshot of any of the other campers. By the time they got aboard the boat, they had decided to pre-empt over three hundred acres, and quickly too, before that guy with the restaurant began to get bigger ideas—if he hadn't already done so. By the time they reached Nelson late next day, they were determined that if the pre-emption went through they would move lock, stock, and barrel to Trail Creek flats as soon as possible.

Well, as it turned out, that guy with the restaurant *hadn't* begun to get bigger ideas, nor had anyone else, and furthermore the samples had assayed very well indeed. So, on Thursday, the 14th of August, 1890—as reported by John Houston in *The Miner*—the Colonel and Frank and Mary Jane Hanna along with their four children set out in the company of others for the promised land of Trail Creek flats, their townsite pre-emption safely filed, their possessions on twenty of Joe Wilson's packhorses, strung out along the trail like some African safari. At Sproat's they loaded everything onto the *Lytton* and were in due course deposited on Trail Creek flats.

Almost immediately Frank Hanna began work on a two-storey log house, while the Colonel went about the business of planning their townsite and seeing to the development of his claim. Mary Jane soon got a good home going in a tent and quickly became a well-loved caterer to the needs of the camp population, just as she had been in Nelson. When the log house was finished she began a meal service for the camp and provided overnight accommodation for men on their way up to the mines. She and Frank ran a small bar and brought in supplies—picks, shovels, and the like—for sale to prospectors. Soon Frank had built himself a blacksmith shop. That way the winter of '90-'91 passed by. In March of '91 twin girls were born to Jane.

When the pre-emption came through, work on the townsite could begin in earnest. The original two-storey log house—now called "Trail House"—had become far too small as the town grew, and the office where the two men conducted business had also become inadequate, while Jane was overworked and needed help. Accordingly, streets were laid out and a large building erected, intended to contain a post office, telephone office, and a few stores, with a big room in the second storey that could be used as an opera house. While that was in progress, the newly formed Townsite Company built a big house for Jane (as its legal owner). Furthermore, a female helper was found for her. Soon, other events, portentous for the future of Trail, began to . . . but we must check this thrust toward the chronicling of further civic developments. This is not the history of Trail. We must leave Frank, Jane, the Colonel, and the town to live out their lives without further attention from us. Suffice it to say, for a few years their fortunes were in the ascendancy, the three friends prospering with the city they had founded. Colonel E.S. Topping entered history as "the father of Trail" and its first mayor, Frank and Jane Hanna as preeminent citizens of its earliest years. And, of course, the Colonel's *LeRoi* claim flourished too.

But human existence is never simple. Other forces were at work on their lives, forces that certain occurrences in their collective history suggest, but about which we—since this is not a novel—must only briefly speculate rather than develop fully. When Jane Hanna's big new house was finished and they had all moved into it, Jane at once began to charge not only the Colonel but also her husband for board and room. To us in our era, this seems a happy development—the woman participating as an equal in the business venture and receiving payment for her part in the undertaking. For all her hard work, Jane Hanna must have been happy at the new excitement of her life, must have enjoyed the sense of partnership in affairs bigger than the running of a home, no matter how well she did that. She must have been pleased that their relationship with the Colonel had led to this Trail flat venture. She must also have felt the stirrings of new ambitions and abilities, and perhaps thought them more in keeping with those of the Colonel than of her blacksmith husband. By this time, the Colonel had been an intimate in their home for over two years, and here he was now, living under the roof of their new house as if he were a member of the family, here where he sometimes showed so favourably in contrast with Frank. Photographs of the two men reveal them as opposite types: Frank Hanna handsome, stolid, unimaginative, a strong-armed uncomplicated blacksmith; the Colonel, handsome too in a lean and interesting way, tall, wiry, with black eyes and black hair, an ambitious, romantic type with tales to tell of an exciting past in the Indian wars, sure to appeal to women. It was proof of Frank's lack of imagination that he was unwise enough to allow such a resplendent cuckoo into the nest, and we don't have to suggest any weakness or lack of virtue in Jane (or the Colonel either, for that matter) when we admit that she must have found him attractive and he her. Thinking over the situation in moments of reflection, she probably became aware of an independence growing in herself, a resentment toward her husband for permitting the intrusion of this emotional ambiguity into their marriage, for so blatantly taking her for granted that he thought nothing of introducing another man into the household. We may, then, explain her motivation in equalizing the two men by making them both pay for board and room as a slight withdrawal from her husband into a secret place of her own rather than as an increased warmth for the Colonel.

Be all that as it may, not much more time passed before Frank and the Colonel broke off business relations and set up separate real estate offices. In autumn of the same year (1896) Frank ran a notice in the newspaper that he would not henceforth be responsible for debts incurred by his wife. A year later Jane went to court to obtain sole custody of the children. The Colonel continued to pay room and board in Jane's house. Frank, sometime between 1898 and 1906, left Trail forever and went to Texas. The year 1906 saw the end of Colonel Topping's fortunes. At the age of sixty-two he was in financial ruin. He and Jane were married, not in Trail, the city they had founded, but in Rossland. After the wedding Jane and "Toppins"—she had always called him that from the earliest days—left on the evening train for Revelstoke, en route to Victoria, where they lived until the Colonel's death in 1917. Frank had long since died in El Paso, Texas. After the Colonel's death, Jane moved to Ventura, California to live with her daughter Estella. She died there at the age of 74.

The story of Frank, Jane, and the Colonel is one of those that seem designed to touch our imaginations deeply—causing us to ponder on the strangeness of human existence, which out of contingency brings purpose for a fleeting moment, only to disperse its elements once again into chaos. Three Americans of widely different origins came together by chance in a foreign country, collaborated for a short time in events that not only raised them to prominence and gave their lives meaning but also brought an important town into existence, then rearranged themselves to pass the remainder of their lives obscurely in widely separated places. As the Roman poet Horace wrote in verse to his friend Bullatius, *Whatever prosperous hour Providence bestows upon you, receive it with a thankful hand.*

William Adolph Baillie-Grohman
among his trophies. KMAHS 623
(Kootenaiana collection)

Kootenay Indians in sturgeon-nosed canoe. KMAHS 85.61.2

Thomas Hammill

The Richard Fry family and other early residents of Bonners Ferry, Idaho. The photograph is thought to have been taken in 1887. Richard Fry is the bearded man smoking a pipe. In front of him is his wife Justine. Standing with her are four daughters and two small sons. To the left of Richard is Arthur Bunting, his son-in-law. The young woman in front of Arthur is his wife. The two men on the right of Richard are thought to be either stage drivers or packers. In the background is Richard and Justine Fry's trading post.

BONNERS FERRY CENTENNIAL 1964 BOOKLET

The Bluebell Mine in later years. KMAHS 69.4.20A

A. S. Farwell.
BCARS 28900

Gilbert Malcolm Sproat.
BCARS 4212

S. S. *Midge.* KMAHS 83.73.1 (Mabel E. Jordon collection)

Above right: Osner Hall at about 50. Above left: Winslow Hall in later years.
(Photographs courtesy Mrs. Pauline Battien, Colville, Wash)

Henry Anderson, 1843 - 1894.

C. W. Busk in later years.

Josephine Ward.
KMAHS 69.88.11

Robert Yuill, centre, in later life.
(Photo courtesy Boswell Ladies Club)

Jim Gilker and his partner Wells. KMAHS 88.41.31

John "Truth" Houston.
KMAHS 59.9.76

Catamaran *Dispatch.*
(John F. Hume collection)

Building the Canal from Kootenay River to the source of the Columbia (Columbia Lake). KMAHS 83.73.5 (Mabel E. Jordon collection)

Mary Jane Hanna, seated at right, and Eugene Sayne Topping, seated at left, with part of Mary Jane's family. TCA 1792

Nelson's first hotel. Owner John Ward is second from the right. The two ladies are the Misses Smith, Mollie on the left, Margie on the right; this photograph alone perpetuates their memory. J. Fred Hume is seated to the left of Mollie. Dr. Hendryx is standing in the doorway, leaning on the right-hand side. Outlined against the left frame of the left window, is Ed Atherton, manager of J. Fred's store. KMAHS 69.18.6

Frank Hanna, early 1890's.
TCA 1569

J. Fred Hume.
BCARS HP 5977

Nelson's fire hall and police station on the southeast corner of Josephine and Victoria Streets, late 1890's. The stone police station remains to this day. KMAHS 94.31.03 (L. Davis collection)

Above right: Newlin Hoover. In 1889 he pre-empted land to the southwest of Sproat's original survey. This later became a part of Nelson and was for many years called the Hoover Addition. KMAHS 69.18.6 Above left: Mrs. John Houston and her daughter. KMAHS 59.9.22

The Phair Hotel, regarded as one of B.C.'s best, on the southwest corner of Stanley and Victoria Streets. It later became the Strathcona, and after a sad decline in status burned to the ground in the 1950's with a loss of several lives. KMAHS 92.95.110 (W. Hall collection)

Above right: Monty Davys and his wife Lucy Bate. KMAHS 93.7.129 (E.L. Affleck collection) Above left: Picnic Group, c. 1901. Dr. E. C. Arthur is standing at the left with his hand on his hip. Dr. Isabel Arthur is seated on a log in front of her husband, holding their daughter Margaret. Isabel's sister Nellie Delmage is standing next to her brother-in-law. The presence of baby Margaret, who was born in 1899, allows us to date the picture fairly accurately. KMAHS 57.12.1

The Mountain Station of the Nelson and Fort Shepherd Railway.

EWSHS L84-423.19.1

Calm after the flood,
S. S. Nelson in
background.
KMAHS 68.36.4

Nelson's first mayor and council. KMAHS 63.1.2

Above right: Narcisse, Indian hunter, who said that his people had no memory of a flood anywhere near the size of the one of '94. KMAHS 68.31.9
Above left: George Owen Buchanan. BCARS HP 90363

Horse Race on Baker Street, July 1st (Dominion Day), 1898. The ornate brick building with the sign on its side is the Clement and Hillyer block, Nelson's first brick business block, erected in 1896. In 1904 it was remodelled by the Wood Vallance Hardware Company to the form it has today. The building in the foreground is the early-day Queens Hotel. Part of the space between it and the Clement and Hillyer is Josephine Street. KMAHS 57.1.36

Above right: Looking down on Nelson from the top of the *Silver King* tramway. BCARS 45901 Above left: H. E. Croasdaile. BCARS 23089

Charles Busk's house at Kokanee. KMAHS 93.7.132 (Photo courtesy Mrs. B. Gillespie)

Boarding house at *Silver King Mine.* The man at the extreme right looks very much like Winslow Hall. BCARS 5215

The Grove Hotel. (Photo courtesy Bob Emory)

# CHAPTER 24

*In which we observe, among other things, the activities of Charles Busk and Dr. Hendryx up on the main lake.*

IN SPITE OF JOHN HOUSTON'S concern over threats to the town's ongoing development, Nelson continued to grow. Or perhaps it was *because* of his concern, for *The Miner* was a leading force in arousing public opposition to threats as they appeared. Public clamour caused the government to rescind, or at least greatly modify, the CPR land reserve that threatened to strangle the town, but only—as John had foreseen—on the condition that that greedy company receive large amounts of land within the town limits. And Van Horne couldn't keep them all guessing forever; Nelson did become the railway's terminus rather than a mere siding. Once that was assured, land sales increased and property went up in price. People began petitioning for the surveying of more streets and improved wagon roads to the mines. Hotels became more numerous and busier than ever, more and more businesses opened—both regular ones and the irregular ones at the east end of Baker—and the streets were noisy with building. In 1891 telephone poles appeared along some thoroughfares as the Kootenay Lake Telephone Company began establishing forty-five miles of line connecting Nelson with the *Silver King*, Robson, Ainsworth and its mines, and Charles Busk's new settlement of Balfour. By '92 Nelson itself had forty "instruments," Ainsworth ten, and Balfour three.

Although Charles Busk had successfully realized his plans for the townsite of Balfour—he had named it after the British prime minister—the new community posed no threat to Nelson. Busk intended it to be the centre of a fruit-growing district and had no other ambitions for it; and now that Nelson had indeed become the railway terminus John Houston need worry no more. After his arrival at Nelson on the *Galena* in the summer of '88 Busk had, as we saw in Chapter 16, surveyed Harry Anderson's pre-emption. Then, after wintering in Victoria, he had hired himself out to Baillie-Grohman, surveying the flood plains at the south end of the lake that B-G had received from the government for his proposed reclamation scheme. Finally, on May 24th of '89, he had got down to the furtherance of his own dream—the creation of Balfour. On that date he filed a pre-emption claim for two hundred acres on the north shore of the west arm where it joins the main lake. By the fall of '90 he had completed the survey of his town and named its streets after his own family members— Charles, Gladys, Madeline, Robert—and friends. In the spring of '91 he erected a two-storey log building which he called the Balfour House Hotel—rooms upstairs and a general store on the ground floor. For himself to live in, he built a house surrounded by acres waiting to become an orchard. There for the moment we will leave him—this upper-middle-class Englishman with the strong urge to be a patriarch, but still at forty a bachelor and fated to be one always—alone in his new house, planning his orchard and arranging for the shipping-in of fruit trees.

We should not, however, leave Balfour without casting a glance at nearby communities—the old ones on the main lake which we have taken almost no notice of for the space of many chapters now. The mines of Ainsworth and Hendryx Camp were still in their ascendancy, producing and stockpiling large quantities of ore. For some time Dr. Hendryx had been toying with the idea of building a smelter on the spot to process all that ore and had begun thinking of possible sites—Hendryx Camp itself, and even the location Charles Busk had chosen for Balfour. On the eastern shore of the lake a few mines south of Hendryx Camp there was a sheltered spot that had acquired the name Pilot Bay. The

Sayward-Davies Lumber Co. of Victoria were already developing a logging reserve and mill on the site, and Joshua Davies persuaded the Dr. to locate his smelter there also. Meanwhile, in the late summer of '91, Eli Carpenter and Jack Seaton made their spectacular discovery at Payne Mountain in the Slocan. At once the hordes of prospectors hanging about the hotels and barrooms of Nelson and Ainsworth removed themselves to the mountains around Slocan Lake, leaving the settlements of Kootenay Lake temporarily bereft of their labour force. A new town developed at the mouth of Kaslo Creek, since it provided the principal access to the Slocan. This new mining rush may also have affected Dr. Hendryx by temporarily impairing his normally unflagging business acumen, for, perhaps thinking of all the ore that would be stockpiling from those new discoveries, he proceeded with undue haste in '92 to the building of his smelter and was checked—the first sign that the poetic Shadow referred to at the beginning of Chapter 12 was ever going to fall between his intentions and their realization—by lack of funds.

Meanwhile, over at the entrance to the west arm that same year, Charles Busk, tired of poor lot sales and far too busy with his other schemes to expend any effort to improve them, sold Balfour, keeping only the house surrounded by its acreage of would-be orchard for himself.

Downstream in Nelson, the slight recession that hit the mining economy of British Columbia in the early nineties was not having too bad an effect. The town was now large enough that its secondary industries kept money flowing. Especially favourable was the fact that Nelson was now the supplier of goods to a wide area of mining activity. Merchants were particularly happy about the opening up of the new Slocan region, and most of them were financing the building of a trail from the Columbia & Kootenay Railway line up the Slocan River to Slocan Lake. (That trail would be replaced by a spur line of the railway before the decade was over.)

But merchants wanted more than just an increased market for their goods. In contrast to the miners, who were an itinerant lot, coming and going as the contingencies of their trade demanded, they wanted their town to take on a look and a feeling of permanency; they wanted churches and schools for their families, better communication with the outside world, improved transportation facilities so they could import more of the amenities that graced the settled towns they had originally come from. This entrepreneurial class, many of them Americans, pushed the town in the direction they wanted, providing committee members and town planners. These were the friends of John Houston. It is astonishing how quickly they urbanized rough-and-ready Nelson, transforming the frontier town into a respectable community filled with civic pride. They were aided by the professional men—architects, for example,—who were coming into town, and by another group, a more aloof class, with strong ties to England—such men as Busk and Croasdaile, the man in charge up at the Hall Mines. By 1891 the process of urbanization had already begun, but the frontier still dominated.

# CHAPTER 25

*Which tells how formal education came to the town.*

YOUNG DR. ARTHUR *did* move into town as John Houston had hoped. In January of '91 he opened for business in a building on the southeast corner of Stanley and Baker Streets, and as soon as spring break-up permitted began building the house we saw in Chapter 21. By May the young couple—Isabel had come out from Ontario to join him—were living in it.

There were now a few children in town of school age, and Dr. Arthur, who had been a teacher in Ontario before going to medical college, was interested in seeing a classroom started. After all, as a young man anticipating a family he would soon have a personal interest in education. For a school two things were needed— a room and a teacher. The room was no problem: there was at least one spare room in his own house, not yet finished and rather bare, of course, but that was nothing to worry about. As for the teacher . . . Dr. Arthur knew where there was one already at work. Among the new arrivals in town was a young Presbyterian missionary student—the Rev. Mr. Thomas H. Rogers, B.A.—whose mission in Nelson was to establish a congregation and then build a church. Noticing soon after his arrival that there were school-age children in town, energetic Mr. Rogers had organized them into a class, using as a schoolroom first the lobby of the International Hotel, then, when the hotel proved too distracting, an upstairs room in R.E. Lemon's store. He accepted eagerly Dr. Arthur's offer of a room in his home. And so it was that on the morning of May 25th, 1891, about a dozen fresh-eyed children of various ages—scrubbed and cleanly dressed for the occasion—found their way up the path to Dr. Arthur's unfinished new residence (where the big brick YMCA building stands today) and were met at the door by the Rev. Mr. Rogers. In the schoolroom they found several long boards (taken from a pile of lumber stored against one wall) to serve them as benches, on which, duly seated, they received instruction from their teacher, who was standing (he had no chair) near a packing case (which was his desk). Behind him, tacked to the rough bare wall, was an old window-blind (which was his blackboard). He had real chalk, ordered specially by R.E. Lemon.

As we can well imagine, this event was the cause of much rejoicing among  the parents of the town (and, we venture to suspect, even among the children of those more innocent times, who would have been well prepared for the occasion with cajolery, and would undoubtedly have absorbed the belief of their parents that their freedom was being given up for a good cause). As the class continued throughout the late spring and early summer, we can be sure that the need for increased formal education was a high priority subject for conversation among townfolk of the respectable kind. By midsummer a petition had been forwarded to the government asking that a school be built. The government answered with a promise to pay the salary of a teacher if the town put up a building. This exchange, of course, must have taken weeks or months, but even before its conclusion was reached a group of men had taken matters into their own hands.

A number of carpenters were busy that spring putting up warehouses and other buildings down on the CPR flats. One rainy morning they didn't feel like working and sat around on the job wondering what to do instead. They were mostly family men, and there they were, lunchbuckets and all, on the job but not feeling like working.

"Well, I can't go home, for sure," said one of them. "The wife's been naggin' me to move the outhouse."

"That'd be one helluva job in the rain," observed someone else.

"Let's build something," suggested a fellow called Archie Fletcher.

"Yeah, let's do that. Why'n't we start buildin' that schoolroom Doc Arthur and that Presbyterian minister fellow want? We could . . ."

"Yeah, good idea! Let's do that. I got a kid needs to go t' school in a year or two. We need to do some . . ."

"Yeah, wouldn't hurt us ta do somethin' good fer the town. If Doc Arthur can give a room in his house . . ."

"An' that preacher can teach school fer nothin' . . ."

"Well, let's go. We can spend the day choosin' a place to build, an' clear the road to it, an' gather lumber."

"Yeah, an' that way we can dodge rain showers an' work in between."

And that's what they did. They chose a vacant spot on Baker Street, down at the unpopulated end, just west of the southwest corner of Baker and Kootenay in today's terms—not that they were exactly sure where Baker Street, Kootenay Street, and the lot *were* down at that end of town. And, since there was no clearing yet for Kootenay Street, they cut brush from Baker Street (itself nothing more than a cleared area then, as the photograph in Chapter 21 shows) as far as where the alley might be some day, and then prepared the ground where the school would be built. Meanwhile, some of the gang scouted for lumber and foundation timbers (we can be sure they asked for donations in the name of a good purpose), and formed a tentative plan in their heads for the building. And when the day was over they had everything ready for a start, and, even better, had built up their own enthusiasm to a degree that would not only keep themselves on the job in their spare time until it was finished but also attract other volunteer labour to the scene. And very soon, a matter of days, really, the simple frame structure was ready for use. The Rev. Mr. Rogers immediately began employing it as a church on Sundays. When Mr. Turner, a Methodist, came to town the two men used it on alternate Sundays. And when the government's answer to the petition finally came, the building was there already built and waiting for use. The classroom in the Arthur home having served its brief purpose in the spring, school resumed after the summer break in the new quarters, where it did not interfere with the building's use as a church on Sundays. The government kept its promise and paid the salary of a proper teacher. She was Miss Jennie Rath, who, when she opened school on the morning of October 1st, 1891, took her place in history as Nelson's first bonafide teacher. Our thanks to the Rev. Mr. Thomas Rogers for acting in the interim. Incidentally, the good Reverend soon got his church, and only a few steps away from the school, on the southwest corner of Kootenay and Victoria Streets. The Presbyterian Church was constructed in 1892. It is still there today.

As for the little schoolhouse built by Archie Fletcher and his friends, it survived for many years. In 1899 the Bank of Montreal building was erected in front of it. During the Boer War it was used as a recruiting station. On the vacant land between it and the Presbyterian Church would-be recruits had to mount and put their steeds through a series of maneuvers to prove their eligibility for enlistment in Her Majesty's Strathcona Horse. When the present-day CIL building was erected in 1905, the schoolhouse had to be moved to the rear of the lot. There, for several decades, it functioned as a storehouse for the fusing used in conjunction with explosives. Finally, on April 23rd 1937, the *Nelson Daily News* announced that CIL planned to tear it down and erect a new warehouse in its place.

On the day they were framing up the walls, either Archie Fletcher or one of the other carpenters left between the boards some newspapers and a small picture of Queen Victoria, one of those cards which at that time were collected from cigarette and candy packages, much as pictures of sports heroes were in a later era—left them there, no doubt, in the hope that some unknown person in the distant future might have the pleasure of discovering them. Someone did have that pleasure of discovery, and so did all the readers of the *Nelson Daily News* of May 3rd, 1937, for the Queen's picture was included in the sentimental farewell to the building printed in the issue of that date.

# FIRST SCHOOL IN NELSON IS DEMOLISHED

### Concrete Building to Rise on Site of Old Building

H.M. Queen Victoria

Victim of the years, a building probably containing more Nelson history within its four walls than any other, has been ripped asunder to make way for a new building. The frame structure, Nelson's first school and church, is no more. In its place and on the site where it is pictured here will rise a new storehouse—the capacity in which the old school has served for latter years—built of modern concrete.

This was the building the construction of which Archie Fletcher, who died last year, liked to tell about. Jim Gilker, peer of Nelson old timers, and Mrs. Gilker, remember the building of it in 1891. R. G. Joy, storehouse of early-day information about Nelson, has considerable data about it in his collection of earliana.

Jim McCandlish remembers that years after it had ceased to be a school, it was used as a recruiting station for the Strathcona Horse during the Boer war, and that would-be recruits had to show they knew how to ride a horse on the vacant lots to the rear.

Archie Fletcher's story of the building of it was that a gang of men—of whom he was one—were engaged in putting up warehouses and other buildings on the C.P.R. flats. On a certain rainy day they didn't want to go to work; and didn't. As they sat about talking, waiting for the weather to clear, someone suggested: "Let's build a school."

The suggestion was all that was required. They opened up a road to the site they chose, obtained lumber and went to work. Shortly after Nelson had a school.

Jim Gilker wasn't sure how the building came to be erected, but he did recall that Rev. Mr. Rogers, a student minister of Presbyterian persuasion then resident in Nelson undertook the first teaching duties. On Sundays he used it for a church; and when Rev. Mr. Turner, a Methodist, came to Nelson they used it alternately. Mr. Rogers was followed by Rev. Mr. Black. Miss Rath —afterward Mrs. John Hamilton—a sister of the Miss Rath who some years later was well known as a primary teacher at Central school, was the first appointed teacher. She was followed by Miss Thom, a sister of Dr. J. B. Thom of Trail.

As to early-day pupils who attended it, Jim Gilker recalls Billy McMorris and Bob McLeod.

When workmen were tearing down the building they found in the walls the picture above of Queen Victoria . . . a small card of the type years ago popular in cigarette and candy packages . . . they found too a number of old newspapers.

# LINK WITH PAST IN NELSON IS GONE

Nelsons first school and church . . . torn down now

Above: Excerpt from the *Nelson Daily News* of May 3rd, 1937 including a picture of the first school and church, and a picture of Queen Victoria found in the school. *Nelson Daily News* Below: The Nelson Presbyterian Church in early days. (200 block, Victoria Street) KMAHS 69.19.46

PRESBYTERIAN CHURCH, NELSON, B.C.

# CHAPTER 26

*Containing a miscellany of happenings and develop-*
*ments concerned with the town's continuing growth.*

THE NEW SCHOOL BUILDING wasn't needed for more than one year. In 1892 the government, having decided that Nelson was now ready for a proper school, let a contract for the erection of a two-room building on Stanley Street, the very place on which its successor stands today. Back in '91 a man called F.H. Latimer had surveyed lots on a whole new section of streets, and in doing so left clear a complete block on Stanley between Carbonate and Mill Streets for the time when a school would be required. Now, with that school about to be built, it was discovered that when the government had ceded many town lots to the CPR in return for the relaxing of the encompassing land freeze, half this block had gone to them. A telegram from provisional school trustees Dr. E.C. Arthur and Owen Buchanan to Minister of Education Colonel Baker of Cranbrook—Nelson's Baker Street is named after him—saved the day. The land was returned and the school was built. And now, leaving the school to its inevitable course of development—enlargement from time to time over the years to meet the needs of a growing population and finally replacement by the building that is there today—we will move our attention to other things.

In 1892 three banks came to Nelson. The first was the Bank of Montreal. Late in the autumn of '91, Mr. A.H. Buchanan, an accountant of that bank in its Vancouver branch, heard he had been chosen to open a branch office in the new town on Kootenay Lake, and was instructed to prepare himself for imminent departure. He set out for his new posting in early December. Because there were serious problems regarding winter travel on the Canadian route— the Columbia, for example, often froze so that *Lytton* and the other steamers couldn't get through, and the new CPR line from Sproat's Landing to Nelson did not even attempt operating in winter— Arthur Buchanan was sent on the American route via Spokane. The American public transportation facilities did their job well, but, somewhere near journey's end, Buchanan learned that more than the Columbia River froze over in winter. There was no steamer traffic running on the Kootenay River from Bonners Ferry to Kootenay Landing either. Unfazed, Mr. Buchanan summoned forth whatever pioneering spirit he had deep within himself and spent the last four days of his travels trekking from Northport to Nelson on snowshoes. He arrived there exulting, we hope, over his adventure and carrying $11.50 as operating capital for his new bank. It opened on January 2nd in the general store of J. Fred Hume, who, we feel sure, used his business abilities to assist the new manager in creating for the public an illusion that his bank had more money in the back room than was the reality. The branch prospered and in a couple of years the head office built new quarters for it on the northwest corner of Baker and Stanley. Finally— in 1899, as we have already noted—it put up the distinguished building on the southwest corner of Baker and Kootenay in which it remains to the present day.

> The contract for the erection of a residence for A. H. Buchanan on lots 9, 10, 11 and 12, block 35 southwest corner of Hendryx and Carbonate streets, has been awarded to George McFarland, and the work of excavating for the foundation was commenced this morning. The building will be 38 x 40 feet, three stories with basement, and will cost about $5000.
>
> News report from *The Tribune*, March 16, 1899

That same year, Arthur Buchanan had a very imposing house designed for himself by a local architect. A year later this residence was bought by the bank for the permanent use of its managers. It is still there today—810 Hendryx Street—but has not been owned by the bank since 1949.

The two other banks that came to town in '92 were the Bank of British Columbia, which opened in March, and a private one, opened a little later that year by Gessner Allen and his new real-estate partner Edward Applewhaite.

Water was becoming an urgent need of the town. Not water *per se*—there was plenty of that, of course—but a system of works that would bring it conveniently to the hotels, businesses, and homes that were being erected at an accelerating pace. Since Nelson was not an incorporated city, the government had to be petitioned for everything, and, of course, the impetus for petitioning and getting things done came from the go-getter type of person, willing to expend time and energy for the common cause without remuneration (except in the form of increased business opportunities). Among the go-getters of early Nelson, John Houston was pre-eminent. In the spring of '92 he and another man from the town, accompanied by one F.S. Barnard—Kootenay country was included in the Cariboo-Yale riding, and Mr. Barnard was the elected representative of that area—went to Victoria to lobby for waterworks and an electric light system. On April 23rd the Provincial Legislature passed a statute incorporating the Nelson Electric Light Company and naming as Provisional Directors of the said Company Mr. Barnard and eight men from Nelson: John Houston, Charles Ink, J.A. Gilker, J. Fred Hume (all of whom we already know), and John McLeod, John Johnson, Thomas Madden, and W.A. Crane (businessmen and hotel-keepers).

Also incorporated that day was the Consumers' Waterworks Company. The list of its petitioners included most of the names of the Directors of the Nelson Electric Light Company but—notably—not that of John Houston.

The Provisional Directors of the Nelson Electric Light Co. had their first meeting within ten days of the company's incorporation—May 2nd, to be exact. They wanted no time wasted in getting started: their charter stated that the lighting system was to be in operation by April 26th, 1893—less than one year from this meeting! The power source was to be a hydro-electric plant, rather a daring venture since there was no such plant in British Columbia yet and, furthermore, the very first one in Canada had been turned on in Pembroke, Ontario only eight years before. Indeed, the first electric power plant in the whole world had become operative a mere decade ago when the Pearl Street Station (steam-driven) in New York was turned on in September of '82—the very month that our old friend B-G, after his successful summer pursuing *haploceri montani* in the company of Darby & Joan, was hurrying southward from Kootenay Lake to inform the outer world about his audacious land reclamation scheme.

So, while the Consumers' Waterworks Company was having trenches dug in which to lay the first underground water pipes in the town and planning the construction of its dams on the east fork of Cottonwood Creek and on the upper reaches of Ward, the nine Provisional Directors of the Nelson Electric Light Company—somewhat dismayed, we can be sure, at the enormity of the task ahead of them—were deploying their energies for the hiring of engineers and the planning of dams, flumes, power lines, and all the other paraphernalia related to the production and distribution of electrical energy. They decided on the site of their plant, placing it just below the falls which—at that time and up until the 1950s—marked the final descent of the creek onto the CPR flats, and when that was under construction turned their attention to the dam which was to be placed a few hundred yards above the falls. When that dam was built or partly built, it was made apparent to the company that they could proceed no farther. A large tract of land along the western bank of Cottonwood was owned by Gilbert Malcolm Sproat and he, for reasons that are now obscure, refused to let the company build a flume over it. It is not to the purpose of this history to become enmeshed in the heated controversy which followed Sproat's interdiction. It was a complicated imbroglio and dominated the local news for months. Finding out why the "father of Nelson" would not allow the Nelson Electric Light Company to cross his property with a flume—or whether he really ever *did* refuse them access; he later denied having done so—is extraneous to our aim. Let another historian concentrate his or her powers on unravelling the many threads that form that tangle and then present us with an illuminating monograph on the subject. It is enough for us now to know that, whatever its cause, the delay in building the flume marked the beginning of a period of company inactivity that kept the town from receiving electric light well beyond the April 23/'93 deadline. In fact, not until the 1st day of February, 1896 did the lights finally go on. (Meanwhile, in '84, electric lighting of a sort was introduced to a small part of the town—R.E. Lemon's store was the first edifice lighted—but it was probably produced by a generator hooked up to one of the sawmills.)

Malcolm Sproat's real or supposed interdiction occurred in the early spring of '92; in May of the same year, John Houston sold *The Miner* and went off to Spokane. The sources, either primary or secondary, tell us nothing of this voluntary absence, which is a surprising one, since John must have been enjoying his editorial battle with Gilbert Malcolm Sproat.

Remembering his earlier thoughts about it being time to take a wife, we might surmise that, tucked away among his busy days, he had found an hour to write a proposal of marriage to a woman he had known years ago in Ontario, and had, in a second letter written after receiving her acceptance, arranged to meet her in Spokane. That seems a plausible explanation of his surprising absence from town at a crucial time, because when he returned in the autumn he did indeed have with him a bride, the former Edith May Keeley from York County, Ontario, a place very near his home. Beyond name and birthplace we have little knowledge of her. By November of '92 the newlyweds were living in their own house on the southeast corner of Hall and Carbonate Streets.

Most people would probably have done all they could to keep an opposition newspaper from coming to town, but not John Houston. He turned his own newspaper, *The Miner*, into the opposition by selling it to someone else, and then at once laid plans to start another of his own. Perhaps his aggressive nature relished the conflict that was bound to ensue between the two, perhaps—now that he was free of partners—he felt supremely confident that he could easily dominate his rival. Whatever the case, he was ready for printing his new paper by mid-November. On November 12th *The Miner*, now under new editorship, published a short notice saying that the "plant" for *The Tribune* had arrived.

*The Tribune*. By using this name for his new paper John proclaimed his bias openly and unashamedly, just as he had always done in the names he gave his newspapers. In Donald it had been *The Truth*. There was nothing equivocal or retiring about that name. It announced aggressively: No cover-up here! In these pages, reader, you learn the facts as John Houston sees them, no matter who gets insulted or angry. And he had kept to his word, building his reputation as a newspaperman on fearless statements of the truth—as he saw it—so much so that the name of his paper had become attached to his person. As John "Truth" Houston, he had gone to New Westminster and finally to Nelson. The name *Nelson Daily Miner* too had clearly announced whose side he was on. And he had justified it that very first year, attacking big capitalist companies like the CPR and capitalist speculators like Baillie-Grohman. And now *The Tribune*. Anyone with a smattering of education knew that in ancient Rome tribunes had been magistrates chosen by the plebeians to protect themselves against patrician oppression. For "plebeian" read "worker" and for "patrician" read "capitalist." That would make it clear where the editor of *The Tribune* stood.

In the second number of his new paper, dated December 1st, 1992, John printed a long news item about the *Silver King*, copied from the *Spokane Review*, saying that Winslow Hall and John McDonald had gone to Scotland to sell the *Silver King* to a "Scotch Syndicate" for two million dollars. No confirmation of this news had yet reached Nelson, but the townsfolk were "on the tip-toe of expectancy" that the sale would go through and usher in "a long lease of prosperity for the town and Toad Mountain district."

# CHAPTER 27

*Which contains mainly the stories of Bogustown and
the phenomenal growth of Kaslo, but also, among other
discussions and divertissements, a description of Nelson's first Courthouse and the first hint of the town's
incorporation as a city.*

LONDON, ROME, Constantinople, Venice, Peking—all
such great and ancient cities must have begun as a few huts erected
by a handful of pioneers. And they also, before they became
ornamented, aggrandized, and so storied with the accretions of
history that to us they seem eternal, must have passed through
dangerous periods in their infancy when some unfortunate turn
of events in the outside world could have nipped them in the bud.
In 1893 Nelson, too, though not destined for such grandeur as
they, was at that vulnerable stage. As a mining town it was particularly affected by frequent changes in the prices of metals, and
potentially disastrous economic declines inevitably occurred. But
the town reacted to slumps by experiencing only a mild slowing
in its growth rate. The *Silver King* was one of the few mines in the
area that produced ore of a high enough grade that it could afford
to ship to American smelters in spite of the high tariff—thirty
dollars per ton on lead ores—imposed by the United States government. And when, in '93, that government repealed the Sher-
man Purchase Act (which it had introduced in 1890 to increase its
silver purchases), thereby causing silver prices to slump considerably, the Slocan mining communities were much affected, while
Nelson—as the district supply centre—easily weathered the

storm. Waiting for better times (which came soon enough), the town never ceased in its forward movement, perhaps, during the most difficult periods anyway, owing solely to that mysterious impetus which often seizes hold of people engaged in a common endeavour and makes them keep going doggedly no matter what the odds.

In '93 the CPR brought the telegraph to Nelson, and during the same year at least two new businesses, both much-needed, arrived in town: a sheet metal and plumbing establishment, and the Lawrence Hardware Co., which in a few prosperous years would build for itself one of Baker Street's most imposing structures. A new architect, W. George Taylor, arrived in town that year, too, and was immediately commissioned to design a firehall and a hospital. There had been a firefighting company, the Deluge Hook & Ladder Co., since the winter of '91-'92, after a big fire had scared everybody the summer before. It was now reorganized with Dr. Arthur as president and J. Fred Hume as treasurer, and at last Nelson had a firehall complete with all the necessary equipment, situated against the hillside on the southeast corner of Victoria and Josephine Streets and paid for by public subscription as well as government funds. Firehalls being places where men like to gather, this new one became a kind of pre-incorporation council chamber where, amid clouds of cigar and pipe smoke, the community's future could be planned.

The new hospital had been another pressing need, not so much for the townfolk—sick people stayed in their homes and were visited by the doctor there, and so did women about to give birth—as for the large population of miners, who were frequently injured on the job. However, since the hospital was really for everyone, its directors called upon all citizens to subscribe one dollar per year, and the cost of building was paid for by public subscription. Some of the names on the committee which worked toward the building of the Kootenay Lake General Hospital are familiar to us: Bob Yuill, Drs. Arthur and LaBau, J. Fred Hume, and R.E. Lemon. Completed in August, the hospital was a frame building big enough for ten or twelve beds, and was placed on the eastern edge of town, just at the base of the cliffs marking the end of the mountain spur that neatly divided Nelson from Harry Anderson's pre-emption. Readers who wish to see where the hospital was placed may look at the picture on page 221.

Harry Anderson's land (which, we recall, had been surveyed by Charles Busk when it was still called "Salisbury" back in Chapter 16) no longer belonged to Harry. He had sold it, probably in '89, to one Joshua Davies, an auctioneer in Victoria. (He was the same Davies who later opened the sawmill at Pilot Bay with his partner Sayward, as we noted a few chapters ago.) As soon as he acquired Anderson's land, Joshua began issuing handbills in Victoria advertising lots for sale. Realizing that the name "Salisbury" would confuse prospective buyers in Victoria, he simply stated that the lots were in Nelson. When real Nelsonites, who knew that the boundaries of their town did not encompass "Salisbury" at all, and, moreover, were suspicious that Harry Anderson had always wanted to usurp their position as the real town, got wind of this, they were both amused and outraged. Then, when Charles Busk designed a wharf for Davies & Co. up at Anderson's Point (now Lakeside Park) and the men from Nelson who constructed it had to wait several months for their pay, amusement waned while outrage increased. (The wharf, incidentally, was not a success. Its poor design made boat captains unwilling to use it.) One day E.R. Atherton, manager of Hume's store, made reference to the area as "Bogustown." The name entered Nelson's language, and as Bogustown Harry Anderson's pre-emption had to wait three decades until, in 1921, Nelson finally legitimized its early claim by annexing it under the more respectable name "Fairview."

In the 8th number of *The Tribune*, dated January 12th, 1893, John Houston made a comparison of the growth rates of the mining camps of South Kootenay by listing the buildings erected in all the towns along with the amounts of money spent on each between April 1st, 1892 and January 1st, 1893. The results were: Kaslo, first place; Nelson, second; Pilot Bay, third; Ainsworth, fourth; New Denver, fifth; and Nakusp, sixth.

On April 1st, 1892, Kaslo, born only a few months before as a jumping-off place to the Slocan, had one "finished" house and two or three others under construction—total cost $2,000. Less than a year later, on the final date of John's time-period, fifty-one buildings had been erected at a total cost of $100,300. Kaslo-ites of that year certainly had every right to expect that their camp would usurp Nelson's premier position on the lake.

For Nelson, John enumerated the new buildings street by street. Front: one building. Lake: two, including a bottling works. Vernon: eight, including a two-storey store and a warehouse built by J. Fred Hume. Baker: ten, including both businesses and residences. Victoria: nine, including the Presbyterian Church and two dwellings valued at $1,000 each built by J. Fred Hume. Silica: nine, including the English Church, valued at $1,000, and three dwellings, the cheapest on the list, built by "unknown" for a total cost of $1,500. Carbonate: two, including the new public school (on the corner of Carbonate and Stanley) value $3,000. Mill: one. Ward: one, the residence of J. Fred Hume (on the southwest corner of Ward and Hoover) value $5,000. Miscellaneous: Electric Light Co. works $6,000, a dry-house for the Nelson Sawmill Co., the government wharf $4,000.

There were, then, slightly under 50 buildings and other structures erected in Nelson during the specified time period, at a total cost of $94,150. For Nelsonites Kaslo's growth was an alarming phenomenon and something to be concerned about.

The Nelson list suggests strongly that J. Fred Hume was seeing his own future as tied to that of Nelson: besides building his new store, he was speculating in houses and putting up a very expensive home for himself. And, indeed, his future *was* strongly tied to Nelson's. He was one of the early go-getters of the town. We already know that in partnership with Bob Lemon, he established one of the earliest local businesses; the present-day Hume School bears his name; and still today some members of the town's older generations will occasionally say "meet me at the Hume for lunch," by which, remembering it is really the hotel J. Fred built a century ago, they mean the Heritage Inn.

As the list shows us, the only structure to cost more than J.

Fred's new home is the Electric Light Company's works. Most residences cost about $1,000. The only other private home to approach the cost of Hume's is one built on Baker Street that year, and it cost a mere $2,000. (It belongs to one Frank Fletcher, a man we will hear more of later.)

Some of the $5,000 spent on Hume's new residence is attributable to the hot-and-cold running-water system that has been installed. It is as yet the only one in Nelson. In building this new home J. Fred has wanted to please his bride of a little more than a year. Only in '91 did he finally make the decision to leave his various business ventures in Revelstoke and relocate permanently in Nelson, where he was already spending about half his time anyway. Accordingly, in the early summer of that year his bride-to-be, Lydia Irvine, left Revelstoke by boat and boarded the new CPR train at Robson. There is a story—disputed by some—that she was one of the two very first passengers on the run, and rode on an open flatcar. Be that as it may, she arrived in Nelson in ample time to prepare for her marriage to J. Fred on Wednesday, July 8, 1891. The newlyweds set up housekeeping in a small house, a "cottage," high up on the east end of Victoria Street, where the street was not yet a street at all, but a footpath—called by Lydia "Bluff Street"—finding its rough way among outcroppings of granite. One day Lydia complained to Fred about being so far from town, with only a footpath, and that uphill, all the way back home. J. Fred answered laughingly, "Yes, but look at the view you get!" then added soothingly, "Not to worry. We'll build a house farther in."

Within a month or two the new house was under construction—the $5,000-house, as reported by John Houston. "Farther in" it may have been in J. Fred's estimation, but on the corner of Ward and Hoover it was actually higher up and farther away from Baker Street than the "Bluff Street" one had been. However, Ward Street was much more than a footpath at that point and much easier to walk up. Furthermore, the house was much grander and had, as we have already noted, hot and cold running water (no doubt because the upper reaches of Ward Creek were not too far away). And the view was even better than the other one.

Though outwardly much changed, the house J. Fred Hume built for his bride is there still, looking down the hill from the southwest corner of Ward and Hoover Streets. It is surrounded by other large houses, some of which are almost as old, attesting that the area in which it was built has since earliest times been an enclave of fashionable residences.

All throughout colonial days Britain made sure that law enforcement agencies arrived early on the scene of any new development. We have already observed—in Chapter 12—how, when the trouble between Hammill and Sproule came to a head in '85, the Law in the person of Harry Anderson was there beforehand, ready to take charge. The same careful government that had sent Harry to Big Ledge in '85 now decided in '93 that the growing mining camp of Nelson needed a courthouse in which itinerant judges could try cases and lay down the law, not only for the town itself, but the whole of West Kootenay country as well. Accordingly, early in the year, construction began on Ward Street just below the northwest corner of Ward and Vernon, about where, in today's terms, steps lead off the street onto the concrete walkway to the "new" Provincial Government Building.

The Courthouse BCARS HP 5203

Apparently the gully of Ward Creek in this particular region fell away in a series of uneven steps, and the new building could not be erected directly at the corner because just at that point there was a deep depression (in which the present-day stone courthouse designed by Rattenbury was built at a later date).

The firm that won the contract had an interesting challenge in building the new courthouse: considering its purpose as the seat of law adminstration, it had to be as dignified and imposing as possible, but it also had to be a simple frame structure made entirely of wood. The building's designer met his challenge admirably. Dignity he obtained, as the picture clearly shows, by the unrelenting use of bilateral symmetry, absolute down to the finest detail. Not even the chimneys—which a less fastidious architect might, forgivably, have been more careless about—have escaped their part in the design. Judging by the aggressiveness of their role in the overall effect, we could easily believe that the designer left instructions to the building's caretakers never to light one fire without lighting the other one too.[31] Be that as it may, we observe that the shape of the building also contributes to its dignity. To offset the lightness of its construction material, its lovely proportions give it a squatness, a satisfying heaviness. But, mindful that his building must also project the Law's full grandeur, the clever architect has ordained that the peak of the projecting entrance-facade shall move the beholder's eye upward to the centre of the tower, whose own peak then pulls that aspiring eye even farther aloft to the top of the flagpole, placed there, of course, for the express purpose of receiving it. And that brings us once again to those chimneys: if we take a ruler and draw lines—but we go too far; this is not a digest of structural aesthetics. Suffice it to say that the new courthouse of 1893 was a tiny architectural jewel, the cold grandeur of whose design was charmingly mitigated by the fussy fretwork and lattice with which its creators so successfully adorned it. It reminds us of the great queen under whose reign it was constructed—a dumpy little old-fashioned lady—Victorian, in fact—who was somehow able to project unerringly the power she embodied.

In seven years' time the building, with its courtroom, jury room, Judge's chamber, prisoners' room, registry, and Gold Commissioner's Office, was considered inadequate, so quickly had the town and district grown. In 1906 work began on the great stone Rattenbury courthouse which is still in service today. For three years both courthouses, the old and the new, stood side by side. Then, when the new one was completed in 1909, the old one was sold to the city and moved down the street and around the curve to the northeast corner of Ward and Front. There, for many decades it served as City Hall. Finally, in the mid-1950s, it was pulled down. We are thankful that someone took this picture of it soon after its construction.

Kaslo, like it or not, couldn't be ignored. Its rapid growth and the aggressiveness of some of its merchants posed a real threat in the minds of Nelson's most zealous promoters, among them John Houston. Early in '93 those aggressive Kaslo merchants had organized a Board of Trade, sent off an application for an official charter, and then held a public meeting. There, one Randall H. Kemp, acting as secretary of the still unchartered Board, made a speech in which he talked of getting ahead in the race for commercial supremacy, a phrase which did not pass over the head of John Houston. John was sufficiently alarmed to report the meeting in *The Tribune* of February 9th, 1893 in a tone of sarcasm bordering on contempt. Already he and his associates, including Dr. Arthur, had been discussing the idea of Nelson's incorporation as a city and had, in fact, organized a planning meeting in Nelson's new first-class hotel, the Phair, to be held the following Saturday night. Now, with Kaslo acting up this way, the need for incorporation seemed more urgent than ever. On the same page—page 1—that carried the report of Randall's speech, John printed an editorial headlined "INCORPORATE!" THE WATCHWORD, arguing for incorporation, urging attendance at the meeting, and ending with the stirring words:  The day Nelson is incorporated, that day will she stand erect and say to her rivals: "Behold the queenliest city in all Kootenay."

In the same issue, John printed yet another article on the subject. Headlined "The Incorporation of Nelson," it explained what must be done to bring about incorporation: a petition must be signed by the owners of more than one-half the value of the real property included within the limits of the area being petitioned for and must state the number of male inhabitants in that area who were fully twenty-one years old and resident for six months. Later issues held articles urging property holders to register their ownership in the Land Registry Office in Victoria, since the records there were the ones used by the government to make their assessment.

John was on the committee to canvass property owners for their signatures. We can well imagine the enthusiasm with which he entered the fray. For all their efforts the members of the committee obtained only one-third of the required signatures. It became known that the failure of both the Nelson Electric Light Company and the Consumers' Water Works was behind the rejection of incorporation. Both those companies were still struggling along, the first with no results at all, and the latter with very unsatisfactory ones. Voters believed that, if incorporation came about, the city—which meant the local taxpayers—would have to face the problem rather than leaving it to the provincial government. Many people held John Houston responsible for the failure of both companies, although, as we know, he had not been a member of the Water Works board of directors. Much controversy developed, including a sniping match between *The Tribune* and *The Miner*. As winter deepened and the end of '93 approached, the three big problems that were dividing the community remained unsolved— the waterworks, electrical power, and incorporation; slightly bothersome in the background—for those who thought about it— was the threat posed by Kaslo, beautiful Kaslo of the eternal peaks, nestled among the trees at the mouth of the creek leading to the rich Slocan.

Meanwhile, as if to give these trouble-making human beings something beyond themselves to think about, Nature was planning an event of her own—one of her regular cosmic events, but a little bigger than usual. People living up at the *Silver King* and the other Toad Mountain mines began to remark that an awful lot of snow was falling this year, and that pathways from cabin to cabin and cookhouse to woodshed were getting harder and harder to clear, each shovel-load having to be thrown higher and higher as the winter wore on. By mid-January the paths were narrow corridors between fifteen-foot walls. In some places tunnels took the place of paths. Still the snow fell—twenty-three feet of it all together—and the icicles hanging from the eaves became sheets of frozen water. And not only on Toad Mountain, but on all the great peaks around the main lake it fell, and over in the Rockies at the source of the Kootenay River, too.

# CHAPTER 28

*In which we put aside for the space of one chapter all those events with which the town's men have been busying themselves in the making of what we usually call history, and turn instead to Isabel Arthur—Belle to her friends—as she muses, on a summer's day in '93, about her recent poor health.*

THE MORNING was a hot one. Through the open window Isabel could hear one of the second-floor maids across Stanley at the Phair Hotel beating a rug against the outside wall. It was nearly lunch time, but Edward had said he wouldn't be home today. Some meeting or other down at the Madden House. She wouldn't bother making anything for herself, better to wait for tea-time at Lydia Hume's. There'd be lots to eat; it was Lydia's at-home day. Meanwhile, she felt a little better now, having just finished the letter to Nellie . . . Oh, how she was missing them all, her sisters, especially Nellie, the one who had always been her confidant. The seven of them had always been so close, even the younger ones, and after papa had died—thirteen years ago; my heaven, how time passed!—they had been a little world of their own out on the farm. . . . All that was so far away now. . . . How long would it take for her letter to cross the prairies to Ontario? . . . and they would have to drive in to St. Marys to get it at the post office . . . and then they'd have to discuss it, her mother unwilling to let Nellie go and yet wanting someone to be with Belle. Isabel placed her elbows on the table and cupped her hands together on her chin, supporting her head. She had asked Nellie to come out west, for an extended visit or even to take a job, now that there was a school here—thanks mainly to the efforts of Edward. . . . But would Nellie think it a good idea? . . . She hadn't, of course, told them she was sick, only *home*sick a little . . . Maybe most of her sickness *was* homesickness . . . she had certainly thought so at first, but it was more than that, much more . . . and it was time she faced it squarely. . . . Marriage just hadn't satisfied her, hadn't made her forget her old dream. *Their* old dream, for, after all, it was all of them, all of the older ones anyway, who shared their mother's dream of *doing* something with their lives. . . . What wonderful conversations she and Nellie had had, curled up under blankets to keep warm in the wintertime . . . planning what they would be . . . Nellie had settled on teaching from the very first . . . nothing else even tempted her . . . of course Nellie had always loved her teachers, and Mama had always held them up as models. . . . But her *own* special heroine, for as long as she could remember, had been Florence Nightingale . . . the Crimean War had been more than ten years before she was born, of course, but they knew all about Florence from Mama, how famous she was, and how she had changed the world. The frown left Isabel's forehead and her features relaxed as she remembered how Nellie had reacted that afternoon she told her . . . "Florence Nightingale! Oh Belle, what a good idea—a *nurse*—that's almost as good as a school teacher!" "But, I don't want to be a nurse, Nellie. Don't you remember those awful, stuffy old army doctors Florence had to battle with to get anything done for all the wounded soldiers as Scutari? I don't just love her for being a nurse, I love her for the *fight* she put up with all those powerful people—with her parents when she refused to get married, then with those doctors, and then with the whole War Office until she changed everything. It was wonderful that one woman could do so much. I want to leave my mark in the world the way she did, in a *real* way, and I could do that by being a nurse, but I could do it much better by being a doctor." "Oh, Belle, you want to be a *doctor*? But you'd never get to do that. There are hardly any women doctors!" "That may be, but there's lots of room for one more. . . . "

. . . How Mama had urged them over and over again, drilled it into them that here in Canada they had every chance to make something *real* of themselves . . . not like what it had been in Ireland for her. Perhaps if they'd had a brother or two among them, Mama'd have pinned all her hopes on *them* and left the girls to grow up more ready for the usual marriage role . . . and maybe if Papa hadn't died . . . maybe the closeness she remembered without any men at all in the house, maybe *that* was what she missed, maybe she just couldn't find room for a man . . . at home it had always been "Make something of yourselves," never "Find a good husband."

Isabel smiled as again she suddenly pictured Nellie and herself alone in their room—this time breathless with the fascination and daring of their conversation—wondering about men—they hadn't even had the experience of a brother—and contemplating the married state. . . . And after, when Edward had come along, and she was awash with all those feelings and emotions, even *then* she had held back, making him solemnly promise—laughingly attaching this proviso to her acceptance of his marriage proposal—that if she wanted afterward to attend medical school he would allow her. Laughing along with her, he had said yes . . . and while Nellie fulfilled her ambition to become a teacher, she had married Edward on the 31st day of July, 1889. . . . And she hadn't really been a very good wife so far. . . . Tears filling her eyes, Isabel got up from the desk and, walking to the window at the front of the room, stood looking vacantly down Stanley, seeing nothing at all of what was on the street, only a tiny dead baby lying in its crib . . . Margaret Isabel Arthur, dead after only three months of life. . . . Edward had never laid eyes on her. The enormity of that fact, the awful gulf it opened in her, made her raise her arm in a gesture of anguish. She never even noticed the woman who, passing up Stanley in a buggy, waved back. . . . What had made that little baby decide to leave? . . . Those reasons the doctor gave . . . Why? . . . all the care and love that had surrounded it. . . . For a long time, she had blamed herself. . . . Maybe she wasn't fit to be a wife and mother. . . . Why hadn't she *insisted* on going west with

Edward? . . . And when she did finally go, after he was all set up in Nelson—everybody thinking this would be a new start—and, really, she had been still in mourning . . . and then, moving into this house . . . and John, born the following summer, almost exactly a year ago . . . and he, too—dead in his crib . . . and Edward comforting her clumsily . . . allowing time to do the healing, while he went back to his man-things . . . and when he had been getting involved in school affairs, she had been getting sicker and sicker, not good for anything. Suddenly remembering her mother's favourite saying: "Don't be just good, be good for something!" she laughed, wiped the moisture from her cheeks, and found herself standing in the room little John had died in. . . . Well, she still wasn't good for anything, not being a wife and mother, anyway . . . Edward was being patient, understanding . . . but what, really, could he know about her feelings . . . a good doctor—a rush of love flushed her cheeks as she remembered him getting up in the middle of the night without even being summoned and hurrying out to see a patient, saying" I know she needs me, I feel it!" . . . and walking to Ymir that day to look after a man injured on the railway they were building . . . a good doctor, a feeling man, but rough-edged and insensitive to inner needs . . . like most men, busy with politics and other male diversions. . . . How often, observing him with a sick person, she had wanted to suggest a gentler approach. Time and again she had seen him minimize the good he did his patients by treading rough-shod over their feelings, gaining a reputation for the very opposite of what he really was . . . how she had wished at those moments he had a little more of the feminine in him . . .

. . . And my God! how, for her part, she had wished to be a good wife. . . . Why were all her friends so happy? . . . What did she lack that made her unable to feel interested in things other women of her social standing did? Lydia Hume, Lucy Davys, Ella Croasdaile, and all the rest of them seemingly perfectly content running their houses, their Chinese servants, leaving calling-cards on each other, planning parties and musical evenings . . . my God! better to be someone like black Mrs. Foster with real work to do, even if it was washing somebody else's laundry—and *she* at least had the satisfaction of being a good midwife!

Isabel's brow furrowed. . . . The *outrage* that someone like Mrs. Foster should officiate at the bringing of children into the world . . . woman's work, certainly, but also *medical* work, the province of someone more knowledgeable like a doctor, but a *female* doctor. . . . Perhaps with better care so many infants wouldn't die. . . .

Standing there where John's crib had been, she suddenly remembered the look on Edward's face when she had made the proviso to her acceptance of his proposal . . . the startled widening of his eyes and then the amused smile that had lit up his face as he agreed. . . . Well, he *had* agreed and she would hold him to it . . . she would become a doctor herself and maybe then a better wife—and mother too. . . .

She began pacing the floor, left John's room, and stood again in front of the window that looked out onto Stanley to gaze unseeingly at the river as it swept out of sight around a curve beyond the CPR flat. . . . There must be a medical college somewhere nearer than Ontario—down in Washington perhaps, Portland or Seattle . . . and now she felt hungry . . . a bite of lunch, then she would get ready for that tea party, and maybe even enjoy it. She moved toward the kitchen.[32]

# CHAPTER 29

*A long chapter containing, among many other things, the story of the arrival of the Nelson & Fort Shepherd Railway to Nelson, an analysis of the cast of a local entertainment called "The Doves and the Ravens," the event of the great flood, the building of the Hall Mines Smelter, and B-G's final exit from our tale.*

For SEVERAL YEARS now a second railway had been in the offing for Nelson, the Nelson & Fort Shepherd Railway Company having been incorporated as far back as 1891, with the intention that it would be open for business in Nelson by April 20th of 1894. The N&FS was an offshoot of Daniel C. Corbin's Spokane Falls and Northern Railway Company, which had already been extended to Northport, just south of the international border. Work on the line had begun at the border in the summer of '91 after much opposition from the CPR, and by September '93 tracks extended along the Salmon River valley to a point only twenty-six miles from Nelson.[33] On November 18th the locomotive pushing the track-laying machine hove around a curve on the mountain and looked down on Nelson. A mile or so farther on it stopped at the site known henceforth to generations of Nelsonites as the Mountain Station. There a small station-house was built. From the day of its completion—well before the agreed date of April 20th, 1894—the people of Nelson had direct access to Spokane. (The station in those days was, of course, a long uphill climb from the town.)

It had been the company's intention to lay rails along the mountain in a gentle descent that would take them to the lakeshore five miles east of Nelson, then turn back westward along the shoreline to a station in town next to that of the CPR. However, when Daniel Corbin visited Nelson in October of '93 to complete those arrangements, his hopes were dashed by CPR officials who presented him with a letter, written by former Premier John Robson, that reserved the whole lakeshore for the CPR. Obviously, the N&FS Railway would have to stop at Five-Mile Point. But even *that* terminus was in jeopardy because the time for cancellation of the company's land subsidy was fast approaching and the tracks were not yet laid up that far.

Clearly, strong measures would have to be taken to meet the crisis, and the ones taken were of the kind that make those earlier times so exciting in our eyes, simply because no one could get away with them in our own day. Orders were given that the tracks from the Mountain Station to Five-Mile Point be laid as fast as possible in a makeshift manner without regard to fine detail. Just get them down on the ground to give the appearance of a proper railway bed. Then, after the inspector had seen them, they could be properly done at leisure. As for the inspector—leave him to company officials.

The inspector, who arrived in town by CPR, was already well acquainted with at least some of the officials and was met by them at the station in the friendliest manner. Wined and dined profusely, made jovial by the attentive officials who were at their most charming, and continually plied with a flask against the cold, he finally arrived at the site in the most expansive and acquiescent of moods, and was easily persuaded that whatever shortcomings he *did* happen to notice along the line were laughable trivialities. The inspection passed just as the company officials desired. The Nelson & Fort Shepherd Railway had officially reached Nelson and, in spite of the failure to get the terminus right in town, the Mountain Station was still there and nobody could take *that* away. And we can be sure that a trail, even a wagon road, was soon constructed up to it.

The year 1894 had hardly started before the Hall Mining Company began using the new railway. One hundred and twenty tons of *Silver King* ore went south in January. The ore was carried to Five-Mile Point by boat from Nelson and loaded onto the train. On March 17th *The Miner* reported a second shipment of forty tons.

Picture of S.S. *Nelson* meeting a train at Five-Mile Point, end-of-the-line for the Nelson and Fort Shepherd Railway. Five-Mile Point later became known as Troup Junction, named for Captain James W. Troup, manager of the Columbia & Kootenay Steam Navigation Company at Nelson. Built in 1891, the *Nelson* was Kootenay Lake's first sternwheeler. EWSHS L84-423 4.2

Things were going well for the N&FS Railway Company, but there was much dissatisfaction over the distance of the terminus from town: people were beginning to speak of the "Fort Shepherd and Five-Mile Point Railway Company." In April Harold Selous and Malcolm Sproat handed around a petition addressed to the government demanding that the company be allowed to bring its rails to a point on the lakeshore at or near Nelson. It was going to take more than a year for them to get their wish.

Newspaper reports of 1894 indicate that, whatever was going on in the noisy houses on east Baker and elsewhere in those parts of town that were still "frontier," there was now a solid population of the respectable middle class, who had undertaken to promote activities of another kind. In early January, G.O. Buchanan held a meeting to organize a curling club. Two musical events oc curred that month as well. The Nelson Band gave a concert at the Phair—widely regarded as one of the finer hotels of British Columbia—and an entertainment, "The Doves and the Ravens" took place one Friday evening of late January at Carney's Hall. This was an amateur local production. *The Miner* of January 27th announced the forthcoming event and gave a list of the cast. Ladies: mesdames Troup, Stewart, Davys, Goepel, Akenhurst, and Stephenson. Misses: Delmage, Scott, Donohue, and Crickmay. Gentlemen: messrs. Robson, Stewart, Chadbourne, Valleau, Hamber, Martin, Turner Elliott, Walstaff, Johnson, and Renwick. Boys: Willie Turner, Sam Stuckey, Percy and Clarence Goepel, Clarence and Morley Grahame—all cast as "curly-headed coons." Orchestra composed of Nelson City Band members, conducted by Thomas Scanlan.

A close examination of the names on that list—particularly those of the "Ladies"—will increase our insight into the town's social structure. Lucy Davys and Sally Goepel are sisters, members of the Bate family, a wealthy and prominent family in the coal-mining town of Nanaimo, and as such are a part of the "establishment" of British Columbia. Lucy is the wife of Monty Davys, whom we have already met a few times, and Sally of W.J. Goepel. Both these highly positioned men and their wives belong to a self-conscious *élite,* along with several other families we have not yet met. Malcolm Sproat, Harry Anderson, and Charles Busk also belong to this class. They have strong ties to Victoria and to England, and they are members of the Anglican Church. Lucy Davys does not live in Nelson, but up at the *Silver King* where Monty is Mine Manager. She thinks nothing of making the journey up and down the thirteen miles of the wagon road (which Monty had surveyed in 1891) to attend rehearsals, and of course she can stay at her sister's whenever there is a performance or concert in town. She is well used to living in out-of-the-way Kootenay mining camps with her husband.

Mrs. Akenhurst is the wife of the rector of the Anglican Church. That denomination first appeared in Nelson in 1891 and initially operated without its own church building. Now in '94 it has a small one.

Mrs. Troup is the wife of Captain James W. Troup, Manager of the Columbia & Kootenay Steam Navigation Co. The C&KSN had its origins in the Columbia Transportation Co. started by J. Fred Hume and two partners during his Revelstoke days back in '88. Their first boat was the catamaran *Dispatch* (we saw Robert Yuill on it back in chapter 16). *Dispatch* was soon joined by a small steamer, *Marion*. The company grew, took on new directors, acquired a big new vessel, the *Lytton*, along with its new name. These steamers were quickly followed by others. In 1891, the C&KSN built Kootenay Lake's first paddlewheeler in Nelson at a shipyard just west of present-day Shirley Beach. It was named the S.S. *Nelson*. Soon afterward the company moved its headquarters to Nelson and hired young Captain Troup (he was thirty-seven at the time) as Manager. Although he is an American, his prestigious position places him and his family on the level of the Anglican *élite*.

The two other ladies on the list are unknown to this historian, although Mrs. Stewart may be the wife of a senior bank clerk, and Mrs. Stephenson that of a CPR official.

Moving on to the "Misses," Nellie Delmage is the sister of Isabel Arthur. In response to Isabel's letter and egged on by Edward Arthur, who was greatly concerned to obtain a really good teacher in Nelson, Nellie has come out west and will assume duties as teacher when school starts in August. (The new school on Stanley Street still has only one room in use.) Nellie has not been slow to enter into the town's social life. She is an accomplished musician.

The Misses Scott and Donohue are not known to this historian but Miss Crickmay is. From a moneyed family down at the coast, she is one of two sisters, Florence and Agnes, who came early to Nelson and left their mark by opening a private hospital which was patronized largely by affluent Nelsonites, leaving the South Kootenay Lake General for the miners. The building which housed this private hospital survives to the present day as a residence on the corner of Kootenay and Latimer Streets.

Judging entirely from the names of female cast members, this historian is inclined to conclude that "Doves and Ravens" was conceived and produced by members of the Anglican Church congregation, with possible forays to the Presbyterians and Methodists for extra singers. The Mr. Turner who sang and accompanied the Bate sisters in their solos may have been either a piano tuner or a young bank clerk. Others of the male singers might also have been young bank clerks, who were among the few accepted by the *élite* and who were greatly encouraged by their employers to mingle in the best society. If these assumptions are correct, the six "curly-headed coons" were most likely children in the Anglican Church Sunday school. Lucy Davys and Sally Goepel were made to sing encores after their solos, and *The Miner* of February 3rd was able to report that "Doves and Ravens" had been a great success.

Activities of all kinds continued. A meeting of ladies of the town took place at Mrs. George Taylor's home on Victoria Street in aid of the Deluge Hook & Ladder Co., a Miss Johnston gave a dance at Lemon's Hall one Tuesday night, a Masonic Lodge was constituted, an athletic association formed, and *The Miner* reported on May 5th that gardens were being started all over town.

Alas, some of those gardens were not fated to reach fruition. As always, that great cosmic event that we paused to observe in Chapter 6 was occurring, and, as always, was not the chief concern of most people. This year was to be different. Inordinate amounts of snow had fallen, as we know, the previous winter; this year, the whole spring had been remarkably cold. The melting of that snow from the peaks into the great basin of Kootenay Lake had been considerably retarded. Suddenly, as is so often the case in late May, the weather turned and became very hot. The snow that should have been melting gradually now melted all in a rush to create the never-to-be-forgotten flood of 1894—of a magnitude unseen previously and unseen since.

By May 24th the whole of the CPR flats was flooded. Six feet of water stood at the depot. The government wharf was submerged, and much of the railway line downstream was either flooded or washed away. Then, on the night of June 3rd the entire Kootenay area was engulfed by a series of violent thunder storms which, as well as dumping uncounted thousands of tons of water into the overburdened basin of the lake, melted the snow even faster. Kaslo, where fierce winds completed the damage begun by the rising water, was by far the hardest hit of all the lake settlements. At Nelson, Front and Lake Streets were submerged, and the rising line of water advanced menacingly farther and farther up toward Vernon. At Five-Mile Point the terminus of the N&FS Railway was under water and the roundhouse barely escaped destruction by the raging torrents of melted snow that gouged the usually tiny creek there into a chasm of mud and boulders. Farther west on that railway, a small tributary of Cottonwood Creek, roused to similar fury, had washed away an embankment. Nelson was completely cut off from the outside world, even by telegraph. Busk's new wharf, built by Robert Yuill up at Anderson's Point in Bogustown, had gone—completely disappeared. So had G.O. Buchanan's sawmill up at Fourteen-Mile.

When the storm subsided, the west arm was strewn with everything from small planks to complete houses. People began salvaging. What had been someone's shack or boathouse twenty miles upstream now became the shack or boathouse of someone in Nelson. New shacks and additions to houses were being constructed entirely of salvaged lumber. And who knows how many planks from G.O. Buchanan's sawmill found their way into buildings away down the Columbia in Northport or Marcus?

We cannot help but wonder what our friend B-G might have thought had he been present to witness this mighty display of power put on by the waters he had for so long sought to control. His dredging operation at the mouth of Grohman Creek would have seemed meagre indeed. He was spared that sight, however, being at this time far away in England, never to return, his troubles having accumulated beyond the point of endurance. In 1891, his canal now unused and filling in at Canal Flat, the town named after him empty, and his dredging operations at Grohman Creek his only hope, he had involved himself in a petition of right against the Crown, just as he was obliged to absent himself from Victoria on other business. Legal documents pertaining to the case, sent to him with insufficient postage, ended in the Dead Letter Office and were destroyed. He returned to Victoria to find that his lawyer had absconded with the five-hundred-dollar retainer fee he had been paid. It was the last straw. Putting the nine years and the personal fortune he had spent on his reclamation scheme behind him, he determined to see the Kootenays no more and sailed for home. His company abandoned his dredging scheme and began work on reclamation of the flood lands by diking. This too eventually failed and the company fazed out.

Time heals all things, but some earlier than others. No more than a fortnight after the flood the Nelson & Fort Shepherd Railway was once more in operation, but the CPR had to wait a full three months before its running stock was travelling the rails. Meanwhile, activities over the whole lake gradually came back to normal as flood waters receded. At Nelson, Dominion Day was celebrated with the usual festivities: baseball, races, tugs-o-war, dance, fireworks, and the big horse-race along the length of Baker Street. This year's race was won by a horse called "J. Beattie."

More important to some than the flood was the news that J. Fred Hume was running for a place in the provincial legislature in the upcoming election. As far back as January 13th a notice to that effect had appeared in *The Miner*. Rumours got about that J. Fred was John Houston's man, part of a "Houston Clique" whose aim was to further the ambitions of John. J. Fred ran a statement in *The Miner* of January 27th denying that allegation. About the same time, *The Miner* gave its approval to Frank Fletcher as a possible candidate. Fletcher (whom we first met, in Chapter 27, as the builder of an expensive house on Baker Street) was a member of the *élite*, or as he later spoke of himself, "one of the better sort." He refused the candidacy, and a short time later G.O. Buchanan was chosen by the Liberals as their man. On June 30th a notice appeared in *The Miner* stating that J. Fred Hume, Conservative, and G.O. Buchanan, Liberal, were official nominees for the south riding of West Kootenay District. During the race John Houston was J. Fred's campaign manager, and Malcolm Sproat, already John's enemy from the earliest Nelson Electric Light Co. days, was

G.O. Buchanan's. Broadly speaking, the election campaign was divided between the interests of the "common man" (backed by *The Tribune*) and those of the "capitalist" class (backed by *The Miner*). John, of course was an outspoken enemy of the latter class, while J. Fred, in spite of his position as a leading merchant and community activist, was also not to be numbered among the "capitalists." Both he and Lydia were Methodists, and Lydia particularly was an aggressive prohibitionist. The more aristocratic Anglicans did not frown upon drinking.

Voting took place in mid-July at the Courthouse. Hume was elected by a majority of 146 votes.

As summer deepened, forest fires proliferated unchecked, and dense smoke filled the valleys. The whole of the Slocan district seemed to be on fire. In some places people had been forced to take refuge in lakes, their heads covered with wet blankets. The town of Three Forks had been destroyed. (Only very old people can still remember what summers were like in those days, and well into the 1930s, when during almost every August people went about their business in a doomsday atmosphere of forest-fire smoke.)

Life in town went on unchecked by the smoke, however. On August 13th the public school opened for the fall term, "no one under six years of age allowed." Miss Nellie Delmage, newly appointed as Mistress of Public Schools, was the teacher. We wonder if the school building was wired for electric lighting that year. Electricity had come to Nelson at last, but only in a few places, since, as we noted in an earlier chapter, the source was probably one of the sawmills. Another year had to elapse before the Nelson Light Co. plant would finally be in operation.

The Courthouse was busy attending to the litigational needs of townsfolk, both prominent and humble. In early September one Patrick Sullivan threw—for reasons unstated—a spittoon at Emma Johnson, coloured woman, resident in one of the "sporting houses" on East Baker. After listening to three different versions of what happened, the judge gave his verdict: a fine of $15 and costs, plus $2 extra for damage done, or one month hard labour. Mr. Sullivan chose to pay the fine.

George Bigelow committed an assault on Dr. Arthur during a July moonlight excursion to Pilot Bay on one of the steamers. One hundred and fifty people were aboard. The cruise was a successful fund-raiser for the school, although Dr. Arthur had to wait until after litigation to experience *his* success—a fine of $30 for Mr. Bigelow.

In October John Houston was brought to court, having assaulted A.M. Johnston. He was fined $20.

Litigation had been in progress for some time now between H.E. Croasdaile and the Hall Mines Company, and the judge had just decided that a trial by jury should decide the issue. Back in the '80s Henry Croasdaile had been a lieutenant on one of the British warships that were resting in the harbour at Victoria. Wanting to stay in British Columbia, he had obtained his release from the navy and taken up various shore jobs of the brokerage kind. In '89 the Hall brothers were in Victoria fighting a case of attempted claim jumping at the *Silver King*. Judge Begby decided in favour of the Halls, but they were left desperate for two things: cash and investors to supply that cash. Looking over the Victoria scene for possible help, they hit upon the promising Henry Croasdaile, whose financial abilities and English connections might be just what they needed. Henry was persuaded to accompany a party of the Halls and Oakes to England in a search for investors. They spent twelve months there and were successful. On their return to the Kootenays the Halls refused to compensate Croasdaile sufficiently for his efforts, hence the court case, which was settled by the awarding of a large sum of money to the plaintiff, but much less than he asked for. A new company with investors and personnel from the Old Country was formed—the Hall Mines, Ltd.—and, all previous enmity forgotten, Henry Croasdaile became its General Manager. As top man at the Hall Mines and with good connections in Victoria and England, Henry Croasdaile was the *élite's* most prestigious figure. In the summer of 1894, while the litigation with the Hall brothers was still going on, he had a big house built for his family in the fashionable area near J. Fred's new home. Located on the southeast corner of Observatory and Stanley Streets, it has survived to the present day very much as it was then.

The summer of '94 was a busy one for that Anglican *élite*. Charles Busk finally made the decision to leave Balfour and buy Bob Yuill's ranch at Yuill Creek (now Kokanee) for $2,000, with the intention of putting in orchards and small fruit plantations there. He also had plans to build a big house high up on the property overlooking the lake, in which he would live the life of an English country gentleman. (Later sold to Charles Hamilton[34], this house survived—a lovely old relic of other times, surrounded by decaying flower gardens, tennis court, swimming pool, and enclosed kitchen garden, and bearing near its imposing front entrance the motto *PAX INTRANTIBUS, SALUS EXEUNTIBUS, BENE-DICTIO HABITANTIBUS*[35]—until it was burned down by government order in the late 1950s.) In the summer of '94, Charles Busk also launched the *Flirt*, a steam launch with a "quadruple expansion engine."

On October 6th *The Miner* reported that Harold Selous was building an office "in the corner of his pretty garden" (on the northwest corner of Stanley and Victoria Streets, where the newly completed Kutanai Building is at the time of this writing) using lumber from two cottages of his which had been swept downriver by the flood. The garden—a "dream, all summer long a mass of bloom covering the whole lot, except for narrow paths between the beds"—was far below street level. The street-level office faced onto Stanley, and Harold lived below it in a basement whose entrance opened onto the garden. This basement was full of tools and other paraphernalia of gardening, but the back part of it was "a windowless cave in which he had his bed and trunk of clothes. His dwelling was revolting . . . " In spite of these unorthodox living arrangements and of a "game leg" that made him unable to bend the knee, Harold Selous was an important part of the social scene, present at every function and dominating the tennis club and the dances, where he was a perfectly acceptable partner for wives and daughters of the *élite*. His particular crony was "old Farwell, a recluse never seen by ordinary people." This was none other than the A.S. Farwell[36] of previous chapters, now living in retirement at the "Bucket of Blood," a boarding house across Stanley Street from Selous' office run by a woman called Mrs. Blood, and very likely "the old Red House" we saw in chapter 21.

Sometime during the year, the N&FS roadbed had worked its way from Five-Mile Point nearly into Nelson, as far as Bogustown in fact, with a station at the terminus below the present-day corner of Maple and Cottonwood Streets. A hotel, the Grove, had been built between Maple and First at Cottonwood to accommodate travellers.

The year 1894 ended with a spell of very cold weather. The Bonners Ferry route to the south was closed owing to ice. The *Silver King* had to cut its staff to fifteen because it was too cold to operate the machines. But the dark days of mid-winter were lightened by rumours of important decisions being made up at the Hall Mines, Sir Joseph Trutch and other directors of the company having been seen in town. There was even a report that certain business firms and property owners were guaranteeing $100,000 toward the building of a smelter in Nelson. Then, in March of '95, it became known that a lot of high-level reshuffling was taking place up on Toad Mountain. One of the visible results of that was the appointment of Monty Davys as Mine Manager at the *Silver King*.

Soon rumours flew that a tramway to bring ore down to Nelson was in the offing. Excitement in the town grew. Some property owners held a private meeting at which a petition was prepared, asking that a number of town lots be donated as part of a subsidy toward a smelter. Up at the *Silver King*, employment suddenly rose from fifty to seventy men. Soon news was forthcoming that tenders would be out on May 20th for the building of an aerial tramway to bring ore from the mines down to Nelson. By May 25th *The Miner* could report that the company had accepted the bid of the California Wire Works Company, the work to be completed in three months. By June 1st everyone knew that Sir Joseph Trutch had been in town to arrange for the tramway right-of-way—and for a block of thirteen acres west of Cottonwood Creek to be set aside for the company. These thirteen acres could be for nothing else but a smelter! Most of the town rejoiced at this irrefutable sign of security; there were a few, however, who wondered about the effect of the smoke from a smelter on their gardens. *The Miner's* comment to them was "The smoke will give dollars to go and buy gardens in Paris, London, or elsewhere."

Now that the town's future was looking so rosy, business, cultural, and all other activities went forward with even greater impetus. A philharmonic society was inaugurated, George Johnstone as president; cries for more sidewalks increased; new houses were built; a local painting of blue irises went on display in a shop window; a concert to aid the newly arrived Catholic Church was held with the aid of performers of all denominations. Miss Sharp played a Mozart sonata and also the encore that was demanded. Mesdames Goepel and Davys sang excellently. Messrs. Jowett and Turner presented a piano and organ duet.

Nelson was declared a Customs Port in July.

Travelling artists Boulon and Gonne gave a musical entertainment at the Oddfellows Hall. Their jokes were "so raw that the coyotes scented them and came down from the hills."

Baseball enthusiasts met to get organized. R.E. Lemon was elected as president.

Mr. Heathcote, clerk of the Bank of British Columbia, left for Nanaimo to get married, and returned to Nelson with yet another of the vivacious and musical Bate sisters.

The Supreme Court of British Columbia held sessions in June—Croasdaile vs. the Hall Company.

Local horse "Jim Beattie" once again won the Baker Street horse race on Dominion Day. All hotels were full for the occasion.

There was not an empty house in Nelson. Among others, two new residences were going up on Stanley Street, one of them for the Misses Delmage and Nelson.

The Nelson Band gave a concert in the firehall. Mesdames Troup, Goepel, Davys, and mezzo-soprano Miss Rhodes all sang, while Messrs. Harper and McIntyre played violin and cello obligato.

The summer months of '95 passed by. Activity around the

construction of the smelter became almost feverish as the whole town seemed to be focused on getting it completed. Throughout early September much blasting occurred just below the smelter site where the CPR was building a connecting line from the flats up to the smelter level. On a day in October the last cable splice was completed on the tramway cable—nine miles of "endless rope" suspended on 128 towers and carrying 200 buckets. Up at the *Silver King* twenty-five men were at work on more ore bins, G.O. Buchanon hard pressed to supply the 225,000 feet of lumber he had contracted to supply for them. By November 16th the *Silver King* had closed down, its ore bins full and 8000 tons more on the dump waiting for the smelter to open.

Work on that had started in early October, granite for the foundations being cut from a nearby bluff. A report in *The Miner* of December 7th stated that Smelter Superintendent Paul Johnson was confident "fires will be lighted" by January 1st. The weather having been good for construction, all buildings were nearing completion. The only sour note at year's end was struck by the Hospital Board, which announced that it had decided to close the hospital because it was in debt. Within days the town ladies had got busy and organized a grand ball at the Phair in aid. It was a success.

The smelter failed to blow in on January 1st as Paul Johnson had hoped. It did on the 18th, however, and no one could complain about that small delay in such a huge undertaking.

# CHAPTER 30

*In which Kootenay Country is visited by the province's
new Sanitary Inspector.*[37]

WHEN JOHN HOUSTON sold *The Miner* in 1892, its buyers were two men by the names of Bogle and Whalley. In the early
spring of '93, they in turn sold it to one Clive Phillipps-Wolley.
Mr. Phillipps-Wolley was owner-editor until the spring of '94,
when he turned the editorship over to Charles St. Barbe (who is
noteworthy as the writer of Nelson's first history). Finally Mr.
Phillipps-Wolley withdrew from the newspaper business entirely
by selling out, perhaps to Mr. St. Barbe, perhaps to someone else,
but that is a matter we will not pursue, since it is Mr. Clive
Phillipps-Wolley himself who is the subject of this chapter.

Clive was one of those newcomers from England who remain
very English. A wealthy man and an ardent traveller, he was also
a lawyer by training and an amateur boxer. Soon after his arrival
in British Columbia he built a house big enough to be called a
mansion in Oak Bay on Vancouver Island, where his wife and family remained during his sojourn in Nelson. Although tiring of his
newspaper stint, he did not tire of the Kootenays and wished to
retain a connection there. He had become concerned over the
threat presented by the incursion of American railways into mining districts along the border of British Columbia, and there was
indeed much in Kootenay country to feed such concern, considering that most of the ore from the *Silver King* and the mines on the
main lake still went south for smelting, and that Trail was being
developed by American money. Looking about for some govern-

ment job that might allow him at least to visit Kootenay country occasionally, Clive was pleased to notice that the provincial government was creating a new office and making a new appointment. He applied, and on August 15th of 1896 was given the job of Provincial Sanitary Inspector.

The government made a good choice in its new Sanitary Inspector. Reading his official reports, we are at once affected by an endearing quality in the writing. Not for him that cold, scientific detachment so carefully cultivated by his modern-day counterparts, who prudently eschew all moral judgement. It is clear he brought a passionate moral fervour to *his* job. *Infamous, deplorable, vile, disgraceful, shameful, dangerous, indescribably filthy* were words he used in noting infringements of the sanitary code. We cringe with him, feel his horror at the sight of *obnoxious drains, terrible deposits, cess-pits,* and *garbage, fecal matter and pigs filth festering in the August sun.* We too experience the intensity of righteous emotion that made him mar his otherwise impeccable standard of punctuation by forgetting the possessive apostrophe after the word *pigs* in that last awful image. Firm in his righteousness, like some knight in shining armour, he strode among these dragons of insanitation bringing havoc to their ranks, ruthlessly using the lance of his office to slay them one by one.

On the very day of his appointment, Provincial Sanitary Inspector Phillipps-Wolley left for Rossland, stopping along the way to give Revelstoke a hurried inspection. Constable Vickers of that town accompanied him on his rounds. Rossland he found in "a deplorable condition." Among many other sanitary outrages he discovered that "water under Columbia Avenue was in a putrid condition, and full of grey slimy growths; that the stench near the Allen House, and at the back of buildings on Columbia Avenue, were [sic] intolerable, and that a considerable number of cases of typhoid and mountain fever existed; and that cases of sore throat were common, and a severe form of diarrhoea accompanied by cramps in the stomach was epidemic." He tended to be forgiving of the community, however, noting that "where a town grows with the feverish rapidity of Rossland, it is inevitable that at first sanitary precautions should be disregarded, . . . " Following his inspection there, Mr. Phillipps-Wolley went down to Trail, where he determined that "for a new mining town" its health was "marvellously good."

On September 16th he paid his first official visit to Nelson, and found it in such "a very bad state indeed, with ten cases of typhoid fever in the town" that he had to remain for nearly a month.

On inspection the principal source of trouble appeared to be in the old wooden flume down Ward Creek, which was being used as a common sewer. This flume was very slightly built, many of the covering boards were off, it leaked so badly that more water ran outside of it than inside of it; the floor of the flume was in no place more than half covered with water; ducks wandered down it, children put their tin cans and wooden ships in it, it was blocked in many places, and the wooden flumes connected with it leaked badly. Pigs were kept at the back of an hotel abutting on it, everyone seemed to use the ravine in which it lies as a common dumping ground; whilst the flume of the principal hotel was disconnected, and a terrible deposit therefrom lay under the bridge, adjoining which are the houses in which three of the ten typhoid patients were living.. A cess-pit at the rear of *The Miner* newspaper office was made at the back of the cribbing of the ravine, its contents showing through it at a distance, and the flume itself was knocked out of plumb by having earth from the foundations (apparently of *The Miner* building) heaped upon it

I found, too, that the water-works system of Nelson was very inadequate. The water is merely the soakage from a bog, collected in a small pot-hole, unfenced and open to all manner of pollution. Very few houses in the town had earth-closets. The slaughter-house is a standing menace to public health, and the stream running past it was full of animal débris, heads and guts whilst the "gardens" in which it is situated were a lair for Chinese hogs. The filth from the slaughter-house drains into the lake. Pigs perambulated the streets; cows wandered up the ravine in which the sewer leaked out its filth; the local hospital had a cess-pit from which an open cut carried the overflow down the hill; the cows of the milk ranch were stabled in the midst of dwelling houses, and wandered at will over the sources of the water supply, and the sewers of some of the hotels were worse than anything in Rossland.

I spent several days inspecting all these things and many other nuisances, and got a slight touch of fever myself, but I shook it off. I employed the prisoners to clear out the ravine, limed it with lime kindly supplied by the Hall Mines Co., summoned various people, and finally broke up and burned the wooden flume as the only way of curing the evil. . . . . . . . . . . .

After making another visit to Rossland and Trail, Mr. Phillipps-Wolley returned to Nelson on October 31st for an additional two weeks. Only a day or so after his arrival in town he became aware that Dr. E.C. Arthur, the town's avowed "health officer," was himself guilty of a certain regrettable laxity in meeting the highest possible standards in sanitation—and not only once, but *twice*. True to his promise back in 1891, the doctor had indeed opened a drugstore in town. On the grounds of both this store and his residence he had installed cess-pits which were not constructed according to code. Learning of these, Sanitary Inspector Phillipps-Wolley approached Dr. Arthur in a friendly enough fashion, expecting that a mere mention of the problem would elicit a cooperative response. For some reason—perhaps the two men had had a falling-out in the past, when Clive was owner of *The Miner*; perhaps the doctor, usually gruff anyway, was feeling out of sorts that day; or perhaps he was missing Isabel, who was still away at medical school and not due back for a month or so—the response was not only uncooperative but downright abusive. Far from being intimidated by the doctor's invective, the Sanitary Inspector was spurred to action. Here indeed was a dragon to be slain! Mounting his steed, armour flashing, lance atilt, Sir Clive thundered to the attack—right down to the courthouse to demand of Stipendiary Magistrate Fitzstubbs that Dr. E.C. Arthur be apprehended and made to answer why he should not be fined or imprisoned for violating one of the Sanitary Regulations. The Magistrate complied, and in due course Dr. Arthur appeared in court to answer charges that he had been "maintaining a nuisance" in two places by having cess-pits instead of the superior "earth closets." The Sanitary Inspector demanded a heavy sentence because Dr. Arthur was the Health Officer and therefore more culpable than ordinary offenders.

Dr. Arthur maintained an attitude of scornful outrage during the whole affair. It was ridiculous, he argued, that Mr. Phillipps-Wolley should demand that people change—during the onset of winter!—what were obviously temporary sanitary arrangements when in a few months the incorporation of Nelson as a city would—he was certain—occur and then a proper sewage system would be installed. This reasonable argument failed—perhaps because of the tone in which it was presented. Magistrate Fitz-stubbs fined Dr. Arthur $50 and instructed the sanitary inspector to "see that the nuisance was abated." Hearing this, Dr. Arthur stated that the inspector had no right on his property and that he would try "in every legal way" to prevent his interference.

We cannot guess which of the two angry contestants had the last word—perhaps Dr. Arthur, for he submitted a letter to *The Miner* admitting that he had been briefly gaoled and stating his opinion of the whole event. Then—we can be sure—he put the incident out of his mind to concentrate on his practice, his many community interests, and, most pressing of all, the need for incorporation. Mr. Phillipps-Wolley left Nelson on other business. On December 5th a notice appeared in *The Miner*: "Mr. C. Phillipps-Wolley left Rossland for Victoria on Friday." We must assume that a sigh of relief went up from many parts of town.

While at Nelson, Mr. Phillipps-Wolley had twice slipped east of the bluff to do an inspection of Bogustown, first at the request of its principal owner Joshua Davies, and again upon the complaint of a Mr. Jiszkowicz, Baker Street jeweller. Only one well was found to be in jeopardy—from the proximity of certain "earth closets." Mr. Phillipps-Wolley "took the necessary steps" to protect it. During the visit Mr. Davies suggested that matters would be simplified "at no additional expense, either to the Government or to the people" if, for all new townsites, "(1) the dedication of a dumping ground, (2) the dedication of a suitable and sufficient water supply, (3) the establishment of dry earth closets from the start" were insisted upon.

It is evident that Mr. Phillipps-Wolley was forthright in pursuance of his duties, speaking his mind fearlessly to both high and low. In one of his reports, referring to his visit to the Slocan, he complained of "Americans, insolently indifferent to our law," and did not hesitate to recommend that, "if sanitary or any other laws are to be enforced a strong Stipendiary Magistrate must be appointed at Sandon at once."

He was unremittingly antagonistic toward the Chinese population: *too filthy for any animal except a Chinaman; Chinamen living like sewer rats; a grave danger to white men's health and by so living at less expense than their neighbours competing upon better terms than the natives in the labour market;* and—the final sentence of his 1898 report— *I have had the honour to assist you in exorcising typhoid; I should take it as a greater honour if I had some share in exorcising a far greater evil, the filthy Chinaman* are expressions of widely-held attitudes at the time. As we know, the CPR had imported hundreds of Chinese labourers to do the hard work of building the transcontinental line. When that job was completed in 1895, all these men had been dismissed and left to fend for themselves. Many of them migrated into the small mining towns of British Columbia, where, bitterly opposed by the unions in their efforts to obtain work in the mining industry, they found employment as servants, market gardeners, and operators of laundries. Their customs and dress often made them the objects of discrimination or even persecution by the dominant population. In 1896 the Chinese population of Nelson had not yet been forcibly removed to a "Chinatown."

This brief interlude with Sanitary Inspector Phillipps-Wolley has added a new dimension to our tale, opening our eyes—and other senses—to aspects of the town not always mentioned in histories of this kind. Perhaps up to now we have been prone to romanticize Nelson too much, to think too uncritically of the "good old days." Now we can smell all that filth and garbage, and feel on our cheeks the flies that are breeding in all those open sewers. And the words of the Sanitary Inspector have opened our ears to the fact that the people there do not always have the kindest thoughts about their neighbours. The Muse that assists historians must be rejoicing that our romantic illusion has been somewhat shattered, and that we can "be there" in a more realistic sense now.

# CHAPTER 31

*In which the burgeoning town bursts its bonds to be-
come a city and elects its first mayor.*

FOR QUITE A WHILE NOW, successful men of the business,
entrepreneurial, and professional class had felt the need to have a
place of their own, where they could congregate and socialize.
Sometime in 1896, during the months when the town was undergoing its cleansing at the hands of the Provincial Sanitary Inspector, a few of these men got together and decided to do something
about that need. The result of their deliberations was the Nelson
Club. There were many men eager for membership, enough that
the building of a clubhouse could begin almost at once. It was an
imposing structure on the northeast corner of Silica and Kootenay
Streets quite close to the Phair Hotel and the Presbyterian Church,
and provided very nicely for the needs of members who dropped
in for relaxation, conversation, or a game of billiards, or even to
spend the night in one of the upstairs rooms.

Readers could quite accurately assume who some of the members were, but we don't have to guess because, many years later
the owner of an old Nelson house found, while renovating one day,
a single sheet of paper inside a wall. This sheet held the membership list of the Nelson Club for the year 1898. Henry Croasdaile,
Monty Davys, A.S. Farwell, Dr. LaBau, Harold Selous, Tom Ward
(we first met him as the ferryman on the trail to Sproat's Landing
but he was now in the real-estate business), Frank Fletcher, and
Charles St. Barbe (editor of *The Miner*) are a few of the local names
on the list of 112 members. Steamboat services on the lake were

represented by Captains Troup and Gore; international high finance by D.C. Corbin, who gave his home address as Spokane, and Sir J. Trutch, who gave his as London, England.

By making visible those differences of rank that no one had thought much about before, the Nelson Club had the immediate effect of polarizing attitudes. Hotel keepers, merchants, housewives, nearly everyone in fact, suddenly became aware that a prestigious enclave had appeared in town and that they—unless they chose to ignore it—must either aspire to belong to it, or accept the truth that they never *could* belong to it. Most men probably did choose to ignore it, but for many the Club became a measure of success. One can imagine, let us say, a rising young businessman contemplating his noteworthy increase in yearly receipts and wondering if he could yet dare to sport a bigger cigar and apply to the membership committee of the Nelson Club; or the pretty young housewife, alarmed that all her friends in the music group are wives of Nelson Club members, nagging at her husband to apply. And how advantageous it would be for business, too.

A man who sought membership in the Club was clearly making a statement about himself—his self-image, his aspirations, his value as a person. But so also was the man who, although well qualified, *refused* to seek it. Such a man was John Houston. Speaking through his mouthpiece *The Tribune*, he was not afraid to say what he thought about the kind of men who populated the Nelson Club. "The whiteshirted hobos" he called them, and "people who think that because they come from a certain locality overseas they are better than others." J. Fred Hume, too was a man who had little interest in becoming a member of such an institution as the Nelson Club, although in time—this historian is uncertain—he may have been pressured into it.

The town was now a divided one. Since the Nelson Club was on the west side of Ward Creek (which neatly sliced the business district in half) and the other extreme of society—represented by the brothels at the end of Baker—was on the east side, people began to refer to West Ward people and East Ward people. We may generalize, then, to say that John Houston of *The Tribune,* battle-scarred from his many quarrels—his latest appearance in court had been only the previous year, when, in his own office, he dealt Mr. Marpole, CPR executive, a severe blow to the head with a ruler during an interview with CPR officials—and allied to the common or "East Ward" man, was lined up against Charles St. Barbe of *The Miner* and his aristocratic associates of the Nelson Club.

Nelson was experiencing a heady period of growth. *The Miner* of Saturday, January 9, 1897 printed a detailed account of the building that was going on all over town. It announced that $138,750 had been spent in construction during the previous year. Over $18,000 had been spent in buying government lots. The most noteworthy edifice constructed in '96 was the Clement & Hillyer two-storey brick block on the northwest corner of Baker and Josephine. This elaborately ornamented structure—a veritable *tour de force* of the bricklayer's art—was Nelson's first brick commercial building. It exists today in a much disguised form. The Lawrence Hardware Company, new in town, built itself a two-storey shop and a warehouse at a cost of $1,750. The Salvation Army, also new in town, put up a two-storey frame block as their headquarters. Among many other constructions of interest to us but too numerous to mention were four small houses built at a cost of $3,500 by the Misses Delmage and Nelson, who appear to have gone into a sideline of building speculation.

In the early months of '97 most of the town's boiling energy went into attaining incorporation. The need for proper sewage and water systems was becoming critical. Streets and sidewalks were in a deplorable condition. Every new building erected simply compounded the problem. Both newspapers undertook to rouse their readers to action. "The time has come when this town must cease to be looked upon as an overgrown village: its duty is to assume the dignity of a metropolitan existence. Here is the chief town of the south eastern part of this province. . . . As a railroad and steamboat centre, it is also the business centre of the great Kootenay country. The time is near at hand when its growth will . . . make it the largest city in western Canada," stated *The*

*Miner.* "In view of these facts, the immediate incorporation of Nelson as a municipality is absolutely essential."

Property owners became convinced that the editorial writers were correct. The general consensus was that incorporation had to take place *at once* and that a way would have to be found to circumvent the laborious process currently in use by government. By February 6th a petition to the Lieutenant Governor was being circulated asking for the incorporation of Nelson under a special act of the Legislative Assembly. A committee was formed to raise funds for the despatch of a delegation to Victoria. On February 13th *The Miner* was able to report that the incorporation of Nelson would soon be a fact. A telegram from J. Fred Hume, member for Kootenay south, stated that he had examined the special bill to be introduced for the towns of Rossland and Grand Forks and would see that it apply also to Nelson. A meeting of the Citizens' Executive Committee in Charge of Incorporation decided to send a telegram to J. Fred asking that a draft of the bill be sent as soon as possible.

Now began a short period of worry about what exactly incorporation must entail. Stormy meetings took place at which people sought the furtherance of their own individual rather than the common good. The problem of water rights became a point of contention. Many people were claiming that speculators were attempting to hold up incorporation until they got control of the Anderson and Cottonwood Creek rights. On Wednesday evening, February 17, a mass meeting was called in the firehall. Robert Lemon was chairman. The evening's most important resolution was proposed by Dr. Arthur. Its main thrust was that the meeting must protest against the granting of any company water rights on Anderson Creek or the east fork of Cottonwood, which rights must be reserved for the City of Nelson. (These were oblique references to the Water Company and the Nelson Electric Light Company.) A copy of this resolution was to be forwarded to J. Fred Hume.

The meeting—a lively one, full of anger and difficult for the chairman to control—ended harmoniously with three cheers for the City of Nelson.

On February 27th, *The Miner* announced that the Incorporation Bill had made quick progress through the Legislative Assembly. Rossland, Grand Forks, and Nelson were now certain of incorporation. The City of Nelson would include only the government townsite, not Bogustown or other outlying areas. Its total area was to be 372 acres.

On March 6th *The Miner*, under the headline NELSON INCORPORATED, announced that the bill, having been given assent by Lieutenant-Governor Dewdney on Thursday March 4th, was now law. By his act "the town had cast off its village swaddling clothes and assumed the dignity of self-government in all local matters and laid the foundations for its future greatness." Amid general celebration, Messrs. Houston and Hillyer gave a small dinner party for a few close associates.

The immediate problem before the new self-governing city was to create a body to *do* the self-governing. Editorial comments in the two newspapers emphasized the great care that must be taken in choosing the mayor and aldermen who were now to run the city. *The Miner* stressed the importance of selecting candidates "by the record they have made in enterprise and integrity" and noted that it would be "particularly unwise to place men in office who are so indifferent to the transaction of public business that the interests of the city would suffer. Equally important is the necessity for crushing those who 'have axes to grind' or who may be expected to abuse the trust that may be placed in them."

By March 13th it was expected that a municipal government would be in office within thirty days. *The Miner,* no doubt with its own choice of candidate in mind, expressed the hope that "the political strife, jealousies and heart-burnings of a contested election will be avoided." This hope for choice by acclamation was dashed when John Houston announced his candidacy for Mayor in *The Tribune*. Shortly afterward the battle-lines were drawn when John Turner, backed by *The Miner*, announced that he reluctantly and entirely out of a sense of public duty would also run for that office.

Reading *The Miner* and *The Tribune* for the following weeks, we can observe the contest building up from a fairly decorous beginning to outright name-calling and dirt-throwing.

Mr. Charles St. Barbe was appointed Returning Officer, in charge of registering voters and conducting the election which was to take place between the hours of 10:00 a.m. and 4:00 p.m. on Thursday, April 15th. He stated he would "be prepared daily until the election to register voters at the court room in the governmental building between the hours of 12-noon and 2 p.m. and 8 p.m. and 9 p.m.

"Persons qualified to vote shall be male subjects of the full age of twenty-one years and who have resided within the city limits for not less than three months preceding the date of the elections and who shall, in due time, have been registered."

John Houston was Manager of the Nelson Electric Light Company and also involved with the Water Company. *The Miner* used this fact to rouse the fears of voters that, if elected, he would attempt to sell both companies to the city, thereby relieving himself of their upkeep and making a gain in pocket. At first the dangers were only alluded to generally. As the campaigns became more heated—the interest of all townsfolk in the election was very high—the allegation became more open.

Attacks on the character of John Houston became frequent. *The Miner* of Saturday, April 3rd evoked the prestige and dignity of classical history when it began an editorial with the statement "If we remember correctly it was Aristides who, many hundreds of years ago, said 'The character of a city is known by the character of the men it crowns.'" and then proceeded to compare the "clearly defined liberal, sound and fixed principals" of John Turner to the "inconsistent" behaviour of Houston in his business affairs.

John Houston did not help matters for himself when, three days before the election, he appeared before Police Magistrate Harold Selous on a charge of assaulting one Michael Tobo. John's defence was that Mr. Tobo had used foul language to him. Witnesses proved that Tobo's language was elicited by John, who had called him a liar. Magistrate Selous found that John Houston had been at fault, fined him $20, and bound him in the sum of $250 to keep the peace.

*The Miner* made the most of the affair. Under the headline AN ELECTION EPISODE it gave a detailed account of the trial, and made the following comment: "In fining the defendant $20 and costs, Mr. Selous evidently recognized the propensity of the defendant for brawls. This is the third conviction that appears upon the police records since Houston has resided in Nelson."

On the evening of Tuesday, April 13th, two days before the election, the Turner faction held a meeting in the firehall. Its purpose was to ratify the Turner aldermanic candidates. *The Miner* claimed it was the "most representative and enthusiastic" meeting ever held in Nelson. John Houston and his aldermanic candidates were invited. Dr. G.A.B. Hall, chairman of the Turner campaign committee, called the meeting to order. The first candidate to speak was Dr. Arthur, who talked at length against John Houston and his policies. During the course of the evening John Houston himself made a short presentation during which he—as usual blunt and given to uttering the "truth" as he saw it—suggested that Turner's supporters had formulated a plan by which the names of 140 miners at the *Silver King* would be placed on the voters list. Mr. Turner very forcefully denied the allegation. After several more speakers had held the floor, the meeting concluded with three rousing cheers for John A. Turner and three more for Her Majesty.

Election day—Thursday, April 15—arrived. Of the 589 voters registered, 519 cast ballots. John Houston received 299 votes, John Turner 204. And all John's aldermanic candidates were elected too. They were: J. Gilker, Alex Dow, J.J. Malone, W.F. Teetzel, Frank Fletcher, and Charles Hillyer.

The votes were counted by 7:00 p.m. At news of the victory John's supporters "fell on one another's necks and wept for joy." John was lifted and placed in a waiting carriage to be conducted along the length of Baker Street, pulled by "six solid citizens, each weighing over 200 pounds," and preceded by a band. Following the carriage came "the Smith-Fisher glee club with their Houston yell," and behind them a long line of citizens carrying torches and intermittently emitting loud cheers. Baker Street was lined with the citizenry, all *"en fete."* It was a night for the "common man," and celebrations lasted until early dawn.

This is the final scene of our history, the moment toward which our tale has been building all this time—John Houston seated in his triumphal carriage, pulled along Baker Street by six solid citizens, surrounded by a raucous mob of adulating partisans. Seeking to end our story on an elevated philosophical note, we could wish that as John sat there he gazed, raptly unaware of the tumult around him, into the future of his city, dreamed glorious dreams of its destiny, dreams that we might record in singing prose. Alas, knowing him as we do—a man of action rather than ideas—we must conclude that no such thoughts danced in his brain, that his triumph took a more earthy and commonplace turn, that he sat there smugly satisfied at the defeat of his enemies, planning plans about waterworks, sewage, electric light, and the council meeting he was going to hold in the firehall next morning. Following his cue, we will end our tale without prophetic flight, and take our leave in a quietly congratulatory mood—happy with John and his fellow citizens that their newborn town has survived its troubled infancy and taken its first step.

# Notes

CHAPTER I

1. This quotation is from "A Paradise for Canadian and American Soldiers," an article in a magazine called *The Nineteenth Century and After*, 1918, volume LXXXIII, pp. 762-78.

CHAPTER 2

2. All the factual information in this chapter comes from "What Happened To The Frys," a 2400-word carbon-copy transcript by Van B. Putnam, in the Colville Museum, Colville, Washington.

3. This letter was published in the *Nelson Daily Miner* of Feb. 3rd, 1894.

CHAPTER 3

4. The factual information for this chapter comes from W. A. Baillie-Grohman's book *Fifteen Years Sport And Life In The Hunting Grounds Of Western America And British Columbia*. 1900. London, Horace Cox.

5. Many of the terms used by Baillie-Grohman to describe the indigenous people are offensive to modern-day ears, and so, indeed, is the contempt with which he often speaks of them. In fairness to Baillie-Grohman, I remind readers that he sometimes spoke contemptuously of Europeans too, and offer the words used by Father de Smet in speaking of the Kootenai Indians, approvingly quoted by Baillie-Grohman in the 1894 appendix he wrote for W.M. Barnaby's book *Life And Labour In The Far, Far West*, part of the DTUC collection now in the Nelson Library. Baillie-Grohman says:

I can in every respect re-echo the old missionary's warm praise of this remarkable tribe, which, as he very truly says, "present a delightful, unexpected spectacle to find in the bosom of these isolated mountains on the Columbia, a tribe of poor Indians living in the greatest purity of manners, and among whom we can discover the beau ideal of the Indian character uncontaminated by contact with whites. The gross vices which dishonour the red man on the

299

frontier are utterly unknown them. They are honest to scrupulosity. The Hudson Bay Company, during the forty years that it has been trading in furs with them, has never had the smallest object stolen from them. The agent of the Company takes his furs down to Colville (two hundred miles away) every spring, and does not return before autumn. During his absence (he being the only white man in the country) the store is confided to the care of an Indian who trades in the name of the Company, and on the return of the agent renders him a most exact account of his trust. I repeat now what I stated in a preceding letter that the store often remains without any one to watch it, the door unlocked and unbolted, and yet the goods are never stolen. The Indians go in and out, help themselves to what they want, and always scrupulously leave in place of whatever article they take its exact value."

## CHAPTER 4

6. This chapter begins the story of the struggle of Robert E. Sproule and Thomas Hammill for possession of the *Bluebell Mine* at Big Ledge (present-day Riondel). As opposed to earlier versions which have Sproule arriving at Kootenay Lake in 1882, accompanied by Meyers and Hunley, this version has him arriving in 1882, but accompanied by a new character, Gay Reeder. The difference is due to the indefatigable research of E.L. Affleck, who recently uncovered irrefutable evidence in a primary source of unimpeachable integrity; namely, that on July 31st, 1882, the *Bluebell* claim was recorded for Robert E. Sproule and, contiguous with it, the *Mogul* claim was recorded for Gay Reeder. Those two facts—the common date and the contiguity of the claims—added to various facts in the history of Sproule, make it—in the mind of this historian anyway— not only possible but extremely probable that the two men journeyed to the lake together.

Mr. Affleck's source is in the Provincial Archives at Victoria: *Register of Mining Claims for Kootenay*, kept by William Fernie, Gold Commissioner at Wildhorse Creek.

## CHAPTER 5

7. The factual information about Bill Feeney and Jerry O'Donnell comes from Bill's granddaughter Bernarene Stedile, Salmo, B.C.

## CHAPTER 6

8. The author as a young man was witness to this phenomenon for several summers while staying at the summer homes of friends just above the nine-mile narrows, and also knew intimately the swamps and ponds in what is now Kokanee Park.

9. This letter was published in *Cominco Magazine*, November 1958, in an article called "The Bluebell Letters," pages 11-17.

10. Bill Feeney did finally settle permanently in the Salmo River valley in a piece of land he named Stagleap Park Ranch. It is still there today, a few miles south of Salmo, and is still owned by his descendants. Bill and his brother Jack, who followed him west later, worked in the timber trade, sometimes cruising for the CPR and the banks, which owned large tracts of land. (See note 7.)

## CHAPTER 7

11. Both these letters were published in the *British Columbia Gazette* of July 12, 1883.

## CHAPTER 8

12. This chapter presents Sproule arriving at Big Ledge with Meyers and Hunley in '83 as opposed to the earlier version, which had them arriving in 1882. With the new evidence of A.E. Affleck (see note 6), we may now take this as the correct historical version. Much conjectural narrative colouring has been used in this chapter—a case of making "it might have been so" become "it *was* so."

## CHAPTER 9

13. One place in which Baillie-Grohman described this trip is the appendix for Barnaby's book. (See note 5.)

14. From *Fifteen Years Sport And Life In The Hunting Grounds Of Western America And British Columbia*. (See note 4.)

15. The letter of David McLoughlin was discovered in Spokane by the indefatigable E.L. Affleck. The news, reaching this author during the writing of the previous chapter, caused the doubts that gave birth to this chapter.

16. There had actually been a much earlier attempt to build a canal there. In his 1894 appendix to Barnaby's book (see notes 5 and 13), Baillie-Grohman states that "some 19 years ago," that is, toward the end of the 1865 gold rush over at Wildhorse Creek (see Foreword map), a group of twenty-five men had begun work on a canal intended to divert the Kootenay (or a large part of it) into the Columbia. *Their* purpose, not quite as altruistic as Baillie-Grohman's, had been to dry up the Kootenay river-bed so they could remove the assumed gold from its gravel. They had expected to complete the work in one season, but gave up for lack of provisions and funds. No wonder human beings have walked on the moon! There seems no limit to the grandiosity of their ambitions.

17. Chief Justice Matthew Begbie: "The Kootenay Mining Appeal," page 44 of *Proceedings of the Supreme Court of British Columbia*, March 28, 1884.

CHAPTER 13

18. The factual material for this chapter comes from "The Dramatic Story of the Silver King," which appeared in *The Spokesman Review Inland Empire Magazine* in four parts: November 30 to December 31, 1958. It was written by Van B. Putnam.

19. In his Journals, David Thompson tells us that on Sept. 27, 1809 he first looked at this river; then, on Sept. 27, 1810, he attempted to follow it to its mouth.

20. On first reading the account of the Hall brothers' expedition, I was not prone to believe that horses—about which I know very little—would have climbed under their own volition up the steep slopes of a mountain to a fairly high elevation. I determined to visit the area to set my mind at rest. The late Jack Steed of Nelson obliged by guiding me—in the late summer of 1989, I believe—up the mountain to the *Silver King* site, where we wandered about for

some hours, examining signs of very early exploratory diggings—perhaps those of the Hall brothers themselves. At one point, we could look down from open plateau-land to Hall Creek. The slopes, still largely open except for clumps of trees here and there, were not excessively steep, nor was our elevation from the creek-bed anywhere near that from the Kootenay Lake side, from which our approach had been made. I was satisfied that horses could indeed have wandered voluntarily up those slopes. But had the slopes been heavily forested at that time rather than open? Near where we were standing were a few stumps of trees that had been sawn down. The size of the stumps indicated that these trees had been larger than any of those still growing. Counting the growth rings, we determined that these trees were less than a century old. It seemed clear enough, then, that the area on which we were standing and the slopes down to Hall Creek had been as open in 1886 as they were now.

The descriptions of the landscape on that mountain are as I saw them that day and also, I believe, as the Hall party saw them. We ate our lunch sitting on the spot where the boys—in the story as I tell it—"standing on a mossy ledge amid rock ferns and small red-leaved bushes . . . found a panoramic view lying below them."

CHAPTER 16

21. This insert and the previous one were used by Malcolm Sproat in a *Tribune* article of 1897.

22. Modified slightly, this map is taken from page 37 of *Nelson: A Proposal for Urban Heritage Conservation*, where it is called "A land use map of Nelson based on Sproat's memorandum of Sept. 3, 1888." This 223-page publication of the British Columbia Heritage Conservation Branch of the Ministry of Recreation and Conservation, published ©1980, has been much used as a source of information by the author, who cannot emphasize too strongly his indebtedness to Donald Tarasoff, his group of students, and all the others who carried out the research for it.

23. Bob, writing in his 1918 "diary," seems to have forgotten the name of this catamaran, but it is the famous old *Dispatch*, built by

J. Fred Hume and his two partners in 1888. The journey Bob speaks of is the maiden voyage of the vessel. Robert D. Turner, in his excellent book *Sternwheelers and Steam Tugs*, 1984, gives us and interesting description of *Dispatch*.

## CHAPTER 18

24. Mrs. Hanna had cooked and served Nelson's first Christmas dinner to a group of men, all invited, only a week before, on Christmas day of 1888. That more well-known dinner party took place in the Hanna cabin and is not to be confused with this New Year's Day one in Hume & Lemon's store.

25. The author has stood there and heard it.

26. The author remembers always knowing, as a child, the first names of the men of his acquaintance (outside of his immediate circle), but never knowing the first names of their wives.

## CHAPTER 19

27. Robert D. Turner, in *Sternwheelers and Steam Tugs*, tells us that Dawson travelled up the Columbia from Sproat's Landing to Revelstoke on July 10th, on board *Dispatch*.

28. The information regarding the occupants of these buildings all comes from *Nelson: A Proposal for Urban Heritage Conservation*. (See note 22.)

## CHAPTER 22

29. It will become apparent to the attentive reader as this chapter progresses that the author has already decided for himself where that elusive building must have been—east of George Bigelow's store, yes, but on the *opposite* side of the street.

## CHAPTER 23

30. Most of the factual material regarding the Colonel and the Hannas comes from *Topping's Trail*, 1964, by Elsie G. Turnbull.

## CHAPTER 27

31. Another photograph reveals that there were actually *four*

chimneys, the precision of whose placement raised the effect of symmetry to prodigious heights indeed.

## CHAPTER 28

32. Information regarding Isabel Arthur came from the following sources: a column written by Jean Baker for the *Nelson Daily News* in 1966, and a letter to Shawn Lamb of the Nelson Museum from Margaret H. Smith, curator of the St. Marys Museum, St. Marys, Ontario. Material to aid in the narrative colouring came from speeches delivered by Dr. Isabel Arthur, recorded in the British Columbia Sessional Papers of 1918. What went on in Isabel's mind is, of course, pure speculation.

## CHAPTER 29

33. Bill Feeney, our acquaintance from chapter 5, was one of the construction workers on the line that year. (See notes 7 and 10.)

34. In the late 1930s, the author's sister lived in this house for a short period as the private nurse to Charles Hamilton when he lay dying.

35. The author, whose knowledge of Latin is rudimentary, translates this as "peace to those who enter, health to those who leave, a blessing on those who live here."

36. The description of A.S. Farwell as "old Farwell, a recluse never seen by ordinary people" presents a picture of this respected man seen through the eyes of a young child. The quotation is from "Memories of Helen Dickson Reynolds," a typescript copy (1965) in the Nelson Museum.

## CHAPTER 30

37. The information for this chapter was obtained from historian Peter Murray of Victoria, who very kindly spoke to me of his own research on Phillipps-Wolley and sent me excerpts from that man's reports to the British Columbia government. All quotations used in the chapter are from Phillipps-Wolley's report for the year 1896 to the Provincial Board of Health, published in the British Columbia Sessional Papers for that year.

# Bibliography

Affleck, E. L. 1976. "Columbia River Chronicles." *The Kootenays in Retrospect,* Vol. 1. Alexander Nicolls Press, Vancouver, B.C.

Affleck, E. L. "Kootenay Lake Chronicles." *The Kootenays in Retrospect,* Vol. 4. Alexander Nicolls Press, Vancouver, B.C.

Affleck, E. L. 1992. *Affleck's List of Sternwheelers Plying The Inland Waters of British Columbia.* Alexander Nicolls Press. Vancouver, B.C.

Affleck, E. L. 1989-1995. *Various unpublished monographs, letters to John Norris and conversations with John Norris.*

Akrigg, G. P. V. & Akrigg, Helen B. 1977. *British Columbia Chronicles. 1847-1871. Gold & Colonists.* Discovery Press.

Akrigg, G. P. & Akrigg, Helen B. 1969. *1001 B.C. Place Names.* Discovery Press, Vancouver.

Baillie-Grohman, W. A. 1918. "A Paradise for Canadian and American Soldiers." Pages 762-778 of an *Unknown Publication.* Vol. 83: April, 1918.

Baillie-Grohman, W. A. (with a chapter by Mrs. Baillie-Grohman). 1900. *Fifteen Years Sport and Life in The Hunting Grounds of Western America and British Columbia.* London: Horace Cox.

Baillie-Grohman, W. A. *Camps In The Rockies.* Vancouver Public Library.

Barnaby, W. M. *Life & Labour In The Far, Far West.* DTUC Library (Special Collection) Nelson.

Battien, Pauline. 1989. *The Gold Seekers.* A 200-year history of mining in Washington, Idaho, Montana and lower British Columbia.

Bealby, J. T. 1909. *Fruit Ranching In British Columbia*. Adam & Charles Black, London, U.K.

Bissett, Priscilla. *Life at the Silver King Mine*. Unpublished 2-page typed account. Nelson Museum.

Bouchard, Randy & Kennedy, Dorothy. August, 1985. *Lakes Indians: Ethnography & History*. Report prepared for the B.C. Heritage Conservation Branch, Victoria.

Busk. *Memoranda of Early Days In Nelson & District, 1888-1889*. Unpublished 2-page typed manuscript. DTUC Library (Special Collection) Nelson.

Christian, J. W. 1967. *The Kootenay Gold Rush: The Placer Decade, 1863-1872*. University Microfilms, Inc., Ann Arbor, Michigan (Ph.D. thesis)

Cone, Michael. *Busk, Charles Westly*.

Cottingham, Mollie. E. 1970. *Kootenay Chronicles*. Unpublished. DTUC Library (Special Collection) Nelson.

Davis, Angus. *The Memoirs of Angus Davis*. Presented serially in issues of the "Western Miner."

Fahey, John. 1965. *The Inland Empire: D. C. Corbin, and Spokane*. University of Washington Press. Seattle.

Fenwick, Arthur. 1946. *Memoirs*. Provincial Archives, Victoria, B.C.

Freney, Rev. T. P. *Parish History of Nelson, B.C.* Unpublished, typed 10-page document. DTUC Library (Special Collection) Nelson.

Gosnell, R.E. 1906. *A History of British Columbia*. Lewis Publishing Co.

Gray, James H. 1971. *Red Lights On the Prairies*. Macmillan of Canada, Toronto.

Graham, Clara. 1963. *This Was The Kootenay*. Evergreen Press, Vancouver, B.C.

Graham, Clara. 1945. *Fur and Gold In The Kootenays*. Wrigley Printing Co., Vancouver, B.C.

Graham, Clara. 1971. *Kootenay Mosaic*. Evergreen Press, Vancouver, B.C.

Howay, F.W. & Scholefield, E.O. S. 1914. *British Columbia*. Vol. 1, Vol. 2. S. J. Clarke Publishing Co., Vancouver.

Hume, R. Fred. *Memoirs*. Unpublished typed manuscript, bound by Vancouver Public Library binding department. 1977.

Hume, John F. Jr. 1973. *Some Highlights in the Life of J. Fred Hume*. Unpublished, typed manuscript, with photographs & maps. Kootenay Museum, Nelson, B.C. Revised April 1975.

Innis, H. A. "The Kootenay Region Before & After the Railway." *Settlement of the Forest & Mining Frontiers*. Vol. 9. Lowrie & Innis.

Jordan, Mabel. 1961. "The Kootenay Reclamation and Colonization Scheme and William Adolph Baillie-Grohman." *The B.C. Historical Quarterly: July-Oct., 1956*. pp. 187-219.

Lee, Helen. 1986. *The Silver King*. Kootenay Museum Association & Historical Society.

Lees, J. A. & Clutterbuck, W. J. 1888. *A Ramble In British Columbia (1887)*. Longmans, Green & Co. London & New York.

Moir, George T. 1947. *Sinners and Saints*. Mimeographed and offset printed. G. L. Wooding, Victoria, B.C.

Morris, Richard B. (ed.). 1953. *Encyclopedia of American History*. Harper & Brothers, New York.

Norris, John. 1985. *Old Silverton, B.C. 1891-1930*. Silverton Historical Society.

Ormsby, Margaret A. 1958. *British Columbia: A History*. The Macmillan Co. of Canada.

Putnam, Van B. *What Happened to the Frys?* A 2400-word carbon-copy typescript written in Inchelium, Washington, U.S.A. Colville Museum, Colville, Washington.

Putnam, Van B. 1958. "The Dramatic Story of the Silver King." *The*

*Spokesman Review* (Inland Empire Magazine in 4 parts, Nov. 30 - Dec 31, 1958).

Riegger, Hal. *The Kettle Valley & Its Railways.* Pacific Fast Mail. Printed in Canada by Evergreen Press, Vancouver.

Sanford, Barrie. 1977. *McCulloch's Wonder, the Story of the Kettle Valley Railway.* Whitecap Books, Vancouver, B.C. (1978). (Paperback 1988)

Scott, David with Hanic, Edna H. 1974. *East Kootenay Saga.* Nuvaga Publishing Co. Ltd., New Westminster, B.C.

Scott, David with Hanic, Edna H. 1972. *Nelson: Queen City of the Kootenays.* Mitchell Press, Vancouver.

Smith, James K. *David Thompson.* DTUC Library (Special Collection) Nelson.

Smyth, Fred J. 1977. *Tales of the Kootenays.* Douglas & McIntyre. First printed 1942.

Spritzer, Donald E. *Waters of Wealth.* Pruett Publishing Company, Boulder, Colorado.

St. Barbe, Charles. 1897. *A History of Nelson & The West Kootenay.* Unpublished. Nelson Archives.

Turnbull, Elsie G. 1964. *Topping's Trail. The First Years of a Now Famous Smelter City.* Mitchell Press Ltd., Vancouver, B.C.

Turner, Robert D. 1984. *Sternwheelers & Steam Tugs.* Sono Nis Press, Victoria, B.C.

Turney-High, H. H. 1941. *Ethnography of the Kootenai.* American Anthropological Association, Menasha, Wis., U.S.A. DTUC Library (Special Collection) Nelson.

Various. 1988. *Kootenay Outlet Reflections: A History of Procter, Sunshine Bay, Harrop, Longbeach, Balfour, Queen's Bay.* Urisco Publishing, Edmonton, Alberta.

Watters, Reginald Eyre. (Ed.). 1958. *A Centennial Anthology.* McClelland & Stewart Ltd.

Webber, Harold. 1975. *People and Places*. Cotinneh Books. Castlegar, B.C.

Welwood, Ron. 1989. "The University Club of Nelson and The Provincial University Question 1903-1910." *British Columbia Historical News. Journal of the B.C. Historical Federation*. Vol. 22, No. 2. Spring, 1989. p. 10.

## GOVERNMENT PUBLICATIONS, GAZETTES, NEWSPAPERS, LETTERS, ETC.

Drysdale, Charles Wales. 1917. *Memoir 94*. Department of Mines & Technical Resources, Geological Survey of Canada.

Cairnes. 1934. *Memoir 173*. Department of Mines & Technical Surveys, Geological Survey of Canada.

Little, H. W. 1960. *Memoir 308. - The Silver King*. p. 177. Department of Mines & Technical Surveys, Geological Survey of Canada.

Heritage Conservation Branch. 1977(?). *Nelson: A Proposal for Urban Heritage Conservation*.

*British Columbia Gazettes* for the year 1883 and other years.

*Henderson's British Columbia Gazetteer and Directory* for the year 1889.

*Cominco Magazine*. Nov. 1958. p. 11. Letter from William Fernie to S. S. Fowler. Nelson *Miner*. 1894. February 3. Letter from R. Fry to J. Fred Hume, dated Dec. 2, 1893.

*Nelson Daily News*. 1982. *Nelson: Historic Pictorial - A Glimpse of the Past*.

Joy, R.G. Letter, Memoirs, Notes. Stored in boxes at DTUC Library, Nelson.

Nelson *Miner, Tribune, Daily News* of the early years.

## INTERVIEWS WITH NELSON OLD TIMERS.

Conversation with Bernarene Stedile regarding material for Chapter 5.

# INDEX

Acton, D.A., 165

Ainsworth, George, 75, 76, 103

Ainsworth, John C.: history of, 51; planning in Oakland, 52, 53; plan for Columbia and Kootenay Rwy., 74-77; telegram sent to, 87; plan for reclamation of Kootenay lands, 103

Ainsworth party: Thomas Hammill, E.W. Blasdel, C.J. Woodbury in 1882, 71-73; Hammill, Woodbury, Maxwell, Brown in 1883, 87, 97, 100

Ainsworth Syndicate, 96, 98, 105, 151, 152, 166, 171

Ainsworth Townsite, 76, 98, 109, 114, 117, 118, 124, 146, 147, 167, 168, 173, 184, 224, 242, 258

Akenhurst, Mrs., 274

Allen, Gessner, 206, 211, 222, 252

Anderson, Henry (Harry), 117-121, 153, 154, 159, 162, 184, 224, 258, 274

Anglican Church, 274

Applewhaite, Edward, 252

Arthur, Dr. Edward Charles, 219, 220, 229, 230, 245, 247, 250, 257, 268, 270, 280, 288, 289

Arthur, Dr. Isabel, 219, 220, 245, 266-270, 288

Astoria, Oregon, 36

Atherton, E.R., 258. *See also* photograph of the Lakeview Hotel

Baillie-Grohman, William Adolph (B-G): arrival at Sandpoint and Bonners Ferry, 21-27; hunting at Kootenay Lake, 38-44; travelling down west arm, 63-66; meets Bill Feeney, 67; with Dick Fry, 67-68; granted land reservation, 77-78; with Sproat and Farwell, 91-96; at *Bluebell* dispute, 98-99; speculations about, 101-104; brings *Midge*, 106-108; at Canal Flat, 113, 149, 224-225; at Grohman Creek, 225-226; return to England, 277-278

Baker, Colonel James, 161, 250

Balfour, 75, 146, 241

Bank of British Columbia, 252

Bank of Montreal, 248, 250

Barnaby, W.H., 77, 91

Barnard, F.S., 252

Bate family, 274, 283

Bates, Mr., 111, 112

Begbie, Judge, 105

Big Bend, 52, 95, 147, 165, 170, 207

Big Eddy, 95, 122

Big Ledge (later Riondel), 34, 42, 45, 47, 54, 60, 61, 68, 83, 92, 96, 97, 116, 143, 147

Bigelow, George, 211, 217, 220, 231

Blasdel, E.W., 72, 75, 103, 105

*Bluebell*, 49, 69, 70, 72, 73, 82-90, 97, 105, 109, 110, 116, 117

Boats. *See Dispatch, Galena, Flirt, Henry Villard, Idaho,* S.S. *Kootenai,* S.S. *Lytton, Lady-of-the-Lake, Marion, Midge,* S.S. *Nelson, Surprise*

Bogle and Whalley, 285

Bogustown, 258, 259

Bonner, Ed, 35

Bonners Ferry, 20, 22, 23-27, 36, 37, 48, 75, 83, 87, 92, 107, 180, 251

bornite, 135

Boundary Commission, British/U.S., 39

Bourgeois, Joe, 234, 235, 236

# ABOUT THE AUTHOR

John Norris was born in Silverton, B.C. and at the age of five years moved to Nelson, where he received his education to grade 13. In 1942 he joined the navy and saw active duty in the North Sea and English Channel. Following the war, Norris attended UBC. He held a variety of teaching positions—from Principal of a three-room school in Blubber Bay, B.C., to college instructor in Vancouver, to founder of an alternative school in New Denver. John Norris has published two previous books—*Old Silverton* and *Wo Lee Stories*. Both grew out of his childhood memories of the west Kootenay country. In 1986 he was awarded the Lieutenant-Governor's Medal for History Writing in B.C. for *Old Silverton*. His interests besides writing are drama and gardening. He lives on his 60-acre property in New Denver.